CRY OF THE URBAN POOR

CRY OF THE URBAN POOR

REACHING THE SLUMS OF TODAY'S MEGA-CITIES

VIV GRIGG

Published in partnership with World Vision Resources

To my wife, Iêda,
beautiful companion, joyful friend, lover of God.

And to those who follow.

For strategizing is a form of loving those
who in the future will walk this path;
a way of fulfilling Micah 6:8
in its command to do justice.
By thinking ahead, one is better able
to create just structures
that deal kindly with future missionaries.

Contents

Introduction

"Blessed are you poor for yours is the kingdom of Heaven," declared Jesus.
"Blessed are you poor, for poverty is blessed," misinterpreted the old priest sadly.
"Blessed are you poor, for you are God's central interest in the historical class struggle," added the new priest knowingly.
"Blessed are who?" queried the uninvolved evangelical naively.
But the true disciples asked in obedience, "How do we bring this blessing of the kingdom to the poor?"
And they went about preaching, teaching, and healing everywhere. And the poor heard them gladly.

Genesis of a book

In an earlier book, *Companion to the Poor,* I dealt with the struggle to find a theology and practical basis for establishing the kingdom of God in the Catholic context of a Manila slum. While preparing to get teams into other Asian cities, I extended this former work, seeking universal principles for church-planting among the poor and integrating data from a worldwide context.

Cry of the Urban Poor is a report on those two years of walking the slums of the great cities of Asia and more recently of Latin America and the United States. It tells of our search for God among the poor. It describes our efforts to discover how the great mission surge of the last decades has established the church among the urban poor.

It is also an introduction for middle class Christian workers who would accept the call to plant churches among the urban poor of the Third World.

These urban poor now constitute an unreached people's bloc that is the third largest in the world, the most responsive to the gospel, and one that is doubling every decade.

The cries of these poor call us to devote every effort to one task—that of finding men and women who can initiate kingdom movements among these poor. But structures need creating to serve such laborers. They need to be taught a theology that will enable them to understand the patterns of such kingdom movements, and they need a demonstration of the demands of life among the poor.

Evangelicals are beginning to understand the needs, but have largely been unable to achieve any practical breakthroughs. At the Lausanne II Congress in Manila, the urban squatters became a central theme. Statements were read to this gathering of 4,000 evangelical leaders from 190 countries, expressly purposing that these poor be reached with the gospel.

Some major questions have needed answering:

1. Where are the men and women who, like Jesus, will choose to live as poor among the poor, establishing and tending newly formed churches day and night, exhibiting what I term the incarnational lifestyle?

2. Is living among the poor a necessary approach if we would establish the kingdom among the poor? Is it the wisest approach?

3. What are other critical factors in patterns of kingdom movements among the poor? What models do we have?

4. Have other groups integrated community organization techniques with evangelism among the urban poor?

What has been written?

Literature on church planting and establishing movements among the urban poor is limited. The most notable is the literature that emerged from Kagawa of Japan (Davies, Cyril, *Kagawa,* Epworth Press, 1960) some decades ago, the journals and subsequent literature about John Wesley, and William Booth's *In Darkest England* and *The Way Out* (Salvation Army, 1890). Various works on the French worker priests (Perrin, Henri, *Priest and Worker: The Autobiography of Henri Perrin,* Holt Rinehart and Winston, 1964), Mother Theresa and other Catholic workers among the poor, such as Sister Emmanuel's work on the slums of Cairo, also give a great deal of understanding as to the incarnational lifestyle of ministering among the poor.

But recent works on establishing the church among the poor are difficult to find. David Wilkerson's literature, Bruce Kenrick's *Come out in the Wilderness* (Fontana, 1965) documenting traditional work, and John Perkins' books (Perkins, John, *With Justice for All,* Regal Books, 1982), deal with church-planting among the poor of the United States. Jackie Pullinger's *Chasing the Dragon* (Hodder and Stoughton, 1980), which describes her ministry in Hong Kong, and some inadequate books about the work of Mark Buntain in Calcutta express two mission approaches. Donald McGavran, in his original masterpiece on church growth, has several chapters that discuss the interrelationships of church growth and issues of poverty and economics.

Much literature exists on development and aid for the poor, but the list is too extensive to document thoroughly here. The number of books on theologies of justice among the poor is growing. They range from extreme Marxist liberationists through the spectrum of more biblical liberationist exegetes, such as Thomas Hanks', *For God So Loved the Third World* (Orbis,1983), to the conservative evangelical theological camp captured in contributions to *Transformation* magazine. William Cook's study on base communities in Latin America forms a bridge between these theologies and the practice of formation of the church in the slums of Latin America.

Limits of this study

In my earlier book, recently re-published, I deal with my struggle to find a theological and practical basis for ministry among the poor in one location. The autobiographical and theological reflections are presented in an almost ethnographic manner. *Cry of the Urban Poor* seeks to extend the former, in non-theological terms, by examining universal principles behind strategies for church planting among the poor. It seeks to integrate data from ten cities with various theoretical approaches.

Since, as I will later indicate, the cause of urban poverty is largely injustice, I would have liked to have tackled the theme of justice only. But I have concluded that the most strategic actions of my life relate to breaking injustice through Jesus' approach—the establishing of movements of disciples in churches among the poor.

Since this earlier writing, my life has been involved in mobilizing men and women into incarnational ministries in the slums, and helping them learn how to plant churches. From among these and the movements they raise up, I would expect a small but significant percentage to move into effective transformation of the injustices, oppression, and oppressive structures that cause the poverty in which they are laboring. This seems to me to be the pattern of history and to accord with the realities of diverse giftings the Lord gives to His church. A book to meet needs at this phase of mobilization seems more appropriate than one on the issues of justice, even if it is less dramatic or popular.

I had hoped for the emergence of a series of studies of different incarnational workers, but the number of these workers is too small to enable this to be very effective. A longer task is needed, covering more cities. But I have included various reflections on the role of incarnation in the work of evangelizing the poor.

While affirming that most developmental approaches are sincere attempts to reflect principles of the kingdom of God, I am committed to the view that establishing the church is the primary objective in developmental activity for those committed to the Scriptures. Kingdom perspectives see the development of the spiritual kingdom as the central element of societal transformation. Economic, social, and political developments are an outgrowth of this spiritual development. They are important, but not central nor primary, even though at times they may assume a temporary priority.

Sadly, few groups exist that have integrated evangelism and community organization. Thus, there is little development of the theme in this book. A number of groups have succeeded in integrating evangelism and community projects, and a good number of groups have developed community organization approaches at the cost of avoiding preaching the gospel. But like the Liberal/Evangelical split, these two areas of ministry seem not to have been well integrated.

Liberation, while a biblical category, is too emotionally connected to Marxist analysis, in the present context, to be useful for Evangelicals. Therefore, I do not utilize this terminology. This book is about setting people free, but it does not begin with baptized Marxist categories. It deals with Jesus' approach to setting people free in the context of sin, oppression and poverty.

Methods used

This book is essentially a composition of anthropological and sociological reflections on church planting among the poor, integrated with principles drawn from practical experience.

I have sought to follow a participant-observer approach where the parameters of the community I have been evaluating are defined in ten cities. Out of this has come a series of case studies that are the basis for the reflective analysis of the book.

This book might also be said to be in process, for insufficient models exist at this time to demonstrate fully or even make possible a statistical verification of the various theses and analyses offered.

Thanks a million!

These ideas have been developed through contacts with a wide variety of persons in all the countries involved, and I am indebted for them to the body of Christ.

I am grateful to the faculty at Fuller Seminary for exposure to a breadth of missiological ideas—particularly to Dr. Paul Hiebert, whose interest in urban issues has expanded new horizons. My thanks also to Dr. Sam Wilson, whose discussions and encouragement have provided some new avenues of exploration.

Much has been learned from co-laborers as I have pioneered the various SERVANTS missions. Of particular note are, Pastor Waldemar of Brazil, who has provided the most amazing model for this kind of work. John Macy, Ruth Cruz, Corrie Accorda, John and Lynn Samaan, Dr. Betty-Sue Brewster, Randy Sperger and many others have all helped with aspects of research.

Thanks are due to World Vision International for funding some of this research work, and to Bob Linthicum whose encouragement has been an important catalyst.

Gene Tabor is the originator of core ideas related to the Four Seasons Chart and Maslow's Hierarchy of Needs. Concepts of church planting have grown from experience with hundreds of different laborers too numerous to mention.

In every city there are a dozen friends who have all contributed to the task. Thank you! This book is yours. May it spur you on to greater effectiveness in the task we share together.

Viv Grigg

PART 1

THE CONTEXT:
NEW MEGA-CITIES

Chapter One

Sorry . . . The Frontier Has Moved!

And the Lord said to me, "Proclaim all these words in the cities of Judah, and in the streets of Jerusalem" (Jeremiah 11:6).

It is a Marxist city of ten million. Two-and-a-half million live in the *bustees* (slums). Most of the middle-class families are poorer than the street people of Los Angeles. Sixty-seven percent live one family per room.

And the church? There are only three churches and ten house churches in the bustees. Some of the middle-class and other individual families from the bustees are involved in the 154 middle-class churches.[1] But the poor of the slums and the 100,000 poor on the streets, while having seen some Christian missionaries, have never known a poor people's movement nor churches of their own. No one proclaims Jesus to them. No holy person lives among them to show them Jesus in word and deed, in acts of mercy and deeds of power.

Once I had the joy of finding such a person. He had been imprisoned for working with the poor. He clearly couldn't face talking of it. But he had gone back to the ragged wretched orphans, widows, and beggars whom he loved and for whom he labored. He was a man who took Jesus' pattern of ministry to the poor seriously.

But where are other such followers of Jesus?

This book is a report on two years of walking the slums of the great cities of Asia, looking for God among the poor, seeking to know how the great mission surge of the last decades had established the church among the urban poor.

The sad report is that after thorough research in ten Asian cities I found only two such embryo movements. The conclusion: *The greatest mission surge in history, aimed at the last frontiers, has entirely missed the greatest migration in history,* the migration of rural peasants in the Third World to the great mega-cities.

Convictions to begin from

Two assumptions in mission seem self-evident. The first is that Jesus is our model for mission. Did he not say, "As the Father has sent me, even so I send you" (John 20:21)? And did not his first declaration of his own great commission tell us, "The Spirit of the Lord is upon me, because he has anointed me to preach good news to the poor. He has sent me to proclaim release to the captives and recovering of sight to the blind, to set at liberty those who are oppressed, to proclaim the acceptable year of the Lord" (Luke 4:18–19).

Surely with these words he modeled the gospel as primarily good news for the poor. And he defined ministry to the poor, declaring that the ministry to the poor is holistic, involving preaching, healing, deliverance, justice, and doing good deeds, but is initiated by proclamation (and reception) of the kingdom.

The second set of assumptions is simply pragmatic missionary strategizing:

1. Urban is the direction of history.

2. The poor are the direction of responsiveness. This is true both in Jesus' teaching and in missions history as well as sociological analysis.

3. The migrant poor are the greatest responsive group across the face of the earth today. I have found this responsiveness among Muslims in Karachi, Hindus

in Calcutta, Buddhists in Thailand, and Catholics in Manila. All are in a state of rapid socio-economic and worldview change and are hungry for the reality of a new relationship to a god.

Jesus commands a focus not so much on the last unreached unresponsive people groups in the world, but on those major unreached or partially reached groups that are *responsive.* The period of time within five years of a person's or family's migration is one of those times of greatest responsiveness.

Dr. Roger Greenway, who has done a great deal to focus people's attention on urban missions, speaks of his ministry to the urban poor with the phrase: "If the streets are paved, move on."

The frontier that moved

The experience of walking through the slums and seeing hundreds of thousands of squatters in destitute poverty is devastating. As history moves towards its climax, the wound in God's heart for this migration of people must make it difficult for him to hold back his judgment. To walk again and again into the destitution of these millions sears the soul with a darkness and grotesqueness that we could not cope with outside of the rest of Christ that comes from the refreshing balm of his Spirit and the hope of the returning King.

If the destitution of the urban poor is staggering in itself, their numerical growth is just as devastating. Since World War II, an endless convoy of smoke-belching, over laden, chicken-squawking bus after bus have careened down newly-constructed highways into the mega-city capitals of the Third World, disgorging crowds of wide-eyed impoverished farmers and teenagers looking for the next step towards affluence (or, more likely, poverty) in the squatter areas.

Wherever land can be found, huts and plywood shacks go up. Few governments have the capacity to prevent it or to provide services for the people arriving. The majority of new arrivals remain in squatter areas. Each capital city will continue to grow exponentially as it exploits the resources of its rural hinterland.

Hardly a church, rarely a pastor, seldom a missionary

More nightmarish than the poverty and the staggering growth of that poverty is to find no more than a handful of God's men and God's women ministering among these poor in each city.

I do not mean that there are no relief and development agencies. They are many, and most of them are doing good work in their roles as diaconal agencies of the church. *But the church has given bread to the poor and has kept the bread of life for the middle class.*

My search has not been for aid programs but for people who are establishing the kingdom of God, for the men and women working and living among the poor to bring them the bread of life by both word and deed.

I have found only a few. In the midst of the darkness, they are some of today's heroes. In each city, a handful of people have followed Jesus fully in his calls to renunciation and involvement with the poor.

There is a pastor in one west Asian city who wears the sandals and blanket of the poor, walking as holy men do. God has used him to mobilize and deploy 300 workers into the slums.

There is a man of God, a doctor, on the streets of one city ministering to the sick. The government has tried to deport him for ministering to the poor. For four years he has remained, by bringing a court case against the government and quietly continuing to serve the poor.

There is a pastor who for some years has chosen to live among the poor in a relocation area of Manila. He has worked to provide housing for the poorest in his community. The official housing manager and gang leaders were curious about this man and his concern for their people. They decided to help him build houses. Ultimately, they were converted because of his obedience in living out the love and justice of God among them.

There is excitement in Bangkok, for a new generation of creative church leaders is seeing new breakthroughs for the gospel. In 1985 there were 97 churches in this city of nearly 6 million. By 2004 there were 143 churches in a city of 7.5 million

Hidden in these statistics is an old, highly successful Finnish Pentecostal church planter. At the age of seventy, he daily spends long hours in a slum area, quietly establishing a church.

Despite all of this, there are only three churches and six house groups in Bangkok's 1,024 slums. Only two percent of churches are among the migrant poor.

Examples of men and women who are following Jesus in his ministry to the poor should not be the exception but the rule, if we as a church were truly following Jesus. We must refocus our energies and make the urban poor the primary thrust of missions.

In an otherwise excellent article by Dr. DuBose on the urban poor, he makes an unusual series of conclusions: "Like the poor who have long gathered in their urban store fronts in America, the Christian communities are proliferating among the urban poor in the wake of an impressive advance of the gospel and are gathering in 'shop churches' and in 'house churches' in all major areas of the world."[2]

This statement simply is not true. Perhaps it is a misunderstanding of the word "poor." To the Americans, the entire world is poor, including the middle class of the Third World. Or perhaps he is inaccurate because he is using Latin American Catholic categories for the church among the poor. I have wondered whether his statement might be true of African Churches, but discussions with missionaries from those countries indicate that though there is more activity than in Asia, the percentage and focus of activity is about the same. My two years of research in Asia do not bear out his conclusions.

The great misconnection

When faced with the sad failure of the great mission thrust to reach these poor one must ask "Why?" and beyond the why, "What can be done to rectify this failure?" The following appear to be some factors:

1. As mission leaders we have failed to foresee both the immensity of urban growth and the fact that most of the urban growth would be in squatter areas. The opportunity to save the cities from many traumas associated with this development, as well as the opportunity to establish a Church in every squatter area that has formed, have been lost almost entirely.

Perhaps it is because these poor are hidden. As we drive through Third World cities we see occasional glimpses of squatter and slum communities, but they are tucked behind houses and buildings and down in the hollows by the river, so that no one sees them. Those who emerge are dressed in their best clothes, soon to blend in with the middle-class people of the city. No one knows that they are poor. The poor do not advertise their misfortune.

People are being thrust out to the last frontier, but the last frontier has moved. Perhaps we could encourage missions researchers to revise their multicolored charts of unreached peoples. Instead of dividing them by religion alone, perhaps they should also be divided into urban-rural and rich-poor. We may find that the largest group of truly "unmissionaried" people would be the urban poor.

2. Some missions have made a deliberate attempt to reach the rich, believing in a sort of religious "trickle-down" theory. This strategic mistake lacks support both in biblical exegesis and in sociological analysis, and already has been competently refuted.[3]

The gospel "trickles up." Any man or woman who would follow Jesus and walk among the poor will affect countless members of the middle and rich classes. People in these classes will come to the slums because they are curious. They hear of good deeds and like Nicodemus, they come seeking for truth and reality.

Despite the failure of affluent missionaries to preach the words of Scripture about unjust wealth and to live simply themselves, the converted rich come because these new believers can read the Bible. They come searching for the person who has chosen the poor, because they know that here is a true answer to the problems of wealth. They come because they are now concerned for the uplift of those they previously exploited. Jesus has an answer for the rich man. The rich middle-class missionary often has only words.

3. The same strategic reasons that led to defeat for an affluent power in the Vietnam war have led to failure in this spiritual war. Depending on affluent and high-powered programmatic approaches, the mission force has been out of touch with the realities of the Third World poor. A missionary living on $2,800 per month in a western-style house and sending his children to a westerners' school while trying to reach people who live on $200 per year is like a B-52 bomber attacking guerrillas.

4. This failure in the great Western mission thrust is, at its roots, ultimately not strategic but spiritual A church trapped by cultural perspectives on affluence rather than adopting the biblical stance of opposition to the "god of mammon" has exported this into missions. We must return to the pattern of Jesus, who chose non-destitute poverty as a way of life, took the time to learn language and culture, and refused to be a welfare agency king. We must return to the way of the apostles and of the wandering friars who have been the key to the conversion of the world in generations before us. Non-destitute poverty and simplicity must again become focal in mission strategy.

5. Some perhaps have concluded that the poor are unreachable. This is a culturally logical conclusion for those of European descent growing up in the capitalism of the United States. Claerbaut, in an excellent analysis on urban ministry, has some penetrating insights into American cultural attitudes to the poor:

> The truths of stratification and self-perpetuation of the socioeconomic system are not widely known or accepted. As a result, negative attitudes towards the poor persist.
>
> To argue that poverty is a self-perpetuating condition in a capitalistic society is to attack the nation's sacred civil doctrine of the self-made person. To suggest that one is poor because of an unequal distribution of opportunities is to suggest that riches are as much a matter of good fortune as of virtue.[4]

The poverty of the Third World urban poor, however, is a direct result of social forces and oppression, not of personal sin. The oppressed poor in the Scriptures are considered to be rich in faith and the ones for whom the kingdom is particularly to be preached.

6. The propensity for the Western church to accept the agenda of aid organizations as focal to the Great Commission has seriously skewed mission. Mission to the middle class is seen as proclamation. To the poor it has become giving handouts or assisting in development as defined by Christianized humanitarian perspectives. It is far easier for churches to give thousands of dollars than to find one of their members who will walk into the slums for a decade.

Vows of poverty

My convictions have deepened and been modified during these months of wandering, preaching to the poor, and research.

1. Apostolic movements

The central conviction remains: we must thrust out groups similar to the devotional communities of the twelfth century preaching friars, or the wandering Irish monks that converted Northern Europe between the fifth and ninth centuries, before the Catholic hierarchy gained control there. In our case we must send communities of men and women, married couples and singles, with commitments to live as the poor among the poor in order to preach the kingdom and establish the church in these great slum areas.

Westerners and upper-class nationals who choose such lives of non-destitute poverty may be catalysts for movements of lay leaders from among the poor in each city. The spearhead of such a thrust will be those who accept the gift of singleness for some years. We must set up new mission structures for this to happen. The key is young couples who will choose to give leadership to these communities of pioneers.

We need men and women who will commit themselves to lives of simplicity, poverty, devotion, community, and sacrifice in areas of marriage and family.

2. Devotional communities

Most missionary teams are not communities, but teams. The focus of most teams is to work. On the other hand, traditional communities in the church are by definition primarily committed to relational caring, worship, and a devotional pattern. These emphases are essential if workers are to survive in the slums. Working and living two by two in various slum areas, they need to come together every two weeks for a day of ministry to each other, of worship and relaxation.

3. Poverty, chastity, obedience

The commitments to non-destitute poverty may be similar to those of the older Catholic orders, without the legalism.

So too is a commitment to singleness—taken not as a vow of celibacy, but for a period of time. We Protestants have lost the concept of the gift of singleness. Marriage has been seen as the only ideal. The biblical blessing on chosen or given singleness has to be recovered. Part of the blessing of that gift is freedom to pioneer in difficult and dangerous places

Obedience for Protestants is democratized by the emphasis on the priesthood of all believers. We obey God within the defined decision-making processes of our organization.

4. New structures

Historically, movements among the poor have consistently been thrown out of the middle-class churches. It is traumatic for one missionary living on $2800 per month to have to be in the same mission team with someone willing to receive only $500 needed for living expenses and all ministry and travel costs.

To avoid such trauma, it would be wise for mission directors to create new orders of men and women called to the poor. These could be within or without their old mission boards. Ultimately this will both create effectiveness and prevent disharmony.

Such orders should only be guided by persons in authority who have lived, for long periods, this kind of sacrificial and incarnational lifestyle. Authority should never be given to administrators who have not lived out this lifestyle. Incarnational workers do not want protection. They want pastoral care from leaders who have been on the front line, who will keep them at the front line, and who will take the "bullets" out when the workers are wounded.

An opportunity lost?

God is offering Western missions the chance to return to a biblical commitment to the poor and to incarnation as the primary missionary role model. The need is urgent: several thousand catalysts in the slums of scores of Third World cities who can generate movements in each city. Two billion people cry out.

If Western mission leaders, boards, and pastors do not heed this call, God will sidestep us and rely only on emerging Latin American and Third World missions to meet this focus of mission in the next decades.

How sad to miss the focal call of the Scriptures to preach the gospel to the poor! For the God who sent his Son to a manger will find a way to send other sons and daughters to those poor for whom particularly he came. He will not leave their cries unheard.

Notes

1. In 1985, of the 143 churches in the city, there were only two house churches and one Pentecostal church, though a number of poor attended three larger churches.

2. DuBose, Francis M., "Urban Poverty as a World Challenge," *An Urban World,* Larry L. Rose and C. Kirk Hadaway, eds. pp 51–74, Nashville, Tennessee: Broadman Press, 1984.

3. See for example McGavran, Donald A., *Understanding Church Growth,* pp 269–294, Eerdmans, 1980.

4. Claerbaut, David, *Urban Ministry,* Grand Rapids, Michigan: Zondervan, 1984.

Chapter Two

The City Beckons

Talk about urbanization with its big, powerful, secular cities: they stand there like giants, iron chariots, enemies of the church. Today one city alone may have 20 to 25 million people. And like a giant, it shouts at the church, "I'm here. Now what are you going to do about it? I don't want the gospel. Just leave me alone!"

—Thomas Wang, AD2000 chairman

What if the size of the Muslim world or of the Hindu population doubled every ten years? Suppose furthermore that these population blocs were found to be among the most responsive to the gospel on the earth? How would this affect our present strategies of Christian mission? Would we take up the challenge?

The answer is a dramatic "Yes!"

Yet the number of urban squatters and slum dwellers in the world's major cities constitutes a bloc as large as either the Muslims or the Hindus, it doubles in size every decade, and all indicators show it to be a responsive group. Logically, missions must swing their strategies to make these their priority target.

The majority of migrants to the mega-cities will move into the slums (Bangkok), squatter areas (Manila), shanty towns (South Africa), *bustees* (India), *bidonvilles* (Morocco), *favelas* (Brazil), *casbahs* (Algeria), *ranchitos* (Venezuela), *ciudades perdidas* (Mexico), and *barriadas* or *pueblos jovenes* (Peru). I will describe these in general with the term *squatter areas*.

These tend to be slums of hope. Their occupants have come in search of employment, have found some vacant land, and gradually have become established. They are building their homes, finding work and developing some communal relationships similar to those of the *barrios* or villages from which they have come. In slums of hope social forces and expectations create a high degree of receptivity to the gospel.

Missions today must reach the last tribes and fulfill prior commitments to the rural poor. But new mission strategies must focus on the crucial point of spiritual warfare for the mega-cities. Within this broad objective, mission to the urban poor becomes a central target, as they are the ultimate victims of the oppression and evil of the mega-cities and nation states. They loom large in the heart of God. They are the key to the elite and the heart of the city. Among the most reachable of people groups today are migrants living in community, groups of peasants who have moved to cities and live in squatter areas.

Over the past thirty years, about one billion people have moved from rural areas to cities. In the next ten years, another one billion will board overladen buses and come to the cities. For most of them, the first step is into squatter areas—centers of great darkness and demonic activity.

Between 1950 and 1980, urban growth in Third World mega-cities rose from 275 million to just under one billion. From 1980 to 2000 it doubled. In the next two decades the global urban population will grow to five billion. Wherever land can be found, huts and plywood shacks will go up. Few governments have the capacity to prevent it or to serve the needs of the people arriving. Even the United States may not remain immune as its economy slows down.

Some of the most destitute of the poor live in mud homes on the streets of modern Dhaka city in Bangladesh, a city that was home to ten million people in 2000, a city that will grow to contain twenty million people by 2015. In 1984 there were 730,000 people in Dhaka's 771 squatter areas. It was estimated that in the coming years, they will make up the majority of the city's population of twenty million. Because of the lack of raw materials and other factors, there is little possibility for the city's industrial growth to keep pace with the migration influx.

Almost all of the world's population growth in the next decades will be in cities. Rural populations will tend to remain at present levels.

There is usually one mega-city per country. It drains resources from the entire country. Its bureaucracy locks up the potential for growth in the smaller cities. The next largest city as a rule is only 10 percent the size of this mega-city. Chiang Mai, the second largest city of Thailand, for example, is thirty times smaller than Bangkok.

To understand the process of bringing the kingdom of God into squatter areas, we need first to live among them and learn their ways. But we must also come to understand the processes that are creating them. The following statement from Sam Wilson rings true:

> Ghettos *per se* (even the most pathological ones) are not the real problems of our times but are visible symptoms of fundamental, systematic processes. To treat ghettos as the basic urban disease, or even to make them special targets of evangelization strategies as the *sine qua non* of urban ministry, is like treating a sick person's temperature, rather than the disease . . . Evangelism is most effective when the passion for evangelistic effectiveness is adorned with broad ranging concerns and goals for the renewal of the whole of city life.[1]

The extent of the squatter areas

Research from Bangkok shows the growth of these slums, from 80 in 1940 to 1,020 in 1982.[2] In other mega-cities, research collated from various sources shows that the number of squatter areas in each ranges from 177 to 1,000. The statistics on the previ-

SQUATTER POPULATION IN SELECTED CITIES [4]
(IN PERCENTS, BASED ON VARIOUS STUDIES)

	1950 -54	1955 -60	1961 -64	1965 -67	1968 -69	1970 -71	1972 -73	1974 -79	1980 -85	1986- 2000
Dhaka							17.5	35	24	
Karachi								23	33	50
Calcutta								33	67	33
Mumbai									45	38
Delhi									36	30
Chennai									25	
Jakarta		25	25			59	24	26	30	29
Bangkok			16	15		19	20	24	19	6
Kuala Lumpur	16	25	25		30	37	35	30	24	31
Manila	1.5	4.9	20	23	35		43	35	38	38
Seoul							30		29	
Mexico City		14			46				46	60
Lima		9.5	17.2			24.4	40	32	50	8
Rio de Janeiro								30	30	
Sao Paulo		0.8			1.2	1.6	5.0	3.9	7	
Bogota									60	
Caracas									42	23
Baghdad									29	
Kinshasa								60	60	23
Istanbul								40		

ous page summarize conclusions from research studies in various cities on the percentage of urban poor.[3]

This chart gives a general idea of the percentages of squatters in various cities around the world. There is a pattern of gradual growth of the squatter areas from the 1940s when the first squatter areas began to appear. These figures exclude the decaying slums of the older city, except in the final column, where they are included to give a more complete picture of the actual numbers of urban poor.

When we include both slum and squatter figures for these Third World mega-cities, all have more than 6 percent of the population in slum and squatter areas. Bangkok has 6 percent. Sao Paulo, perhaps one of the world's most productive cities, has a *favela* population of only 7 percent but another 17 percent live in *corticos* (decaying inner city buildings). In many cities, over 60 percent of the people live in slums or squatter areas.

With an urban population in the Third World of 793 million in 1980 and a conservative overall estimate of 25 percent of these living in squatter areas, we are looking at a people group of 200 million. When one adds the slum areas and street people of the cities, 35 percent of the people in these cities are the urban poor—277 million people. By 2002 this had risen to 31.6 percent in the slums or 924 million.[5] This is in a world that is about 15 percent squatters in 2001—a bloc nearly the size of the Muslim or Hindu populations, doubling each decade. Squatters thus constitute an immense people group—a distinct entity deserving specific strategies for evangelization.

If one includes the less reachable, decaying inner-city slums as well as the street people in these cities, a reasonable estimate of the urban poor in the year 2000 was one billion people—40 percent of these cities or 16.8 percent of the world's population.

The urban poor as an entity cannot, in contrast to the squatter communities, be generalized as a broad reachable bloc with cultural commonalities. They do not identify themselves as communities with shared characteristics, nor do they have an affinity for other types of urban poor. The urban poor as a larger class are defined in contrast to the people of the city rather than as an entity in themselves.

Most responsive international cultural bloc

Not only do squatters share a common economic history and system, they also share universal religious characteristics—an animism that is far stronger than prevailing "high" religions. Also, cultural characteristics in the slums are as much universal as they are related to the prevalent cultures in each city. We may define squatters as a cultural bloc with as much ease as we define Muslims or Hindus, even though they span a broad range of ethnicity and culture. Animists in general are more reachable than people who believe in high religion.

Socially, each squatter community of reasonable size perceives of itself as a distinct social entity, linked to the city, but with a life, society, and subculture of its own. In any city the squatters have coping strategies independent of middle-class life, including middle-class religious life, to which they have little or no relationship. If you have ever been present when two squatter churches met, you understand the affinity evident between these people as a social class with similar occupations and patterns of residence.

Language in the squatter areas tends to draw migrants together as all learn to speak the *lingua franca* of the city. Yet almost all realize they cannot read and write properly and, unlike the middle class, are uneducated. As a result, ethnic barriers are lower in the city, but a strong class barrier between the lower class and the middle class emerges.

Such communities are more responsive than the closed rural village or the isolated middle-class person. Poverty creates a positive responsiveness to the gospel, according to the apostle James (James 2:5). The changes migrants go through also create a responsiveness.

Faced with high responsiveness in the international subculture of poverty in these squatter areas, we must develop specific missions and plans for evangelization. Hence, while agreeing with Dr. Wilson about the need for a broader approach to the problems of the poor, these statistics and trends would indicate the necessity of a specific plan for evangelization of the squatter communities, while not neglecting other urban poor.

Where did such growth come from?

Estimates of rates of growth of the squatter areas indicate they are growing faster than the cities at annual rates of about 6-12 percent. The squatter areas of Kuala Lumpur, for example, grew at an average annual rate of 9.7 percent from 1974 to 1980.

AVERAGE URBAN ANNUAL GROWTH RATES (IN PERCENT)

	EAST ASIA	SOUTH ASIA	LATIN AMERICA	NORTH AMERICA	EUROPE	AFRICA	WORLD
1950-1975	4.06	3.93	4.29	2.16	1.56	4.89	3.11
1975-2000	2.60	4.07	3.45	1.38	1.16	4.56	2.76
2000-2010			1.83	1.16	0.04	3.66	2.05
2010-2020			1.45	1.10	0.07	3.26	1.85

Much of this may be attributed to the growth rate of the cities. Worldwide urban growth has been pegged at 2.76 percent a year. At that rate, city populations will double every twenty years. But the mission field among the squatters will double about every ten years. The following chart shows the worldwide urban growth rate per year.

The processes of urbanization are not new phenomena. They have been occurring since Nimrod and Babel. But there are historical differences occurring today that have resulted in the world rapidly becoming urban and more of the world's people becoming the urban poor.

The vital and occasionally magnificent cities of the past existed as islands in an overwhelming rural sea. Less than 200 years ago, in the year 1800, the population of the world was still 97 percent rural. At that time only 1.7 percent of the world's population resided in places of 5,000 or larger.

By the beginning of the twentieth century, the proportion of the world's population in cities of 100,000 or more had increased to 5.5 percent. England was the first country to undergo an urban transformation. In the second half of the nineteenth century, it was the world's only predominantly urban country.

In 1975, by contrast, 24 percent of the world lived in large cities of 100,000 or more. By the year 2001, 48 percent were living in cities.

What is behind the mushrooming of the cities since the 1940s? Many assume that migration from the rural areas is the primary cause. But migration has always occurred. It is not the only cause of growth. The growth of cities is made up of both migration (called explosion growth) and natural increase within the cities (sometimes called implosion growth). Migration represents only some 30-50 percent of this urban increase. Causes of migration are described as push and pull factors.

Push factors behind migration

1. Rural poverty

The primary driving force behind migration is the rural economy. In a study on migrants in slums in Dhaka, 39.7 percent indicated the cause of their migration as poverty, 31.5 percent as unemployment, 23.3 percent as famine.[6] There are other less significant factors that modify the primary driving forces to the city slums mentioned above.

In an increasingly cash economy, the same levels of agriculture provide a declining level of effective cash. It becomes increasingly rational to migrate to the town, even if there is only a one in three or a one in two chance of getting a job.

2. Political unrest and warfare

Unrest in the provinces often creates an influx into the cities. Stable political government in the city acts like a magnet in such times. The partition of India and Bangladesh sent a million new urban poor to Calcutta. The subsequent war in 1971 between Pakistan and Bangladesh sent another wave.

3. Weather factors

Weather also affects migration. Dwyer shows that urban migration in the Philippines is directly related to areas where productivity is constantly hampered by typhoons.[7] In a study on Dhaka, 9.3 percent of migrants indicated they came because of river erosion and flooding.[8] The diagram on the following page illustrates some of the structural factors involved in urban migration.

Pull factors behind migration

Throughout the centuries men and women have needed permanence, security, community, and achievement. The city, good in its reflections of the godhead, in its communality, opportunity for creativity, and creation of order; and evil in its infiltration with the demonic components of abusive power, exploitation, and arrogant rejection of God, has always been the Mecca for such aspirations.

Santos talks of a demonstration effect—when the impact of radio, television, films, magazines, and newspapers results in

STRUCTURAL FACTORS IN URBAN MIGRATION

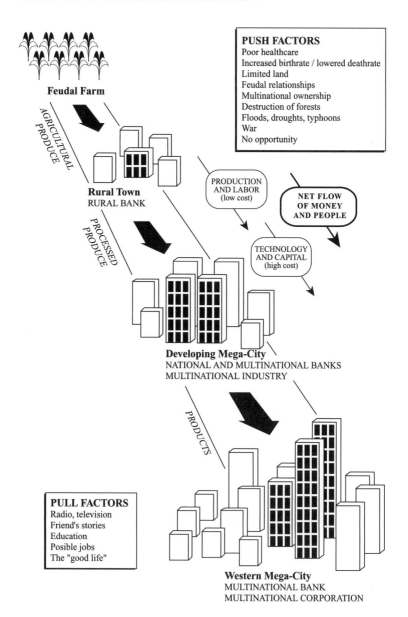

Feudal Farm

AGRICULTURAL PRODUCE

Rural Town
RURAL BANK

PROCESSED PRODUCE

PRODUCTION
AND LABOR
(low cost)

TECHNOLOGY
AND CAPITAL
(high cost)

**NET FLOW
OF MONEY
AND PEOPLE**

Developing Mega-City
NATIONAL AND MULTINATIONAL BANKS
MULTINATIONAL INDUSTRY

PRODUCTS

Western Mega-City
MULTINATIONAL BANK
MULTINATIONAL CORPORATION

PUSH FACTORS
Poor healthcare
Increased birthrate / lowered deathrate
Limited land
Feudal relationships
Multinational ownership
Destruction of forests
Floods, droughts, typhoons
War
No opportunity

PULL FACTORS
Radio, television
Friend's stories
Education
Posible jobs
The "good life"

rising expectations among the rural population. These, plus the new highways into the rural towns, open up a bewildering array of alternatives for people who for centuries have lived at subsistence levels. This is a prime reason why those who live in rural areas that are closer to centers of politics or economics migrate at a greater rate.

The desire for education and health are also factors. Rural schools often prepare people not for rural lives but for the modernizing influences of the city.

The family I lived with in the favelas of Sao Paulo, Brazil, for five months was typical. The mother told me, through tears, that they had come from the hills, like most people in this favela. There, only two of her six children had survived. There was no hospital, no doctor, and not enough sustenance in the food. In despair, they moved to the city, where for 15 years they had lived in the favela, and the father working long nights in a low-paid job. But life was infinitely better. Three more children had survived. The children went to school. They had a roof over their head and the possibility of a permanent piece of land.

RELIGIOUS DIVERSITY IN CALCUTTA (IN PERCENT)

	1951	1961	1971	1981
Christians	2.98	1.82	1.40	1.36
Hindus	83.41	83.94	83.13	81.89
Muslims	12.00	12.78	14.20	15.34
Buddhist	0.37	0.31	0.29	0.32
Jains	0.46	0.58	0.60	0.62
Sikhs	0.56	0.51	0.36	0.45
Other	0.22	0.06	0.02	0.02

Who are the migrants?

Cities are primarily for the young. Seventy-five percent of migrants are less than twenty-four years of age. In the year 2000, 666 million children under the age of fifteen lived in Third World cities.[9]

Interestingly, some cities are for men and some for women. For example, we may look at the city of Calcutta as a primarily male city, with a male/female ratio for the total population of 100/61, for Hindus, 100/65, and for Muslims, 100/40.[10] In contrast, Latin cities are primarily female. Data indicates the importance of specific targeting of male populations in New Guinea, part of Oceania.

Migrants come from diverse religious backgrounds into a melting pot of religions, as the figures on the previous page show for Calcutta (they also show the decline of Christianity within Calcutta).

The figures for Calcutta do not reveal the fact that most migrants into the city are more animistic and do not have a clear understanding of "purer" forms of Hinduism. The figures do reveal, however, the possibility of significant Muslim conversions in a context of religious plurality.

These figures also show the great decline of Christianity in this city since the British left. Anglo-Indians, who made up the bulk of the city churches, suddenly found they were no longer a privileged caste within Indian society. They began to integrate back into their Hindu culture. At the same time, the decline in economics caused a migration of middle-class people to other cities in India. The church contained many of these.

Migrants are generally illiterate. But cities facilitate increasing literacy. In India, about 30 percent of the population is literate. In Calcutta, about 67 percent are literate.

There are also patterns as to where the migrants first find vacant land on which to live. Squatters may be found up the rivers in older townships that have been surrounded by the city, places where modern land titles have never been fully obtained. There is also land along the railways. Generally, a ring of squatters surrounds the city as it was in the early 1950s and another ring is emerging around the satellite cities. Swamps are commonly left for squatters, and along the coastline there may be houses built four-deep out into the sea.

Implosion: natural urban growth

1. More rural and urban natural increase

In ancient cities, the rate of in-migration plus birth rates in the cities nearly equaled the death rates. Cities had relatively stable populations. In English cities during the Industrial Revolution, cities grew almost entirely by migration. Life in the cities was grim. More people died than were born.

But natural increase has quickened since the late 1930s, with the rapid technological and organizational advance of modern medicine resulting in increased birth rates (more babies live) and longevity (more people live longer). Improved patterns of plumbing, modes of transportation, chlorination of water supplies, and other innovations have also played a part.

Since many in these emerging cities are trapped in poverty, the reproductive rate is high because birth rates among the poor are higher than among the educated.

2. Increased affluence

Because of modernization, incomes have risen in most areas of the world. The more rapidly incomes rise, the faster urbanization occurs.

3. Technological development in agriculture

The faster productivity in agriculture increases, the faster people move out of the agricultural sector. This negates the fallacy that somehow we can reverse migration to the cities by improving the lot of the agricultural areas. This is particularly true in nations with high birth rates, where increasing productivity requires fewer workers on a limited supply of land.

The historical context of underdevelopment

The Industrial Revolution in England and Northern Europe generated the first major wave of modern urbanization. Those countries had their slums. Theory based on historical analysis of this growth indicates that as industrialization continued, the extent of urban poverty decreased.

The development of Third World cities, however, is totally different from the development of Western cities both prior and during industrialization. The differences can be described in social, spatial, and economic terms.

Today's Third World mega-cities were established primarily as trading centers for colonial powers. Their industrialization, infrastructure, and legal systems were established in situations of dependency on Northern or Western cities. They were the exporters of their countries' raw materials, and recipients of advanced technological processes and foreign legal and bureaucratic systems.

The economies of the advanced countries, on the other hand, had not been dependent on other nations. Their economies and politics were not distorted by dependency, but rather were integrated. These cities were the centers to which the goods of the world were delivered.

As a result, contemporary urban growth in the Third World is characterized by fundamental differences from the growth of large cities like New York or London some generations ago.

High urbanization vis-à-vis low industrialization

Third World cities are developing capital-intensive industry that provides few jobs for the influx of new people, whereas the European growth of cities drew people because of the massive new employment growth that outstripped the labor force.

The industrialization of developed countries required rural labor to supplement inadequate urban supplies; in the Third World, the process of capital-intensive industrialization attracts far more labor than it can possibly absorb. Part of Hoselitz' thesis that has been substantiated is that urbanization is outpacing industrialization in the Third World, in contrast with the relationship between the two that prevailed at earlier times in currently developed countries. In short, more people enter the cities than jobs can be created for them.[11]

In most cities, industrial growth ranges from 1-4 percent per year in contrast with slum population growth, which ranges from 6-12 percent. Those unable to enter the industrial life of the city remain trapped in lives of service and patronage without ever acquiring the capacity to gain their own land or housing.

For example, to accommodate rising populations in Central America and Mexico, 1.2 million jobs need to be created a year. In contrast, the USA creates only 2 million jobs per year with an economy fifteen times as large.

Today's Third World tertiary sector (government bureaucrats and services such as insurance, banking, and publishing) is numerically larger than the Third World manufacturing sector. In nineteenth-century Europe, levels of productivity were roughly similar between the two sectors.

In Western urbanization, agricultural development led to industrial development. Industrial development directly fed back into the development of agriculture. Later came the increases of service industries and bureaucracy. In the Third World today, the primary growth of the cities is from agriculture to bureaucracy and services (such as car-washing, hand-carrying letters across a city), supported by a weaker industrial sector.

The infrastructure of skills, the value systems outlined by Max Weber and others, the legal structures, and city organization that created an environment for entrepreneurial activity in Europe have been transplanted from the West, and in many contexts, fit poorly and malfunction badly.

As a result, some Third World cities are almost entirely non-industrial. Ray Bakke comments on Dhaka:

> An Urbanologist would view Dhaka as a pre-industrial city, a kind of urban village. It does not have an urban structure or infrastructure like Western cities. It has a huge population and a rapidly growing one.[12]

The response

Chapter two of this book presents an analysis of the need in slums and squatter areas. Chapters three to five are a discussion of the nature of these squatter areas and causes of their poverty. In chapter six, the extent of the church within them is analyzed. Chapter seven and eight tell of our personal and organizational response to these needs. Chapters nine on, by means of case studies and analysis of anthropology, economics, and theology seek to define what the church in such contexts will look like.

The argument in the following pages is that at the core of any response to these processes is the development of the kingdom of God in these slums; that movements at the grassroots are a key to long-term change; that as the church has done through history, we must reach the victims of oppression and in the process we will generate life that will transform the oppression itself.

The church in the city must therefore attack the issue of evangelizing the urban poor at several levels:

1. Establishing movements of churches among the poor that are genuinely churches of and by the people, expressing their leadership and style of worship, and addressing their needs.

2. Establishing movements of disciples among the educated elite, or non-poor, who have a biblical theology of justice, economics, and society. These probably will come from student ministries where students are exposed to ministry among the poor and forced to develop a strong biblical basis for dealing with the issues of such a ministry.

3. Seeking to mobilize the affluent church to open its doors to the poor and become directly involved in confronting the international issues of unjust economic structures by speaking the word of God into these arenas.

4. Developing a holistic kingdom-oriented theology, with a strong emphasis on Christology—Christ's incarnation, his miracles, his chosen suffering on the cross, his Great Commission, and his kingdom.

This book will concentrate on the neglected first aspect—establishing movements among the poor—while not neglecting the others. These are being addressed by other mission strategists and authors.

Cry of the Urban Poor

Notes

1. Wilson, Samuel, *Unreached Peoples 1982,* Monrovia, California: MARC, World Vision International, 1982.

2. Pornchokchai, Sopon, *1020 Bangkok Slums: Evidence, Analysis, Critics,* Urban Community Research and Actions School, 688/56 Jaransanitwong 68, Bangplad, Bangkok, 1985

3. *The Challenge of the Slums, Global Report on Human Settlements, 2003,* Nairobi:UN-Habitat, has extensive analysis of the nature of slum growth.

4. Extensive references to sources are available in a manuscript copy of this book and the Urban Leadership Cities Database, P.O. Box 20-524, Glen Eden, Auckland, New Zealand.

5. UN-HABITAT, 2003, *The Challenge of the Slums,* p 14.

6. Dhaka Municipal Corporation, Centrer for urban studies, *Slums in Dhaka City,* 1983.

7. Dwyer, D.J., *The City as Centre of Change in Asia,* Hong Kong University Press, 1991.

8. Center for Urban Studies, slums in Dhaka city.

9. U.N. Population Division, 1980 statistics.

10. Siddiqui, M.K.A., editor, *Aspects of Society and Culture in Calcutta,* Anthropological Society of India, 1982.

11. Hoselitz, Bert F., "Urbanization and Economic Growth in Asia," *Economic Development and Cultural Change,* Vol. 6, Oct. 1957.

12. Bakke, Ray, "Evangelizing the World Class Cities," *Together,* Jan-March 1984.

Chapter Three

The Migrant Poor:
Who Are We?

The way to the Celestial City lies just through this
town, where the lusty fair is kept; and he that will go
to the City, and yet not go through this town must
needs go out of the world.
—John Bunyan, The Pilgrim's Progress

One was a big man with a good education, speaking
English fluently with an English accent. The other was a
Nepalese, small in stature but full of big dreams.

"What business would you get into if you were to make it off
the street?" asked my friend, a Kiwi businessman.

"We would establish a tea stall," they replied.

Several further discussions led to a conclusion that it was
a worthy goal for $100. But to find a piece of unoccupied
street took ten days. They only had to pay the police a
reasonable two rupees each day for protection. But paying
the local mafia cut their profit margin to zero.

A daughter fell sick from a fever. She had been caught in
the rain without good blankets in the cold Calcutta winter.
This crisis slowly consumed their financial capital.

Unable to pay the mafia, members of the family were
beaten up.

City of joy

Calcutta, oh Calcutta! City where the powers of darkness
have so gained control over the political and judicial leadership

that only darkness prevails, and a mafia rules the city's people. Poverty and evil triumph and infest the lives of ordinary people until they go crazy with the pain.

Calcutta has more poverty and more grades of poverty than any other city in the world. I walk down the street, and a well-fed wraith-like figure, baby on hip, comes after me pleading, pleading. There are four of them fighting each day for this territory. An amputee shakes his cup on the corner, an old man lies on the path further along, near death.

In 1984, Geoffrey Moorehouse estimated that there were 400,000 men in town without a job;[1] the 1981 census put it at 851,806. Ganguly comments that perhaps no other city has one million educated youth registered with the employment exchanges.[2] There is beggary all over India, but nowhere is there beggary on the scale of Calcutta's.

Beyond the beggars are anywhere from 48,000 to 200,000 people who live permanently on the streets. One survey shows that two-thirds of them have some kind of regular employment, while 20 percent are beggars. Most have some kind of part-time work or have earned money by selling vegetables, paper, firewood and scraps.

More than half of the 3.5 million living within the metro core are slum dwellers. Two-thirds of Calcutta's families earn 350 rupees or less a month (the poverty level is Rs600 or US$50 per month for a family). Less than 20 percent of its workforce works in an organized industry. Agriculture and small crafts, not major or modern manufacturing, are the principal occupation of the people. In as much as 80 percent of its extended land surface of 1,350 square kilometers, there are 3.15 million bustee and slumdwellers.[3]

There is a level of poverty still lower than that experienced by beggar, street-dweller or bustee-dweller—the poverty of those who are approaching death. The dying are faces along the streets.

An old man, his eyes fixed. Some passers-by leaving a few coins. A visit with the Brothers of Charity to the street-sleepers under an unfinished overpass. A plaintive plea from a silver-haired mother shivering violently with fever for some coins to buy medicine. Behind her, two pot-bellied little boys displaying their first-degree malnutrition.

Calcutta daily demands that we face not just poverty, not alone inhumanity, but this gray face of approaching death. The burden is increased by the knowledge that the continued over fertility inherent in poverty will force five times this number of people off the land in the next generation (about twenty years). The fact is that there is no more land, no more subdivision of farms possible. Increased agricultural productivity will only add to the migration, for it will increase the number of living children without bettering the quality of rural life.

The constant bickering of Bengali politics is death for these poor, as is the economic dislocation introduced by a theoretically Marxist state government—in reality a continued domination by a rich ruling class. The perpetual bondage of Hindu caste and culture adds to the death.

The task ahead

Into this scene Jesus speaks the words, "And this is eternal life, that they may know you" (John 17:3 NRSV). The confrontation with death involves aid, development, organization, politics. But as the brilliant Francis Xavier learned early in life, the issues of this world are not determined by politics and force, but by the mysteries of grace and faith. In the preaching of the cross comes the vanquisher of this slow death that grips the city. Eventually it must be movements of the righteous who can turn the flood tide. The question is how to generate movements of disciples among these poor and subsequently among the rich.

Defining poverty, its types, causes, and potential responses, is an important step in the process of generating such movements. An understanding of the breadth of need and the range of potential responses enables us to reflect both on theology—that is, God's responses—and on strategic possibilities to implement as we walk with God.

Some levels of urban poverty

It would be a mistake to consider that the poor are to be found only in slums or squatter areas. Or that the people in the slums are necessarily all poor. Slums and poverty are not to be equated. And even among the poor there is a class structure or ranking. What then are the relationships between squatters and poverty?

Differences between first and Third World urban poor

Absolute poverty is a term used to describe poverty when people have an absolute insufficiency to meet their basic needs—food, clothing, housing. Indeed, many who are in absolute poverty starve to death. Within this category there are many levels. For example, we may talk of first-, second-, and third-degree malnutrition.

Relative poverty is found in the developed world and is measured by looking at a person's standard of living relative to others in the community or nation. It is sometimes called secondary poverty. It is a measure of the extent to which people are on the margins of society.

The measure of this relative or secondary poverty is often in terms not of a material or economic level, but of capacity to own and consume goods and services and to have opportunities for development. It is often an exclusion from opportunity and participation, a marginalization from society.

This marginal status is associated with and caused by (or causative of) a low material standard of living in relationship to present social perspectives of how one should live well. To be without a car in a New Zealand city, for example, means one is poor and largely unable to participate in society. This is not true in Lima, Peru. An International Labor Organization study uses a measure of disposable income to establish the standard poverty line, dividing the total available income in the country by the population, thus determining this level relative to others within the nation.

Thus when talking of poverty in Third World squatter areas, we are generally talking of something that occurs at a level not even to be seen among the poor of a Western country. The middle class of Calcutta are poorer than the poor of Los Angeles.

The definition of poverty is also, to a large extent, a historically perceived issue. The poor of Manila are not as poor as the middle class of England even 400 years ago. But they are poor

FEATURES OF FIRST AND THIRD WORLD POVERTY

First World	Third World
Relatively few of society	Significant percentage of population
Objects of discrimination	Originates in lower and middle classes
Upward mobility difficult	Upward mobility from urban and rural roots
Job mobility limited	Flexible and adaptive labor
Hard to find permanent employment	Self-inflationary employment generation
"Secure" poverty/welfare	Daily subsistence search

compared with the present-day middle class in any country in the world. Our definition of poverty has changed with the availability of technology that enables us to enjoy a healthier, happier life.

Poverty can also be defined in terms of what man and society could be, in terms of a future vision of a reasonable, or ideal, lifestyle. Biblical scholars have recently clustered their definitions around the theme of *shalom* in the Old Testament—peace that comes out of a just and secure society.

Reachable communities of urban poor

The physical characteristics and culture of each squatter community differ from country to country. Yet the processes that generate them and the resultant evils are universal among the major cities of the Third World countries.

We may talk of three major international categories of urban poor: inner-city slums, squatters, and specialized groups.

Inner-city slums are decaying tenements and houses in what were once good middle- and upper-class residences. They may be described as slums of despair where those who have lost the will to try and those who cannot cope gravitate. Yet here too are the recent immigrants, living near employment opportunities, and students in their hundreds of thousands, seeking the upward mobility of education.

In Sao Paulo, approximately half of the migrant poor that come to the city find their first residence in favelas, or shanty towns. The other half move to the corticos (rundown, inner-city housing), then within four years move down into the favelas. In Lima these are called *tugurios*.

In inner-city slums of despair there is little social cohesion or positive hope to facilitate a responsiveness to the gospel. Since they are older poor areas of several generations of sin, they are not responsive, and hence do not constitute a high priority for church planting.

In terms of response it is more strategic to focus on squatter areas, which tend to be slums of hope. Here people have found a foothold into the city, some vacant land, jobs, and some communal relationships similar to the barrio back home.

Slum of hope

Tatalon, in Manila, is an example of one of the many slums of hope that have sprung up since the 1940s. A total lack of facilities and services did not deter provincial migrants flooding into Manila. In the unoccupied lands of Tatalon, they found an ideal site to establish footholds in the big city. In 1976, the average home in Tatalon contained 12.3 people. There were 14,500 people in about six square blocks—approximately 57,500 people per square kilometer. By 1985, the number of residents had doubled.

Tatalon is one of the more fortunate squatter areas. The government in the last few years has established a "sites and services" program, gradually upgrading the area. It has put in roads, a number of toilets, some water pumps, and surveyed the land. It has organized the people so that those longest in residence may buy the small lot on which they live. This upgrading has been done at a cost of between 70 and 120 *pesos* (US$3.50-$6.00) per month over a 25-year period.

Tatalon is a place of hope, a slum in which to dream, to aspire. It is a community that is beginning (with a little help) to come through decades of suffering into a little economic security. In such a context the gospel is welcomed as one more part of the social changes people are going through. It can move like wildfire.

The incarnational patterns outlined in *Companion to the Poor*[4] are applicable in Catholic contexts such as the Philippines and Latin America. They are probably applicable as well in any context where the culture has a positive direction towards Christ. In contexts moving away from Christ or under severe political control, the principle of incarnation still holds, but foreign workers may need to work closely with and train national people while they themselves live outside of these poor areas. This will lower the profile of the foreigner.

There are other situations where squatter areas are so destitute that living in them is not a viable option, such as the squatters in Calcutta (the next three million lower than the bustees). Geoffrey Moorehouse describes the street people in the heart of Calcutta:

> For five hundred yards or so there is a confusion of old packing cases, corrugated iron, straw matting, old bricks and wads of paper arranged in a double Decker sequence of boxes. Each box is approximately the size of a small pigeon loft, with room to squat and only just to kneel . . . each box is the sleeping and living quarters of a family. The rest of their life is conducted on the pavement where they cook and play and quarrel together.[5]

Among these poor the poverty is so intense that the primary response may have to be aid, given in such a way that Jesus shines through and their dignity is sustained. Mother Teresa's Missionaries of Charity reflect the patterns of Christ in ministering among such poor more than any other ministry I have seen.

Specialized groups

To these categories of poor communities may be added other groups of poor that do not make up a natural community for church planting, but may be reached by specialized ministries. These would include the street people of Hong Kong, Calcutta's 48,000 pavement dwellers, the 600,000 drug addicts and 500,000 prostitutes of Bangkok, the deaf and lame outcasts of these societies, and the white slave trade between many of these cities.

Some groups of urban poor are likely to be more open than others. Sam Wilson sums up an aspect of this by relating it to the concept of an unreached people:

> The urban poor do not necessarily exist as a meaningful group, even in a given locality. Some sense of belonging and community which affects one's sense of identity will

be necessary if the category listing is to be verified as a group that needs a strategy for evangelism.[6]

Some questions for verification come from this kind of thinking: Is this really a people group in the sense of belonging and community? Do they meet and change one another? Is there a mutual influence on behavior because the individuals sense likeness? Is there a viable church ministering within the people group? Can it carry witness forward? Some of the people groups within the urban slum and potential responses to their needs are listed below.

1. Street vendors

Hawkers, illegally eking out their existence along the road-sides of the crowded streets, pose special problems because of the logistics and the long hours of work they must endure. A strategy based on small groups that reaches a cluster of two or three stalls could be effective. Search would have to be made to determine which hawkers live on the streets with their stalls, which ones are the truly poor, and which ones come from various squatter areas. With this knowledge, it may be possible to locate reachable and responsive clusters. These could then be linked together in monthly fellowships at some inner-city location.

Generally, street vendors work from early morning till late at night, so the time for Bible studies and fellowship have to be carefully defined. It would seem perhaps wiser to reach street vendors from churches planted in the squatter areas.

2. Marketplaces

Public preaching and celebrations should be held in market places two or three times weekly during the early afternoon when the stalls close for siesta. Again, most vendors live in squatter areas, so a squatter ministry would be a better starting point.

3. Street kids

City officials estimate that there are 10,000 abandoned children in Lima. In Sao Paulo, estimates range from 8,000 to 300,000. Antioch Mission in Brazil is a Christian mission giving good leadership in approaches that meet some of these children's needs, establishing contacts with them on the streets, and then developing programs for them with the hope of integrating them into Christian homes.

4. Drug addicts

Of all urban ministries, a ministry to drug addicts requires the tightest authority structure and discipline. The one-to-one discipling process involved will result in a network of disciples, many of whom, as they become stabilized, will return from the rehabilitation retreat homes (outside the city) to their squatter areas and may become foundational for churches. Among the drug addicts, a discipline movement developed comparable to a Christian gang is possible. This kind of ministry, often linked to a prison ministry, is operating in a number of cities.

5. Alcoholics

Years of experience has been acquired by Alcoholics Anonymous concerning the philosophy and strategy of reaching alcoholics. Its patterns are derived from Christian ministry and Christian values. We need to seek dynamic Latino and Asian equivalents.

6. Prostitutes

The problem of prostitution is at heart related to demonic in-filtration of a city's leadership structures and to severe economic exploitation. It requires a justice-oriented ministry that begins with a grassroots attack through rescuing girls from the houses in which they are trapped.

After working with single mothers in New Zealand for years, Pat Green was called by God to work with prostitutes in Bangkok. During a year of language study, she formed many relationships with girls in Patpong, the streets that are at the center of prostitution in Bangkok. Over one hundred go-go clubs, beer bars, discos, massage parlors and restaurants line the streets and alleys. On any given night approximately 4,000 women work here as bartenders, waitresses, go-go dancers and masseuses. Most are prostitutes, and indeed many are forced by their employers to "go with customers."

From these contacts, and through God calling other missionaries from Singapore and elsewhere, a team called Rahab Ministries formed. Pat also has a gift of relating with women in high places. Many of these are appalled at the sex and slave trade, and are eager to work together, bringing public and legal pressure to bear. In her last letter, Pat said she was considering whether they should rescue, even by buying back, a girl sold for $5,000 into a closed brothel in Japan, as part of international sex trafficking.

7. Deaf, blind, and amputees

Specialized ministries for deaf and blind are needed. In Manila, for example, many blind people are balladeers, going from house to house seeking events at which they may sing and earn their keep. I often have encouraged rich Western performers to take two years to live among them, seeking to generate a movement of Christian blind balladeers in the slums. The sense of dignity that could be generated among these people and the potential impact of such a ministry are great. There is a good man in Calcutta who has developed a card-making shop for amputees. They sell their cards around the world. He has assisted scores of poor in this way.

8. Prisoners

A number of poor people's churches have formed through ministries to prisoners in different cities. Real conversions and training within prisons can prepare tough men for their return to the squatter areas where churches are then formed through their testimony. It was a thrill to walk back into a community where I had labored years ago and find one of the first converts, Boy Facun. He used to be a man well acquainted with jails. When we were reunited, he had become an associate pastor and was forming a jail ministry team. He preached one evening and fifty made commitments to the Lord. His joy and mine knew no limits, as he told the story.

Finding a responsive community

To initiate ministry among the poor in these cities, it seems wise to begin movements that first focus on responsive slums of hope. All kinds of poverty can be found in such a place, but there is an atmosphere of hope, there is some degree of community relationships, and communities of Christ that can minister to each other's needs are easier to establish.

Within cities we can analyze the responsiveness of squatter communities according to criteria developed by Edward C. Pentecost.[7] Other criteria may be developed. For example, Paul encourages the believers to pray for peace that the gospel might move unhindered. Thus, finding a community that has a history of peace is a factor.

The following are some criteria we developed to select a community that was likely to be more responsive—a community where the first Servants workers in Bangkok would minister.

1. Size of the slum

About 100 to 500 families (500–2,500 people) would provide a big enough community so that the responsive sectors could be reached. These can then influence other sectors. In smaller communities, the whole community becomes involved in decisions. If they reject the gospel immediately, there is no encouragement or modeling that will easily reverse their initial rejection.

2. Peoples from responsive rural areas

In Thailand, we knew that northeastern and northern Thai are responsive to the gospel. In Bangkok, we focused on areas where these people had migrated.

3. Age of the slum

The younger the slum, the more responsive it will be. When people live in a slum for more than five years, their senses become dulled by sin. Younger age groups are more responsive. In new squatter areas, people are more open to new relationships. In older slums, web relationships are more tightly developed.

4. Homogeneity

Slums where there are ethnic or other divisions may not be places where the gospel will easily move.

5. Religious background

Previous exposure to Christianity, outside help and programs, is a factor to be considered, as is proximity of a temple, mosque, or other religious site.

6. Direction or discernment of the Holy Spirit

7. Education, home, and family

Schooling for workers' children is a priority for families. The level of education in the city is important. In Bangkok, the level of education in the public schools is high. Other family criteria include peace and security, economic level, area for children to play, proximity to buses and other services.

8. Spiritual receptivity

While evaluating some of the natural factors regarding responsiveness, one is able to press on in the task of discerning the spiritual receptivity of a community. Jesus wasted little time on surveys. His commission was to go and to preach. Where there is obvious receptivity, remain in that place. Where there is obvious opposition, move on.

We need to remember, however, that we are faced with the difficulties of entering new cultures, whereas he was dealing with a known cultural context and responsiveness. For us, then, some degree of survey work is appropriate, if it is not overdone.

It is useful to find out the history of the community from the people. The community's name often indicates a spiritual connection to past events. Is there a history of covenants between people and their gods?

During prayer, and while preaching in these communities, the Lord often reveals, through gifts of discernment, some elements of community history, present spiritual warfare, or future strategy.

Lima: desert capital

The various categories of the poor may well be demonstrated by a look at Lima, Peru.

Once, like Calcutta, it was the center of an empire—Spanish-speaking Latin America. Now it is a city in decay, yet with new life emerging. It is built on a desert, which is a positive factor for the poor, as land is not so restricted a commodity as in other cities. There are several classes of poor in the city, including three classes of settlements:

1. Asentamientos

Asentamientos are homes made with straw matting (*estera*). The people occupy a vacant area of mountain or desert and build their homes. They are quickly organized so that basic necessities become regularized.

2. Pueblos Jovenes

Pueblos jovenes, also known as *barriadas* and *barrios margi-nales,* spring up and develop without preplanning by government agencies. Initially there are no telephones, streets, or water.

Official figures from 1980 placed pueblos jovenes at 40 percent of the city. Tito Paredes and others estimate 60 percent in 1987, with an added influx due to the terrorism in the Quechua areas.[8] Extension of the 1980 statistics with consideration of the depression in the economy in the early 1980s would give a conservative estimate of 50 percent of the city presently as pueblos

GROWTH OF THE BARRIADAS OF LIMA, PERU

	Total City Population	Number of Barriadas	Population of Barriadas	% of City Population
1922		1		
1940	645,172	11		
1956	(est) 1,200,000	56	119,886	9.5
1961	1,652,000		316,826	17.2
1972	3,302,523		805,117	24.4
1981	4,492,260	408	1,460,471	32.5
1983		598		
1985				40
1990	5,860,000		5,500,326	38

jovenes. This figure, as for many figures from different cities, does not allow for the rapid movement into more middle-class levels of many within the oldest barrios as they become *urbanizaciones*.

Barriadas or pueblos jovenes began to multiply rapidly in 1950, as they did in most other world-class mega-cities. In 1961, legalization of these areas began to occur. In 1970, there was promotion of land title registration. Since the late 1980s, with much political assistance from the new president and the Mayor of Lima, people have been able to get land titles.

In fifteen districts of Metropolitan Lima, the population in barriadas ranges from 50–100 percent of the total population. Four of Lima's 47 districts have over 90 percent squatters. For more detailed data, see the chart below.

3. Urbanizaciones

Urbanizaciones, or well-planned suburban communities with water, drains and electricity, develop from *asentamientos* and pueblos jovenes. After five years, the government taxes those houses in a pueblo joven that are not constructed permanently. Then development occurs, as lights, water, and roads are brought in. Twenty percent of the city's residents live in regular planned suburbs. Eighty percent live in popular settlements, of which 23 percent live in popular urbanizaciones, 37 percent in barriadas, and 20 percent in the *tugurios.*[9]

4. Street people

Over the last decades there has been a conversion of the economy of the city from a more formal industrial economy (of legally incorporated businesses) to an informal, unofficial street economy. Main players are typically street vendors, or self-managing vendors, with the whole family participating in this economic enterprise. This unofficial sector represents 67.4 percent of the total productive economic activity of Lima. Some vendors pay as much as US$500 per month rent for a piece of sidewalk six feet wide.

Lack of housing: universal squatter concern

The major criteria defining squatters is the nature of their housing. The chart on page 57 lists the cities of the world that have the worst housing situations. Housing gives an indication of the extent of peasantry in the city. Yet if a city is 90 percent squatters, are they then actually the people of the city? Are cities indeed middle-class, or can there be functioning cities of the poor?

Stratification of squatter and slum poverty

The fundamental economic factor defining squatter poverty is land. Using Hong Kong as his context, Abrams[10] has typified squatters partly by their economic relationships to the land:

The *owner squatter* owns his own shack, though not the land. He erects the shack on any vacant plot he can find. Public lands and those of absentee owners are the most prized. The owner squatter is the most common type of squatter.

The *squatter tenant* is in the poorest class, neither owning nor building a shack, but paying rent to another squatter. Many new in-migrants start as squatter tenants, hoping to advance to squatter ownership.

The *squatter holdover* is a former tenant who has ceased paying rent and whom the landlord is afraid to evict.

The *squatter landlord* is usually a squatter of long standing who has rooms or huts to rent, often at exorbitant profit.

The *speculator squatter* is usually a professional to whom squatting is a sound business venture. He squats for the tribute he expects the government or the private owner to grant him sooner or later. He is often the most eloquent in his protests and the most stubborn in resisting eviction.

The *store squatter,* or occupational squatter, establishes his small lockup store on land he does not own, and he may do a thriving business without paying rent or taxes. Sometimes his family sleeps in the shop.

The *semi-squatter* has surreptitiously built his hut on private land and subsequently comes to terms with the owner. The semi-squatter, strictly speaking, has ceased to be a squatter and has become a tenant. In constructing his house he usually flouts the building codes.

The *floating squatter* lives in an old hulk or junk which is floated or sailed into the city's harbor.

The *squatter "co-operator"* is part of the group that shares the common foothold and protects it against intruders, public and private. The members may be from the same village, family, or tribe or may share a common trade.

Government responses to housing needs

Generally the first attempt by governments when the problems of squatters emerge is to bulldoze down these areas. Political considerations then lead to the possibilities of relocating them—usually on cheaper land outside the city. For example, 900,000 squatters have been relocated outside of Manila's boundaries onto land that has a few water wells, with a toilet for each family. Between 1964 and 1974, an authoritarian government in Rio de Janeiro relocated 80 communities.

Squatters, while appreciating the new land, although it may be without water or near shops, cannot build houses in such places because they are too far from their places of work. Most return to the city.

The next approach governments have tried is to provide high-rise apartments at low rentals for the poor. In Chinese cities, with ia of urban experience, this has worked. Elsewhere, it has astrophic. High-rise apartments are too expensive for the poor to rent, so they are rented by middle-class officials, and the poor again are forced to find new squatter areas. A variation on this has been to construct low-cost, single-story dwellings.

PERCENTAGE OF URBAN POPULATION LIVING IN SLUMS AND SQUATTER SETTLEMENTS

(52 CITIES THAT HEAD THE LIST)

Addis Ababa, Ethiopia............ 90	Lusaka, Zambia.................... 50
Yaounde, Cameroon 90	Maracaibo, Venezuela.......... 50
Douala, Cameroon................. 87	Monrovia, Liberia................. 50
Buenaventura, Colombia........ 80	Recife, Brazil....................... 50
Mogadisho, Somalia............... 77	Guayaquil, Ecuador.............. 49
Ibadan, Nigeria...................... 75	Mexico City.......................... 46
Lome, Togo............................ 75	Phnom Penh, Kampuchea..... 46
Santo Domingo, Dom. Rep...... 72	Bombay, India....................... 45
Casablanca, Morocco............. 70	Colombo, Sri Lanka............... 44
Nairobi, Kenya....................... 70	Tunis, Tunisia 43
Calcutta, India....................... 67	Caracas, Venezuela............... 42
Chimbote, Peru...................... 67	Barquisimeto, Venezuela....... 41
Mombasa, Kenya.................... 67	Brasilia, Brazil...................... 41
Izmir, Turkey......................... 65	Arequipa, Peru...................... 40
Accra, Ghana......................... 61	Ciudad Guyana, Venezuela ... 40
Abidjan, Ivory Coast 60	Istanbul, Turkey 40
Agra, India............................. 60	Lima, Peru 40
Ankara, Turkey 60	Kuala Lumpur, Malaysia....... 37
Bogota, Colombia................... 60	Delhi, India........................... 36
Dakar, Senegal....................... 60	Manila, Philippines 35
Kinshasa, Zaire...................... 60	Antananarivo, Madagascar ... 33
Rabat, Morocco...................... 60	Makasar, Indonesia............... 33
Blantyre, Malawi.................... 56	Pusan, South Korea.............. 31
Port Sudan, Sudan................. 55	Cali, Colombia...................... 30
Quagadougou, Upper Volta..... 52	Guatemala City, Guatemala ... 30
Dar es Salaam, Tanzania........ 50	Rio de Janeiro, Brazil 30

The emergence of various forms of self-help development has been the most effective long-term solution. Either the squatter area itself is upgraded, by introducing legal titles to land, water, sewerage and electricity, by encouraging the people to construct their own homes of solid materials, or by locating a new site and introducing these basic services before the people are relocated. The World Bank recently set aside large sums of money to assist governments in this latter kind of program.

Possessions of the poor

It was her first full-time job as a secretary. The income upgraded the family's diet, then carefully week by week a little was set aside to buy the TV set. It took two years of skimping and saving before it was bought. They proudly showed it to me each time I returned to the community. This was the first step into the middle class—a status symbol and a source of delight after years of struggle.

Oscar Lewis'[11] work gives us a concrete glimpse of the poverty of the slums in a study of the possessions of the poor. He noted how short a length of time possessions are kept.

Substantial proportions of people's possessions had been bought secondhand. Often, even beds had to be pawned in order to provide more basic needs. The average ownership of a bed was only four years and eight months. Jewelry was pawned more often, so little remained. Toys were few. There were several articles of furniture considered essential: a bed, a mattress, a table, a shelf for an altar and a set of shelves for dishes, a chair, a wardrobe, and a radio. The wardrobe was often a wedding gift from husband to wife (I have observed this also, both in Manila's slums and Calcutta's slums), and represented a relatively large investment. It was the longest held piece of furniture.

Eleven of the fourteen families studied by Lewis had kerosene or petroleum stoves. In the other three, cooking was done over a brazier or earthenware hotplate.

This type of cooking is a common pattern in many cultures. The poorest use wood fires (or dung in South Asia and the Middle East) in earthen hearths or firepots of various kinds. Charcoal is a step up from this. The next step up is the use of kerosene. In many countries the next step up for those with jobs is to use a two-ring gas burner connected to a small gas tank.

Nutrition of the poor

Another perspective on the absoluteness of poverty is to consider the malnutrition in a community.

Malnutrition may be caused by bad hygiene and health practices or by lack of food. Health services are generally better in cities than in the rural areas, even for squatters. There is generally a good supply of food in the city. Malnutrition in the slums is caused not by the lack of food, but by the lack of finances and the nature of a new urban diet—a diet without the traditional combinations developed in rural cultures through the centuries to give a healthy balance of nutrients.

The problem becomes one of adaptation to new patterns of packaged city foods. The migrant squatter is thus affected by the kind of food, the quality of food and its quantity. Advertising has a further negative effect.[12]

Employment in the slums

While lack of housing may be the fundamental definition by the middle class of what are the squatter areas, the most important issue in the minds of the poor is not housing but the reason for their coming to the city—the possibility of finding a solution to their poverty in work.

Attractive financing, donated land, and subsidized transportation to and from relocation areas are insufficient incentives for many squatters to relocate out of the city. They will accept the land or house, and return to the city again to live as a squatter. They must be near their work. They cannot afford the time or money to travel long distances. The problem is that there is no work for many and inadequate work for others.

Non-employment

The squatters are largely unemployed or underemployed in terms of traditional definitions of work in a modern city. A study of one community in Manila showed the fathers of households as 20 percent unemployed (half of these because of physical disabilities), and 80 percent underemployed.[13]

The source of the problem lies in the slow growth of the modern sector relative to the population increases in the "traditional" sector. Employment opportunities do not expand and per capita income remains low.

There is employment within the squatter areas, and the poor find employment within the city. But it is of a different kind than that of the middle-class city. It is easiest to understand by perceiving the city as a duality with two coexistent economic systems that are interlinked but have different characteristics.

One way of analyzing the extent of unemployment is to discover the length of time that people are out of work. For example, while living in the dynamic context of Sao Paulo, I asked my friends, the favelados with whom I stayed, how long it had taken them to find jobs when they were unemployed. In general they were able to obtain work within about four weeks. In the less buoyant context of Manila, it was not unusual for people to wait one or two years between jobs. Unemployment maims the spirit, dulling its ethics with an overarching anxiety, and generating the other evils of the slums.

Kinds of work

Types of work generally include services, domestic activities, trades, artisans, small-scale businesses, hawkers, and self-employed generally categorized as unemployed.

Small-scale businesses are characterized by low capital and turnover, limited stocks, a small number of persons in each establishment, little space which is usually in a home, and dependence on credit as the mainstay of the business.

In certain cases, especially where demand is uncertain, the transformation of a family enterprise into a capitalist enterprise would lead to bankruptcy.

Hawkers are the lowest level in the commercial structure. Often they are not self-employed but part of micro-chains controlled by bosses.

Financial mechanisms of the squatter areas[14]

Some of the characteristics of a poor people's economy have been analyzed. It is built around family enterprise and self-employment. There is limited capital investment. For example, the average number of loans to the informal sector in Calcutta in one program varied around one thousand rupees (or US$80). Outdated or traditional technologies are used. There are high profit margins, and many available jobs. Classical unemployment is unknown. There is a pattern of non-institutional credit, with cash being in constant demand, no advertising, and no bookkeeping. While good management facilitates larger profits, it is not essential for a business to survive. Obsolete transport powered by both animals and men is used, and poor quality equipment and recycled commodities are prevalent.

Cash Economics

The spread of monetary commerce makes squatter areas cash economies. There are no checking accounts. Small denominations of currency are necessary, but scarce. Storekeepers will bargain hard in order to end the day with the types of currency that are least available. As the capital is in circulation, little of it can be accumulated, so the poor remain poor.

Cash primes the credit pump and then keeps the mechanism "lubricated" through its function as a means of payment.

The major obstacle to the acquisition of capital, however, remains the need to pay accounts on fixed dates. The rules of the upper circuit-banking sector are incompatible with those controlling the lower circuit. People turn to more flexible wholesalers and moneylenders—the middlemen.

Middlemen

With their access to bank credit, middlemen are an integral aspect in this economy playing a privileged and strategic linkage role. The middleman furnishes credit in goods or cash, operating as a wholesaler with connections to the upper circuit and the ability to store large quantities of stock. The poorer an individual, the more dependent he is on this middleman.

Credit

This is essential to entrepreneurs and consumers, but leads to an increased indebtedness at all levels. Thus usury becomes generalized. A lack of money supply in the lower sector necessitates credit, increasing the rapidity of monetary circulation.

Credit for the poor consumer is possible through this lower circuit trade. This trade also breaks up goods into small quantities within the budget of the poor.

Bank accounts and entrepreneurial credit are available to wholesalers and middlemen but not to artisans and small-scale businesses. People involved in these small-scale activities cannot offer enough guarantees, cannot pay bills on time, and would lose all if they defaulted. Hence the banks turn to wholesalers, who then extend a flexible credit to the smaller businesses, which is mutually advantageous. The loans are flexible. If the poor cannot pay, debt may be extended. Neither party wishes to lose the mutually advantageous relationship. To cover such loans, the further one goes down the economic ladder, the shorter becomes the duration of the loan, and the higher the risks and interest rates.

CATEGORIES OF URBAN POVERTY

Level	Housing	Employment	Social Issues	Nutrition
0	Good.	Several in family have work.	Stable family. Reasonable social ethics.	Basic food.
1	Decaying tenements Inner city slums.	Poverty level. Stable work. No catastrophes.	Broken family & social structure.	1st degree malnutrition.
2	Bustees, Squatters, Favelas.	Employed but below poverty level.	Orphan, Widow, Handicapped.	2nd degree malnutrition.
3	Relocation areas. Refugee camps.	Occasional work. Professional begger.	Deliquent, Drop-out.	3rd degree malnutrition.
4	On streets. No house.	Unemployed.	Addicts. Alcoholics.	

Effects of inflation

Deflation does not benefit workers. Inflation is no better, for it acts as a mechanism to exploit the poor, increasing prices faster than wages. But it increases employment in the lower circuit. And it benefits homeowners in the slums.

Comparing levels of poverty

These complexities in the nature of poverty, caused by or resulting in deprivation in several areas of life, make it difficult to compare poverty between cities.

The chart on the next page is an attempt to understand four of the above categories of poverty in any city. Any number of combinations from different columns are possible.

Any family could be classified on a scale that is the sum of the four variables at the different levels. For example: a bustee family in Calcutta that has a small industry and is stable would rate 2+0+0+1=3, while a dropout on the streets of L.A. may rate 4+4+4+1=13, even though he has more money in relative and real terms. Perhaps one should add in a measure of opportunity (a factor that could be defined by its relationship to the economic growth rate of a city).

This kind of analysis, while it should not be allowed to consume inordinate amounts of time in excessive surveys, does give indications of which groups of poor may be more reachable, responsive, and able to be discipled within the resources of the city and the mission. Each area of poverty must be addressed.

A study of 50 categories of poor in Calcutta

Calcutta provides a situation where all forms of poverty and of response can be seen. The following are several groups of poor in this city that require Christian response. The responses listed here are responses to their poverty. If a church were to be planted among any one of these groups, it would have to address these economic issues in the process of its maturing and discipling of these poor.

1. Pavement-dwellers

There were officially 48,000 at the last census. These 48,000 were found to be: permanent (45.6%), migrants (such as those intending to return home, 18.5%), seasonal (24.1%), regular visitors (for odd jobs or business, 4.5%), casual visitors (4.7%), and others (2.6%). 66.5 percent cook on the pavement. 36.5 percent eat once a day, 52.1 percent eat twice a day.[15]

These 48,000 may be also considered in terms of their occupations: beggars/on charity (22.0%), casual day-laborers (23.4%), thelawala or hand-cart puller (6.5%), rickshawala or rickshaw puller (7.3%), hawkers (3.1%), paper/ragpickers (4.8%), regular day laborers (8.6%), vegetable sellers (3.6%), maid-servants (4.2%), and others (16.5%).[16]

Further classification may be made in terms of deviant behavior, such as delinquents, criminals, prostitutes and street gangs; or of special cases such as street children (orphans, deserted or runaways), the blind, lame, deaf, dumb, leprosy patients, older widows, and deserted women.

Responses to this diversity of needs may include emergency relief (such as food, medicine or clothing), short-term rehabilitation or long-term rehabilitation. Short-term rehabilitation focuses on employment, because poor people need work more urgently than they need accommodation, or anything else. Short-term rehabilitation programs may thus provide specialized training to upgrade skills, vocational and non-formal education to street children, and perhaps shelters for *rickshawalas, thelawalas,* and day-laborers. Sometimes a local social club can become a starting point to assist people with solutions to their problems of survival. Long-term rehabilitation in Calcutta and the region surrounding the city includes the development of rural agriculture, the establishment of cottage industries, and the formation of a government planning committee to focus on this problem by creating any necessary legislation and by influencing public opinion.

2. Refugee colonies

These embrace a population of about 500,000 (CMDA, 1981), and include government-sponsored colonies, squatter colonies, and private colonies. The responses should be similar to those of the bustees below, with the proviso that unemployment is greater in the refugee colonies.

3. Squatter areas and bustees

The residents in squatter areas and bustees are either of a permanent type (with potential land rights or legal tenancy) or of a temporary nature (with no land rights or tenancy possible). They may live on unneeded government land, on government land needed for development, on private land with tenancy contracts, or on private land that they illegally occupy. In any of the above cases, the responses would be the same:

a. Government legislation to secure land rights;

b. Slum upgrading, sites and services, environmental development;

c. Development of small-scale and cooperative industries using low-interest loans;

d. Development of community organizations to enable the people to tackle their various problems;

e. Vocational training; and

f. Preventative medical work.

4. Overcrowded downtown multistoried housing

Responses to this situation would probably include re-housing the people in middle-class developments in suburban areas or inner-city redevelopment.

5. Oppressed workers and servants

To help oppressed workers, trade unions need to be developed, Christian businessmen and professionals encouraged to get involved, and forums planned to consider issues of justice for workers.

6. Women in oppressed roles

Responses could include a publicity campaign for change of values and the focusing of women's organizations on specific issues.

7. Oppressed minority groups

Among oppressed minority groups are Muslims, the Anglo community, lower-caste people, certain traditional (but no longer useful) trades groups, the disabled, the aged, and widows. For these, an adequate response would include one or more of the following: permanent welfare programs, specialized schools, retraining in useful trades or professions, and psychological reorientation to God's perspective on their status.

Notes

1. Moorehouse, Geoffrey, *Calcutta,* Penguin Books, 1984.

2. Ganguly, Tapash, "Pains of an Obese City," *The Week,* Nov 17-23, 1985.

3. Calcutta Metropolitan Planning Organization, *A Report on the Survey of 10,000 Pavement Dwellers in Calcutta: Under the Shadow of the Metropolis— they are citizens too,* Sudhendu Muukherjee, ed., 1973.

4. Grigg, Viv, *Companion to the Poor,* Waynesboro, Georgia: Authentic, 2005.

5. Moorehouse, *Calcutta.*

6. Wilson, Samuel, *Unreached Peoples 1982,* Monrovia, California: MARC, World Vision International, 1982.

7. Pentecost, Edward C., *Reaching the Unreached,* Fuller School of World Missions thesis, Pasadena, 1979.

8. Paredes, Tito, ed., *PROMIES Directorio Evangelico: Lima, Callao y Balnearios,* Concilio Nacional Evangelico del Peru, 1986.

9. Mar, Matos, *Desborde Popular y Crisis del Estado,* Institute de Estudios Peruanos, 1986.

10. Abrams, C, Man's *Struggle for Shelter in an Urbanizing World,* Boston: MIT Press, 1964.

11. Lewis, Oscar, "The Possessions of the Poor," *Cities: Their Origin, Growth and Human Impact, Readings from Scientific American,* San Francisco: W.H. Freeman and Co, 1973.

12. Arnauld, Jacques, "Urban Nutrition: Motor or Brake for Rural Development? The Latin American Case." *Ceres,* Mar–Apr 1983.

13. Decaestekker, Donald Denise, *Impoverished Filipino Families,* Manila: UST, 1978.

14. This section based on Santos, Milton, *The Shared Space,* tr. from Portuguese by Chris Gerry, London and New York: Methuen, 1979.

15. Calcutta Metropolitan Planning Organization, *A Report on the Survey of 10,000 Pavement Dwellers in Calcutta: Under the Shadow of the Metropolis— they are citizens too,* Sudhendu Muukherjee, ed., 1973.

16. Ibid, table 8.

Chapter Four

Who Made Us Poor?

Slum children
Longing for a piece of bread,
Abandoned,
No-one reaching them, touching them:
Broken homes,
Lack of love,
Slum billions needing a Saviour.
Go, live down, among,
Proclaim Calvary's love song:
Salvation of the suffering . . .
Lies in him.
For in him the structures
of the mega-cities integrate.

The same kind of analysis with which we looked at the conditions of poverty may be applied as well to its causes. Gunnar Myrdahl's *Asian Drama* suggests twenty-nine categories in which he defines macro-level causes.[1] Michael Harrington suggested other causes in his analysis that sparked the "War on Poverty" in the United States.[2] Both of these lead us to theories concerning the causes of urban poverty at micro and macro levels.

The worker among the poor must be conversant with the range of causes and types of poverty. At the same time, he or she must somehow not be overly preoccupied with analysis beyond that which facilitates effective non-destructive action. This chapter seeks to present some of the major patterns of thinking that have emerged concerning the squatters.

Myrdahl drew heavily on Max Weber's lifetime monumental works. They are perhaps the most useful source for an analysis of the relationships of poverty, culture, and religion. The religious-cultural roots are apparent when contrasting the general levels of poverty between poor Catholic areas of the world and those with significant Protestant inputs or those of Hindu background. His works are important as one looks at poverty in any given city.[3]

But the church planter must not only deal with these religio-cultural causes. International patterns of urban poverty have their roots in places other than local religious values, as has been seen. These causes also require responses. Within the broader context of Western modernization and its correlated urbanization, a number of theories of poverty, explanations of causes, and identification of potential solutions have been developed. None is complete. Each situation requires a model and response appropriate to the factors that impinge on it.

Poor of the city, or city of the poor?

Louis Wirth, building on Weber, defines the industrial city as one that is "achievement-oriented and prizes a rationally-oriented economic system. It is predominantly a middle-class city."[4]

But within the Third World city are the pockets of migrant poor we call squatters, often known as "peasants in cities." They make up from 20-90 percent of the urban population, and many are now second or third generation residents of the city. But are they seen as part of this middle-class modern city? Are they a people in their own right with a separate identity from middle-class city people? Are they the poor of the city or are the cities, cities of the poor? How do squatters, poverty, and the city relate to each other?

Squatters, poverty, and cities

Let us turn more specifically to our target communities of squatters. Early approaches to the study of the squatters viewed them negatively. Later approaches developed which perceived them positively and developed themes of self-improvement and acculturation of "peasants in the city." These were in conflict with the negative problem-solving, city-planner approach which saw squatters as a blight on city planning and political stability.

Later approaches derive from a concept of culture in transition. The city-planner approach has an inherent dual-level perspective on the city. McTaggart[5] highlights these issues of social dialectics in the city. Others developed the theme of "marginality"—people on the margins of society and power.

1. The acculturation theme

Generally, squatters are viewed as a manifestation of urbanization and modernization processes. In spite of distortions, squatter areas provide necessary social and economic functions. They continue to exist because they meet the needs of the poor and provide a place for adaptation to the culture of the city. This is known as the acculturation process. Squatter areas become a zone of transition from peasant society to urban. This perception minimizes the problem of conflict between dual economic and social systems in the same city. It perceives them as providing a cushion and geographic stability.

The degree of acculturation is dependent on local conditions and is neutralized by physical and environmental disorder or difficult relationships to bureaucracy.

Within this school of thought numerous studies have been developed about mechanisms of adaptation to the "transitional" society. A typical path followed by the migrants is outlined by Meister:

a. The individual brings from the country the sum total of standards and values that prevail in his own environment and clings to the same traditions in town.

b. The new mode of life and rural values clash. The migrant fails to find steady work. The children fall under the influence of other displaced urban children; the father loses control and former values are repudiated. With heavy drinking and desertion, the family unit disintegrates.

c. The migrant comes to accept urban life. He has some job successes and begins to develop urban goals in terms of desirable places to live, consumer goods preferences, and begins to participate in formal groups. Although some migrants adapt by delinquency, and others through participation and leadership in migrant development programs, it is important to emphasize that in most cases, there is successful urban adaptation.

McCreary[6] summarizes discussion on the experience in Oceania, following the same lines. First, there is loss of direct contact with indigenous social controls and missions influence, and a non-acceptance of responsibility for collateral kin. The extended family loses its supportive function, although kinship networks continue to function, placing additional strain on traditional values. A new urban social structure develops, with the mother moving into the center of the family and the father becoming a declining figure. Youth form marginal groups and tend to lose direction. Disorientation at the personal level is expressed in delinquency, violence, prostitution, and excessive drinking.[7]

2. Poor peoples' perspective

Anthropological studies tend to be more sympathetic to the views of the poor than do those of sociologists or planners. Ethnographs such as Jocano's *Slums as a Way of Life* show how squatters perceive their lifestyles as positively and gradually integrating into the city, yet not without turmoil and breakdown.[8]

Dominique LaPierre's *City of Joy* tells of a priest's longing for his people to return to the romantic countryside. Eventually a couple does return, only to be brought back to the city and to reality when they lose all to a typhoon.[9]

The poor will not go back. This indicates how they feel about their lives in the city. They are hooked. For all of the deprivations and depravity, they are better off. They have hope. They have access to health and education for their children. They are city dwellers, urbanites who no longer fit back in the home town. They have come from being hopeless, landless farm laborers. They are moving into the city of gold. The momentary problems of the slums can be suffered for such a glorious dream—even for a generation or two.

3. John Turner's self-improvement model

Growing out of a sympathetic understanding of the squatters and the reality of limited finances governmentally for housing programs, squatter areas are seen as providing a context for self-improvement housing. These meet the standards of the squatters but not the unrealistic housing standards of the bureaucrats that telescope the development process and require high finance.[10]

This approach leads to flexible, progressive development, with minimal use of government finances or expansion of government bureaucracy—encouraging an optimum use of resources. The approach of self-help housing for the poor has grown from this conceptual view.

Dwyer, while sympathetic to this approach, criticizes its omission of the cost and alternative-use aspects of land.[11] This is quite a reasonable position for a professor in Hong Kong, where island land use is at a premium. In the deserts of Lima, it ceases to be an issue. There, we find some of the most extensive and successful examples of self-developed communities. There are mixed analyses of the extent to which self-improvement occurs, and these tend to be determined by the geographical and historical relationships that have emerged in each city.

4. *Slums as a problem*

Despite a sympathetic anthropological approach, Oscar Lewis agrees with Juppenlatz's perception of the slum as a place where poor people live in subnormal conditions.[12] This view is predominant among policy makers. Slum dwellers are perceived as people who flout the law and live in areas that are unsanitary, fire hazards, and full of crime—barriers to development that can paralyze city planning.

This perspective results in forced relocation. To help them is to condone illegal behavior. The squatter is not perceived as going through acculturation to socially acceptable behavior. Instead, he is perceived as being exposed to continual erosion of family control, of community and traditions, accompanied by loss of identity and importance. The result is social disorganization, chaos, crime, and prostitution.

5. *Class conflict and social dualism*

Squatters are inevitably pushed into a political situation of class conflict by the unsympathetic approaches of the city bureaucracy. McTaggart talks of the squatter areas as being the "anti-system" that soften the blows of socio-economic dualism.[13]

Oscar Lewis developed the concepts of duality of Lampman[14] and Harrington[15] into the *culture of poverty* thesis.[16] His analysis set the stage for a concept of dual cultural systems within the city. Portes views the matter less from a cultural perspective and more from a social analysis of structures, explaining that the aspect of self-help is dependent on strong *social cohesion* resulting from long conflict.[17] It is the dialectics (going back and forth between two extremes) of the system, the official hostility and opposition to squatter activity, that is a prerequisite for self-improving elements to emerge.

Alinsky develops this concept of cause and effect into a mandate to increase tension at points of conflict in order to effect change.[18] And indeed, this thesis finds general acceptance in most literature built around class-conflict theories.

As Christians, we immediately are aware of ethical problems with this pattern of thinking. It directly contrasts with the reconciliation the gospel offers to conflicting groups. We should be aware, however, that many social workers among the poor, both Catholic and Protestant, have this as their underlying framework.

The class-conflict thesis is not vindicated by research on relationships between squatters and the urban middle and upper classes. Research by Hollensteiner, Laquian, and others in Southeast Asia shows a strong relationship between the poor and the middle and upper classes, upon whom squatters depend for patronage.[19] There is no strong sense of antipathy between the two classes.

Class conflict theory predicts the squatter as being potentially radicalized. This is not evident in first generation squatters. It may be with their children and grandchildren—second and third generation squatters. In Brazil, for example, there has never been a revolt or insurrection from a favela, despite the violence of the *marginales* in the favelas.

Squatters tend to be conservative, not revolutionary. They are too absorbed in problems of survival and of their own security to be interested in anything else. Laquian, Mangin, Turner, and others confirm this, associating squatters with the conservative ideologies of the *petit bourgeousie*.[20] Lack of a revolutionary spirit is also the result of their rural conservative roots.

While we do not observe a generalized conflict between classes in Third World cities, there are localized and limited conflicts between squatters and landowners over the legitimacy of squatter land rights. Christian responses are essential. They are extensions of a theology of reconciliation in the context of defending the poor against injustice.

6. Political participation

Squatters soon learn that exerting pressure on the political system is to their advantage. Even where they have no legal voting rights, they can bring strong pressure to bear through community organizations. Political opportunism and symbiosis are part of the ethos of the slums. On the other hand, often the power of the landowning elite neutralizes any pressure squatters might try to exercise.

Politicians have little choice in these cities. They are faced with both conflict and chaos or with securing cooperation between upper and lower classes—rich and poor. This cooperation enables gradual development, utilizing the resources of the poor and, to a large extent, according to the desires of the poor. Political wisdom can lead cities away from conflict, marginality, or other extremes developed from the dialectic philosophies mentioned above.

7. Marginality

While the classes in the city are not necessarily in conflict nor totally separate, the rift between them leads to the squatter being viewed as a citizen of the city but denied all the rights of the city. Thus squatters can only become marginally productive—culturally, socially, and economically.

Park used the term "marginality" to refer to cultural hybrids—people living on the margin of two cultures and societies.[21] Cuber spoke of "those who occupy a peripheral position between two unrelated cultural structures, complexes, or units."[22]

This perspective juxtaposes the problem of poverty and the variable rates of modernization within a society. Joan Nelson asks three questions: Do the urban poor recognize themselves as marginal? Is the urban poor population a surplus from an economic point of view? Or rather, have they been prevented from economic participation?[23]

Andre Gunder Frank comments, "These poor are not socially marginal but rejected, not economically marginal but exploited, and not politically marginal but repressed."[24]

The sheer size of the populations of the urban poor in cities like Lima or Calcutta mitigates against this marginality thesis. As John Maust comments, "No longer is it accurate to call the newcomers and slum-dwellers 'marginalized.' Rather than being on the fringes of Lima society, they have become the majority."[25]

8. Modernization and marginality

McGee understands that there is a relationship between the degree of modernization in a city and the marginalization of the squatter economic system. As a city modernizes, squatters become less marginal, that is, more integrated, and there is a greater degree of justice. In other words, the faster the rate of modernization in a city, the shorter amount of time a migrant spends in "transition."[26]

Johnstone, along the same lines, defines various cities into three categories:

a. Those such as Hong Kong and Singapore, where rapid industrialization predicts continuing uplift and integration of the squatter communities.

b. A second group such as Manila or Bangkok, where the gross national product is rising and urbanization is rapid, and yet there are institutional problems to hinder progress. Here older settlements will become integrated, and newer and structurally unstable ones have the potential in time for uplift.

c. A third group, where there is economic stagnation, such as in Saigon, Calcutta and Lima. Here there is a far larger dualism, a traditional *bazaar* economy, and potential conflict.[27]

Interestingly, of the ten cities surveyed in this book, Bangkok and Sao Paulo are two of the most modernized, industrialized and prosperous cities in the Third World. Squatters are integrated into the work force with high levels of employment. Economically they become well off, with high levels of comfort in their squatter homes. But in both these cities, land-rights laws preclude ownership and self-help upgrading of the areas of slums.

In Lima or Calcutta, where there is economic stagnation, the majority of the populations are squatters. These cities have almost entirely become the slum. The poor are city-dwellers with rights, and there is social integration (if the continuance of caste can be considered a form of social integration).

Obviously the issue of social integration is more complex than the macro-economic condition of the city. Land rights are a major factor. The size of the city and percentage of squatters is another. Prevailing cultural patterns and historical experiences are also involved.

Some personal observations may be included here from walking through these cities. Where industrialization has increased more rapidly, there is a lower percentage of slum population. Smaller cities have a lower percentage of urban poor in the city. Cities in tribal societies have a higher percentage of urban poor because tribal peoples take more time to make the cultural and technological transition needed when entering urban society. Capitalism is significantly better for the poor than a Marxist society. This last statement has been adequately argued by Peter Berger.[28]

9. Economic dualism

There are economic theories built on dualistic perspectives. Geertz differentiated between two economies in the modern Third World city, the *firm-centered economy* and the *bazaar economy*.[29] In the late 1960s and early 1970s, the World Bank and United

Nations-related agencies talked freely of *formal* and *informal* sectors.

Perhaps Santos' well-documented study is a zenith of these economic analyses. Santos defines his thesis this way:

> At a national level, new economic demands are superimposed over existing "traditional" ones. The economic system is thus forced to accommodate both new and inherited social realities, and faces the need for dynamic modernization. This applies equally to the productive and distributive systems. Two economic circuits are created, responsible not only for the economic process, but also the process of spatial organization.
>
> The upper circuit is the direct result of technological progress and its most representative elements are the monopolies. Most of its relations take place outside of the city and the surrounding area and operate in a national or international framework.[30]

Santos defines the lower circuit economy as:

> The maintenance alongside the modern circuit, of a non-modem economic circuit consisting of small-scale manufacturing and crafts, small-scale trade and many varied services.[31]

It is not independent of the upper circuit, however, but locked into it in a relationship of cause and effect. This thesis clearly is dualistic in basic premise, and Santos does not seek to define these as two poles of a spectrum but as two separate systems. In his native Sao Paulo, his analysis might be accurate. In other cities, the patterns may not be as clearly dualistic. My own experience would be that more affluent cities tend to have a clearer differential between upper and lower circuits.

In Calcutta, for example, where the percentage participation of the labor force has fallen from 67 percent in 1901 to 37 percent in 1971, one may talk of two circuits. But the lower circuit takes on the role of the significant economic circuit in terms of the numbers of residents employed in it. This lower circuit, or informal sector, accounted for 82 percent of economic units and 30 percent of the employment in 1971.[32]

McGee has a theory about the self-inflationary nature of the lower circuit. A continual influx of people creates an expanding market. The division of labor within the lower circuit stimulates the productive use of capital and the speed of transactions, thus raising profits. The lower circuit creates its own service sector.[33]

In a context where there is decay and retraction in the upper circuit, such as in Calcutta or Lima, we would expect a similar lack of growth in the lower circuit. People in the lower circuit, unable to provide services to people in the dwindling upper circuit, have to make an income by providing services to others within their own impoverished circuit. The number of hours worked, however, must increase to make the same income. The number of transactions must also increase. As a city becomes more and more impoverished, it also becomes a hive of increasingly useless and rapid activity.

Notes

1. Myrdahl, Gunnar, *Asian Drama: An Inquiry into the Poverty of the Nations,* 1968

2. Harrington, Michael, *The Other America: Poverty in the United States,* Penguin, 1965.

3. Weber, Max, *The City,* New York: The Free Press, 1958; and *The Protestant Work Ethic and the Spirit of Capitalism,* tr Talcott Parsons, London: Unwin.

4. Wirth, Louis, "Urbanism as a Way of Life," *American Journal of Sociology,* Vol. 44:1–24, July 1938.

5. McTaggart, W.D., "Squatters' Rights or the Context of a Problem," *Professional Geographer* 23(4), October 1971, pp 335–359.

6. Meister, A., "The Urbanization Crisis of Rural Man," *Ceres,* 1970.

7. McCreary, J.R., "Urbanization in the South Pacific," *Living in Town: Problems and Priorities in Urban Planning in the South Pacific,* John Harre ed., Suva,

Fiji: South Pacific Social Sciences Foundation and School of Social and Economic Development, University of the South Pacific, 1973.

8. Jocano, F. Landa, *Slums As A Way of Life,* Manila: New Day Publishers, Box 167, Quezon City 3008, 1975.

9. LaPierre, Dominique, *City of Joy,* Doubleday, 1985.

10. Turner, John F., "Barriers and Channels for Housing Development in Modernizing Countries," *Peasants in Cities,* W. Mangin ed, Boston: Houghton Mifflin, 1970

11. Dwyer, D.J., *The City as Centre of Change in Asia,* Hong Kong: University Press, 1972.

12. Juppenlatz, Morris, *Cities in Transformation,* University of Queensland Press, 1970.

13. McTaggart, W.D., "Squatter's Rights."

14. Lampman, Robert V., *Poverty: Four Approaches, Four Solutions,* Eugene, Oregon: University of Oregon Press, 1966.

15. Harrington, Michael, *The Other America.*

16. Lewis, Oscar, "The Culture of Poverty," *Scientific American,* Vol. 215, No. 4: 3–9, October 1966.

17. Portes, A., The Urban Slum in Chile: Types and Correlates," *Land Economics,* Vol 47(3) 1971, pp 235–247.

18. Alinsky, Saul, *Reveille for Radicals,* New York: Vintage Books, 1969.

19. Laquian, A. A., *Slums Are For People,* East-West Centre Press, 1971.

20. Mangin, William, "Squatter Settlements," *Scientific American,* Vol. 217 No. 4, October 1967, pp.21–29; and *Peasants in Cities: Readings in Anthropology of Urbanization,* Boston: Houghton Mifflin, 1970.

21. Park, Robert E., "Human Migration and the Marginal Man," *American Journal of Sociology,* Vol. 33, no.6, May 1928, pp 881–3.

22. Cuber, John F., "Marginal Church Participants," *Sociology and Social Research,* Vol. XXV, No 1, 1940, pp. 57–62.

23. Nelson, Joan, "The Urban Poor: Disruption or Political Integration in Third World Cities," *World Politics Vol.* 22, 1969, pp. 393–414.

24. Frank, Andre Gunder, *The Sociology of Underdevelopment or the Underdevelopment of Sociology,* paper, 1974.

25. Maust, John, *Cities of Change,* Latin American Mission, 1984.

26. McGee, T.G., *The Southeast Asian City,* London: Bell and Son, 1967; and *The Urbanization Process in the Third World,* London: Bell and Son, 1971.

27. Johnstone, Michael A., "Squatter Settlements in Southeast Asia—An Overview," *Working Papers on Comparative Sociology* #5, University of

Auckland, Dept. of Sociology, 1975.

28. Berger, Peter, *The Capitalist Revolution: Fifty Propositions About Prosperity, Equality and Liberty,* New York: Perseus Books, 1988.

29. Geertz, Clifford, *Peddlars and Princes: Social Change and Economic Modernization in Two Indonesian Towns,* Chicago, 1963.

30. Santos, Milton, *The Shared Space,* tr from Portuguese by Chris Gerry, London and New York: Methuen, 1979.

31. Ibid.

32. Sivaramakrishnan, K.C., "The Slum Improvement Programme in Calcutta: The Role of the CMDA," *In the Indian City,* Alfred de Souza, ed., Manohar Publications, 2 Ansari Road, Daryaganj, New Delhi,110002, 1978.

33. McGee, *The Urbanization Process in the Third World.*

Chapter Five

International Causes of Urban Poverty

As Jane Jacobs points out from a secular point of view, there are powers at work today beyond our control creating these great mega-cities. "It seems as though some force is bent upon transmuting multi-city nations with very different histories, populations and geographical sizes into something resembling city-states—that is states overwhelmingly dominated by single city regions and their cities."[1]

One of the ultimate results of international political and economic structures is the spawning of the slums with all their chaos, tears and bawdiness. They are the final result of all of the major powers that have come to dominate the world in the last decades—urbanization, technology, industrialization, modernization, capitalism, multinationals, nationalism, colonialism, the United Nations, World Bank—all are what the Scriptures call powers that have contributed to the process.

Dependency theories

As we discussed in chapter two, there is a historical pattern of industrial development beginning in an outpost of an empire, and developing into an industrial mega-city that exploits the wealth of the city's hinterland. This pattern has led to what is commonly known as dependency relationships between Third World cities and Western cities.

Changes caused by the demonstration effect between Western cities and their Third World dependents result in changes in balance of trade. Modernization is dependent on imported capital goods. Third World cities then have three paths open for continued industrialization: import substitution (local production) of imported goods for domestic consumption; export of a percent of national minerals and agricultural production to pay for more imports; or manufacturing sectors set up to produce exclusively for developed countries, providing finance to pay for more imports.

1. Substitute imports

Historically, the primary means of growth for industrial cities was the process of copying and producing imported goods within the city itself, and then exporting these to other cities of the same or smaller size. In modern times, this process changes the nature of the imported goods. Production requires the technology and tools of production. As a result, the manufacture of new products creates further dependency on the already modernized nations that provide the technology and tools. Since Third World cities lack the capacity to generate these tools and technology needed for the new products, they must be imported. These tools have a high capital cost.

Import substitution thus requires increased dependence on imports. The developed countries profit at every point. Jane Jacobs indicates that the way to break this pattern is to trade with other underdeveloped cities.[2] But existing dependency relationships between former colonies and their ex-colonist country prevent this.

2. Export raw materials and industrial goods

The second option is to increase export of raw materials. But this leads to tragedies like the rape of the forests in India and the Himalayas for sale abroad. The consequence is extensive flooding, an increasing loss of good farmland through soil erosion, and the destruction of the delicate balance between forest and farmland.

Exacerbating this problem is the relatively slow increase in agricultural prices (an almost linear increase) in contrast with the exponential rise in the price of industrial goods.

3. Set up manufacturing sectors to produce goods for developed countries

A third option is to develop industrial areas for the production of goods specifically for export to modernized countries. To create such industries is not to industrialize, since they so often do not become part of the host country's development program.

Furthermore, export-oriented commerce leads to concentration and monopoly that benefit multinational corporations. The future under such conditions is frightening: "In a generation 400 to 500 international corporations will own two-thirds of the world's fixed assets."

The positive result is transfer of capital and technology to the developed countries. The negative is that, "Underdeveloped countries merely represent the land on which the seeds of foreign capital bear fruit; however the fruit is sent back along with most of the seed to the metropolis."[3]

The country becomes more and more dependent as goods pour into a stunted and unsatisfied internal market. These expenditures result in a growing need to export, but under continually deteriorating terms of trade because industrial goods continue to increase in value faster than agricultural goods or earlier industrial goods. To pay the bills, the country reduces the value of its currency and Third World industrialization begins to be linked to the developed countries' import needs rather than to local needs. The result is dependence.

Santos comments, "We will be working in a situation of bankrupt economies with running inflation, countries that will not significantly develop further into industrialization because of the worldwide economic trends, dependency on the West, repayments of economies of other settlements."[4]

Mediating role of the banks

Foreign banks prefer to focus on high turnover trade activities, including trade in agricultural products. They operate within the export-oriented sectors of the society. Since few local businesses can satisfy the requirements for loans, the banks tend to loan to multinationals. This fosters a flow of credit from rural to urban to overseas and discourages local initiative.

Role of the government

National governments are relatively powerless to deal with growing international dependency. They are often dwarfed by the multinationals and are as dependent on them as they are on the foreign cities.

The State is weakened in three ways: first, it becomes incapable of independent decision-making because of foreign dependence and collusion with the monopolies; second, it becomes handicapped by increased debt and reduction in its investment capacity, forcing it to limit investment in certain sectors; finally, the State in its role as an investor finds itself less and less able to orient the country towards maximum growth and authentic national development. Under these circumstances, it is hardly surprising that the State is allowed to take increasingly authoritarian steps towards the establishment of a strong, even military, government without fear of outside intervention from the supporters of monopolies and multinationals.

A new international order

In response to an increasing understanding of these issues, the NEIO (New Economic International Order) concept emerged in 1974 at the Sixth Special Session of the United Nations. There, Third World nations (known as the "Group of 77") joined to express their opposition to the prevailing international economic system, which they claimed was unfair to their interests. Leaders of the Group of 77 were instrumental in the Sixth Special Session's adopting a declaration for the establishment of the NEIO.

Julius Nyerere, former President of Tanzania and one of the most vocal Third World leaders, described the Group of 77 as a "trade union of the poor."[5] It represents many of the 141 African, Asian, and Latin American countries that belong to the United Nations and are defined as the Third World. Containing 70 percent of the world's population, the Third World commands together no more than 12 percent of the gross world product. Eighty percent of the world's trade and investment, 93 percent of the world's industry, and almost 100 percent of the world's research is controlled, in the words of Barbara Ward, "by the industrial rich."[6]

It is the very system, the proponents of the NEIO argue, that must be restructured. Historical wrongs must be righted, wealth must be transferred from rich to poor, and developing countries must be given far more voice and power in the world.

The dispute between these two blocs of poor and rich nations—the latter being the United States, the European Economic Community and Japan—has continued now for conference after conference, with little to give the poor nations hope. They are trapped in an emerging world urbanization controlled increasingly from a few powerful cities in the West and North, linked by global technologies, dominated by a few multinational corporations and banks.

Macro-economic development and slums

The consequence of dependency and these processes of modernization is the emergence of slums and squatter areas. The implications for a ministry to the poor are obvious. One may work extensively for the uplift of the urban poor through spiritual transformation, and this is primary. But the issues of unemployment, macro-level oppression, and economic injustice in the fabric of the society must be dealt with at that level for the eventual freedom of the poor from their bondage.

Thus we may work hard to uplift the poor in the local community and completely fail, for the critical factor in terms of job production is primarily determined by the macro-economic development of the city.

A biblical response to urban oppression

What is a Christian response to these issues? What does it mean to walk with the God of justice in these cities? How do we manifest his love? An awareness of such oppression must be the foundation of any theology to deal with the issues of the urban poor. As Hugo Assman states, "We are beginning to realize what we are in history: not merely underdeveloped peoples in the sense of 'not yet sufficiently developed,' but 'peoples kept in a state of underdevelopment': dominated and oppressed peoples—which is a very different thing."[7]

Interestingly, oppression is a basic structural category of biblical theology. In a biblical word study in the Old Testament, Thomas Hanks concludes that, "Oppression is viewed as the basic cause of poverty (164 texts). In the case of the other 15 to 20 causes for poverty indicated in the Old Testament the linguistic link is much less frequent—not more than 20 times."[8]

In the New Testament, James places himself firmly in the ranks of the prophets who viewed oppression as the basic reason for poverty (James 2:1–7; 5:1–6). Never does he blame the poor, attributing their poverty because of racial inferiority, laziness, vices, or other reasons. The rich bear the guilt because they exploit and oppress.

To recognize oppression as the basic cause of poverty implies the need of a corresponding Christian response. At the core of any response to such oppression is the development of communities of the kingdom in these slums.

Movements at the grassroots are a key to long-term change. As the church has through history, we must reach the victims of oppression. In the process we will generate life that will transform the oppression itself. Parallel to these movements must be movements among the educated political-military elite who rule the nations.

A just urbanization

As a Christian responding to injustices within the urbanization process, I am affirming some moral views:

1. A transition from a two-level economic and social system to a unitary system is a desirable goal (based on the principle of being our brother's keeper, of reconciliation between peoples, of the equality of people before God).

2. Modernization is a desirable and biblical goal (based on the mandate to manage the earth).

3. Urbanization is a desirable goal, for God is a community and seeks community. Scripture begins in a garden but ends in a city. Although there is conflict between the city of Babylon and the city of Jerusalem in the Scriptures, we may still affirm there is a godly pattern of urbanization implied in the Bible.

4. Something similar to a middle-class lifestyle is a just goal (derived from the principle of every family having enough for their needs and development).

5. Each family has the right to own its own land and to have a place of security.

6. The flow of economic wealth from farm to the city is a result of the fruitfulness of the earth, and is a good process, but such a process requires justice at every step.

There are theological reasons for such assumptions that will require another book. Sufficient has been said, however, to indicate that our role is to move with these processes, apply the

Scriptures to them, modify negative effects of change, and bring positive change with a human face that reflects the face of God. At every step, we must seek just and fair processes, structures, and relationships.

Given this positive attitude towards urbanization and the reality that today's urbanization creates squatter settlements, the question for us as Christians is how to bring justice into the process of peasants migrating to the city.

The primary step is to establish churches—communities of the kingdom among these poor. But as we form churches, we are to respond to spiritual, cultural, economic, and justice issues from thoughtful biblical perspectives and deep levels of understanding about the nature of poverty in the slums and squatter areas.

Justice is a grand theme to evoke positive emotions and elect politicians. But in reality, it involves thousands of little acts accumulating into processes and systems and relationships that are felt by the participants to be right and fair.

The application of this aspect of justice in understanding the urban poor in a city is to think of a "just urbanization gradient"—of increasing levels of integration into the city from the rural peasant or tribal background. This would involve increasing levels of integration into the culture of the city, the economics of the city, the legal and institutional structures of the city, the social relationships of the city—in short, into the power of the city.

In some cities, migrants go through a more gradual process of integration. In others, there is an abrupt barrier between two economic classes, caused by the inability of the poor to obtain work and rights to the land on which they are squatting. Specific legislation and controls by the rich may also create such an environment.

For example, we may contrast Mexico City with Bangkok. In Mexico City, the law of the land does not permit a Mexican to be homeless in his own country. Within a year of invading an area of land in Mexico City, the *paracaidistas* (who descend on the land as if by parachute) are usually able to gain some initial legal basis towards land rights. The result is that people build good houses, requiring good building materials, requiring someone to supply them, producing more jobs. There is a gradual integration into the city.

While there are injustices, it is a reasonably just city compared with Bangkok, where slum dwellers may obtain rights to their land after seven years—unless their shacks are burned down. Fire is the main fear of the squatters in Bangkok. And it is a favorite pastime of rich landowners. Consequently, there is no incentive to develop these areas. Fortunately, the economy of Bangkok, for other reasons, is growing, providing work for migrants. But a two-tiered society has emerged.

Transitional phase or permanent?

This raises the question as to whether the squatter areas are a passing phase, a transition to an integrated urban society. The answer may be affirmative or negative, depending on the macroeconomics of the mega-city state to which they belong. But as Christians, we must work for harmonious integration and social, political, and economic justice in either case.

If squatting and the problems of adaptation listed above are part of a transitional society, we need to have clear definitions in mind concerning the ends towards which the transition is leading. Likewise, we need to know what kinds of Christian responses are important at each phase in the transition.

We must not only seek to facilitate integration into the city. We must seek at the same time to redefine the city, to establish the city of God within the cities of men. We look forward and are building towards that city of God that is yet to be revealed from heaven. We seek his kingdom now in the city. Yet in the midst of imperfection and failure in this task, we set our hopes on its future coming in fullness.

These biblical themes lead us towards the acculturation perspective and away from a dualistic class-conflict or viewing-squatters-as-a-problem approach.

But where dualistic or conflict situations occur, we find ourselves affirming the squatters' entrance to the cities. We defend their rights to unused land. We stand against authorities that would oppress them, yet in a spirit of reconciliation that leads to equality within the city. As Christians, we find that we are biased towards the protection of the poor, to the use of justice as a means of rectifying inequality, and against the use of justice solely to protect the rights and privileges of the rich. We look at justice from a perspective of equity.

The legal conundrum

> He was a lawyer. His strong commitment to squatters had caused him to leave his job and become involved in development but there was also a nagging doubt. "Are we legalizing them into poverty? How can I, as a lawyer, be assisting illegal persons?"

The answer was to refer him back to historical analyses of the emergence of cities. In general, new patterns of living in cities emerge among a large sector of people; are at first legislated against; and then, as the extent of the pattern grows, politicians change legislation to accommodate the people. This was the case during the emergence of guilds, labor unions, citizenship laws in Europe, banking structures, and many other present urban patterns.

Squatters are, by definition, illegal inhabitants—even when they constitute 60 percent of a city. Yet for the majority of them, this is the first time they have ever knowingly broken a law, and then it is only because there remained no other options.

An understanding of the nature of law in the Scriptures and in reality is important to deal with the ethics involved. The relationship of law on paper and law as it is implemented in a given culture is important. Perceptions of law vary greatly from the system of law introduced by Western colonial powers. The relationship of law and political decisions is also an important factor.

The issue also involves citizenship. In Manila and Bangkok, simple processes are in place for slum dwellers to obtain citizenship and obtain the right to vote, even while residing illegally. Politicians need their votes. It is to the benefit of the city to recognize the reality of squatters, even if they are formally illegal. Recognition opens the way for planning, education of children, and rationalization of land rights—ways in which politicians can "buy" votes.

The ethical issues concern both the right to stay and the right to own. In Mexico, they say that no one can be a squatter in his or her own country. The Bible affirms the right of every family to own a plot of land and a house. This universal right is reflected in the whole process of apportioning the promised land, and in the jubilee requirements that enabled the poor to regain land every fifty years.

Then there are the historical issues of ownership. In Manila, three families owned most of the land on which the city is built because of an immoral law passed last century by the Spanish. The law took the land from the Filipino people and gave it to 400 families who have since ruled the nation. Three families were given the land that is now the city of Manila.

Legal ownership on paper has little moral validity before God in this situation. It is stolen land, despite legal titles. And the poor have a moral right to be on land stolen from them. What then should a pastor among the poor or a godly politician do?

These are complicated political issues. Urbanization is an existing phenomenon, as is the growth of the slums. Squatters are not there because of their fault, but because of processes far beyond their control. Their sheer numbers make it politically expedient to voice their concerns.

Working on behalf of people that are breaking an unjust law is not evil. The history of cities is one of evolution from existing illegal situations to legalization of those situations. In the process, there is conflict—often violent conflict. As Christians, we are to diffuse confrontations, but at the same time seek an improvement of the situation with a bias towards the poor.

Notes

1. Jacobs, Jane, "Cities and the Wealth of Nations," *Atlantic Monthly,* March/April 1984.

2. Ibid.

3. Santos, Milton, *The Shared Space,* (tr from Portuguese by Chris Gerry). Methuen: London and New York, 1979.

4. Ibid

5. Nyerere, Julius K., "A Trade Union for the Poor," *Bulletin of the Atomic Scientists,* Vol. 35, No. 6, June 1979, pp. 38-39.

6. Ward, Barbara, *Rich Nations and Poor Nations,* Norton, 1962.

7. Assman, Hugo, *Theology for a Nomad Church,* Maryknoll, New York: Orbis, 1976.

8. Hanks, Thomas, *For God So Loved the Third World,* Maryknoll, New York: Orbis, 1983

Chapter Six

Where Are the Churches of the Poor?

Abraham prayed for a city.
God heard.
Nehemiah prayed for a city.
God gave.
Jonah spoke to a city.
God moved.

Where are the shepherds among the poor and where are the flocks? The chart on the next page[1] summarizes recent research into the extent of the church in the slums in various cities. This research deliberately has not analyzed Christian social programs in the slums.

Asian cities

The principal target of world evangelism—the greatest unreached areas—are in Asia. Here we find slums in cities still unreached by the love of God. From 1996, for the first time in Asia, with the exception of the Korean revival, we are seeing movements of urban poor churches reaching scores of thousands. First in Manila, then in Chennai, and now in Mumbai.

While not wishing to offend anybody, I need to state that the urban church of Asia is a middle-class church. Extending a call to "urban mission" unfortunately increases this bias. The call needs to be redefined urgently as a call to "urban POOR mission." Let us look at some representative cities.

THE CHURCH IN THE SLUMS

	Slum/ Squatter population	Slum/ Squatter % of Population	Number of Slums in City	Number of Churches in City	Number of Churches in Slums	% of Churches in Slums
Asia						
Calcutta, India	6+ million, one family per room 3.15 million in bustees, 48,000 on streets	57% 33% in bustees	1000+	145	3 plus 10 house churches, several middle class churches where poor people attend	4
Manila, Philippines (first city in Asia where an urban poor move-ment of churches is happening)	3.3	38%	1000+	15,000	677 in 1998, 1000+ in 2004	6
Bangkok, Thailand	1.2 million in slums now being rehoused in housing projects 600,000 prostitutes 500,000 drug addicts	17% in 1885, 6% in 2004, with 11% hused in concreate high rises, one fam-ily per room	1024	156	3 + 6 house churches 2 ministries among prostitutes 3 ministries to drug addicts	2
Chennai, India (Madras) (1st city in India turning to Christ)		43%	2000	4000	1500	37%
Latin America						
Sao Paulo, Brazil	3.4 million in corticos, 1.5 million favelados, 700,000 street children	31% in slums and corticos, 24% poor	1086	15,000	10,000	60%
Lima, Peru	2.7 million	55%	598	610	594	90%
Mexico City, Mexico	2.7 million	15-25%	500	2500	1500-2100	60-80%

1. Bangkok

Thailand is a productive country that has never been colonized. There is great pride in Thai culture under the leadership of the king. Bangkok, its capital, is a beautiful, rapidly developing city, dotted with Buddhist temples. All roads in Thailand lead to Bangkok, which is *the* city—the industrial and political center of the nation.

About 6 percent of Bangkok's 7.4 million people live in 1,020 slums. Some of these slum areas are crammed with different sized shacks, arranged roof-to-roof and constructed from second-hand crating wood and galvanized iron. Many communities in the slums are reasonably well off, living in well-built Thai houses, but without rights to the land on which they are living. Crime, drug addiction, smuggling, and prostitution are common. There are 600,000 prostitutes and 500,000 drug addicts in the city. Many of the slums have been cleared to make way for construction, and people have been housed in high rise apartment buldings, in one room per family—better than a slum but with no space for expansion.

The Church Growth Committee estimates that there are 156 churches in Bangkok, about 25 of which are relatively small and new (one church for every 60,000 people). They estimate there are 6,000 Christians. The number of Protestant Christians in all of Thailand is about 20,000 (one Christian for 3,000 population). In Bangkok, there are six Bible schools, 30 ordained ministers and an unknown number of unordained ministers.

The church in Thailand has faced much resistance in the past, but over the last decade, there has been an increasing openness in the city. As people move into endless high-rise flats, traditional communities break down, and people become more open to the gospel. They experience more hope that they will be able to climb upward socially and economically. Student ministries are particularly productive. Northern and eastern Thai are responsive to the gospel, but few have tried to reach the southern Thai in Bangkok.

In the 1,020 slums, however, there are only three churches and six house groups. That is, only two percent of churches are among the migrant poor. For the 600,000 prostitutes, there are only two ministries, and for the 500,000 drug addicts, only one drug center, which was initiated only in early 1986.

A dark demon of sensuality has plagued the kingdom of Thailand for centuries and is woven into the fabric of her palaces, idols, and symbols of state. This demon needs to be overthrown in major power confrontations. The immediate tactic in the battle for this city must involve women working with the 600,000 prostitutes and breaking the power of the prostitution and slave trade. Only two Christian ministries at this cutting edge of spiritual warfare for this city are not enough. Who will venture into such a dangerous task?

Rich man, poor man, beggar man, thief

One day, searching for the God of the poor, a rich man who had chosen to be poor walked with a friend through several of the 1,020 slums in prosperous Bangkok (for 19.3 percent live in the slums). They stopped to talk with a man, who told them he was a thief.

To find out about the needs of the community, the poor-rich man told stories of how God had changed a community in another city and asked many questions. As he and his companion were about to leave, their new-found friend (for stories generate friends), laid a hand on his arm.

"Nobody has ever come and asked us these kind of questions before. No one, not even someone sent by our own king—and we know that he cares for the people. How is it that you, a *farang* (foreigner), have such a concern?'

The poor-rich man replied: "Because one day, a number of years ago, I met a king, a king who does justice, and particularly cares for the poor. I loved that King and decided to follow him. He asked me to be his ambassador. His kingdom is one that is being established in every kingdom in the world . . . "

In the ancient kingdom of Siam, people understand about kings and kingdoms. "Please come back and tell us more about this King," begged the thief.

"I cannot come back, for I have many squatter areas to visit, but I will send others to you," said the poor-rich man.

As he walked away, he thought about how the good news from God, bringing salvation from sins and then social justice, is truly good news to the poor.

"Jesus, all I ask from you is a movement of men and women who will choose to walk into these slums. Some will take a martyr's crown in death. Others will bear the marks of identification with the poor in suffering, sickness, and failure."

So a rich man, following a poor Man, became a beggar in the throne room of a King, because of a thief.

2. Manila

Manila is more evangelized than any other Asian city because of the influence of a Catholic heritage. There are 15,000 churches in the city. At last count, there were 677 church-planting ventures among the more than 500 squatter areas that contain over 38 percent of the 12.5 million people in Manila. There is still the need for someone to develop a church-planting pattern that will generate a movement among the urban poor, as has occurred in Latin America.

3. Kuala Lumpur

Kuala Lumpur in Malaysia is a dynamic city, growing rapidly, exploiting well the natural resources of its hinterland, and putting money pouring in from Muslim brothers to good use. Twenty-four percent of its two million people were squatters in 1986. Of these, 52.5 percent are reachable Chinese, and 14.9 percent are reachable Indians. It is one city in which there has been a consistent and reasonably humane program for uplifting these poor.

Chinese and Indian communities are open to the gospel. In general, however, the Chinese Malaysian church has been locked into an older style of church-growth-oriented evangelicalism that does not understand issues of poverty, or into a newer Pentecostalism dominated by a theology of affluence. As a result of the last decade's charismatic renewal, the church has become more open to ministry among the poor.

An older leader formed an organization called Malaysian Care to enable the churches to begin to focus their ministries to the poor. A former rock musician turned accountant-evangelist heard the cries of the poor from the heart of God and is building a church of emaciated poor.

4. Dhaka

The destitution of the poor in Dhaka is greater than in any city, even Calcutta. This is perhaps because Bangladesh is one of the most bereft nations on earth, despite its luxuriant agricultural resources. Houses are made of mud thatch, a few feet tall, and the people possess virtually nothing. Dhaka is home to three million people. By the year 2010 it is projected to contain twenty million people.[2] The majority of these will be squatters.

There are Hindu converts in the 771 bustees. But the majority of people are Muslim and have never heard of Jesus. The country is open to many forms of foreign development assistance, opening doors to respond to the cries of the poor.

5. Calcutta

Sixty-six percent of Calcutta's twelve million inhabitants live one family per room. More than three million live in 5,511 bustees. Between 48,000 (officially) and 200,000 (generally accepted figure) live on the streets. There are no figures on the numbers in squatter areas, but it is estimated that three million live in tents and mud and thatch huts in such areas.

Of the 143 churches in this city, many contain poor people, but only one is a church of the poor reaching out to the poor. The church *has* given bread to the poor of this city. There have been many aid and development programs in Calcutta. But it has not really given them the bread of life.

Jesus has sometimes been seen in these slums in a few saints in *saris,* but his voice has rarely been heard for two generations, and his body has not yet been formed.

In the slums of Calcutta, communists control many areas. Indeed, slums were the base of their rise to power. This does not lead to openness to the gospel. The urban poor of Manila, in contrast, are more open to the gospel because of the advocacy of the Catholic Church in political issues.

The prototype of Christianity, or standard of reference that people have in their minds—a concept defined by Barnett—is a major factor in evangelism. In Calcutta, the concept of a Christian is based on the gambling, partying, dissolute British rulers, and those who gained their favor, including their illegitimate offspring. How can the gospel be received when the prototype is not desirable? New prototypes have to appear.

African and Muslim cities

1. Nairobi

Outside of the skyscrapers of Nairobi, Kenya is a slum containing 200,000 poor people—the Mathari Valley. It is one of the most destitute situations in the world today, with an air of aimless ambition, prostitution, illicit brewing of liquor, drug peddling, and thuggery.

Into this slum stepped Pentecostal Bishop Arthur Kitonga in 1974, to form the Redeemed Gospel Church, evangelizing at meetings with anywhere from 5,000 to 20,000 people gathered. At the same time, he established vocational training, feeding programs, a small-scale business scheme, a program that helps resettle families, as well as emergency aid for fire victims.

2. Cairo

Cairo is the capital of Egypt, a country with the longest recorded history of any nation, spanning some seven thousand years. Tomorrow, there will be 4,166 more Egyptians than there are today, causing the population to increase by 1.5 million per year. At this rate, Egypt's population which topped 70 million at the turn of the century will double again in thirty years.

Cairo, the seat of Muslim culture and learning, is the largest city in Africa, the Middle East, and the Muslim world, with 9.46 million people.

About 40 percent of Cairo's population lives below poverty level, earning up to $35 per month. An extreme housing shortage and inflationary prices are causing great hardships for the poor. Limited medical care for slum dwellers leads to 40 percent of children dying in their first year of life. Forty-three percent of the people are less than 15 years old, and 60 percent are illiterate. The problem of the slums is growing as the slums rapidly expand north and south along the Nile River and deeper into the city dump and cemeteries. There are 10,000 to 15,000 in each of the seven garbage-dump communities.

The Coptic Church has ministries in over fifty of these areas. Most missionaries are working among the middle and upper-middle class.

Latin American cities

In contrast with Asia, Latin America's cities are centers of amazing growth of the kingdom. The majority of the churches in Latin cities are among the poor. Why this difference? And what are the implications for missions?

1. Lima

In 1940, 35 percent of Peru was urban. By 1984, 65 percent lived in urban areas. In 2000, 72.8 percent of Peru lived in urban areas. Of these, 50 percent of the urban population lived in the coastal desert city of Lima, and 30 percent of the total population of the country. Today, Lima is a city of 7.4 million. It was founded by the Spaniards in 1532 and was once a capital of South America, a city of power and wealth. Migrants from rural areas are slowly erasing the Hispanic face of Lima, bringing more of the face and language of the Andes. More and more migrants speak their native language as their first or only language. New cultural forms, economic options, and systems of organizing reflect rural patterns.

The wave of landless, homeless people coming into the city has also resulted in the sprouting of *pueblos jovenes* (young towns) or slum communities that now comprise 55 percent of the city. Most pueblos jovenes spring up unplanned and without government assistance. Only after a period of time are facilities such as water, roads, and light extended to them by the government. There are 598 pueblos jovenes, mostly on desert or mountains surrounding the city. There are also hundreds of thousands in overcrowded inner-city tenements known as *tugurios*.

Despite massive problems of land ownership among the rural areas of Peru, it is relatively easy to acquire land around the city because it is either desert land or mountainous—not useful for either industry or agriculture. This is in contrast with other world-class cities. The marginal Lima that emerges is pluralistic—culturally and linguistically. Lima's slum economy is informal and subsistence-level, moving back to more of a mixed bartering system with reciprocal patterns of relationship. At the same time, it is dependent upon and interrelated with the formal sectors of urbanized society. Within this informal world, there tend to be grassroots, popular religious movements outside of the framework of the formal church structures. These include some of the old indigenous religious practices, and grassroots Catholic movements as well as Protestant movements.

Royal Spanish power subjugated the deity of the ancient Inca culture. Both traditions held the people in bondage to a ruling class of some lineage and power. The oppression of both remains. One is overt and public. The other lies deep and unmentioned within the psyche of Peruvian culture, religion, and custom. The emerging evangelical church stands against deep-rooted Catholic Spanish pride among the rich. On the other hand, among the poor, it must deal with deep-seated traumas of millennia under oppression of powerful empires.

The 1986 directory, *PROMIES,* lists 610 churches in the city. As the directory itself admits, this is an underestimate. The number of baptized members was reported as 35,345, and the evangelical community 106,035 out of an estimated population of 5,500,326 in 1985. The percentage of evangelicals in the population was conservatively estimated as 1.93 percent.[3]

Of the 610 churches, 60-90 percent (or 366 to 541) are in pueblos jovenes. In Lima, a movement among the urban poor is much larger than in any Asian city or in Mexico. Despite this, there are still many unreached areas in the city. The tugurios are probably largely unreached, as no church leader I talked with was aware of believers or churches in these areas. Tugurios are older, poor areas, witness to several generations of sin, and therefore probably not as responsive nor as high a priority to the church as the newer barriadas.

2. Mexico City

The rich and poor among the 18 million of Mexico City often live side by side on the same block. Other poor live in the *ciudades perdidas* (lost cities), where rundown and abandoned buildings become home. In 1984, Mexico City's School of Civil Engineers counted 500 of these ciudades perdidas, home to 2.7 million people. There are also areas of squatters known as *paracaidistas* (parachutists), where 200 families suddenly descend overnight onto unused land, moving from the ciudades perdidas. The 1985 earthquake left 40,000 families relocated into what has become for them permanent-temporary housing.

The prevailing symbolism in the motifs of the Mexican Catholic church is the symbolism of a sun god, whose millennia-ancient temples are at the center of the city. Although somewhat obscured by the Virgin Mary, the pervasive spirit of that ancient deity remains throughout the culture. There are still sacrifices to the old god. The story of the conquest by the Catholic Virgin, however, is a central one in the folklore of Mexico City. Both powers hold control of the minds of the Mexican populace.

Of Mexico City's 1,200 churches, the majority are among the poor. A major evangelical alliance of churches in the city aimed to establish thousands of new churches by the year 2000. The churches are capturing a vision for sending their own people as missionaries to the world. Perhaps some will hear the cries of the poor.

3. Sao Paulo

Sao Paulo is a vibrant, sprawling metropolis that covers an area of 1,400 square miles, home to seventeen million people who speak a variety of 106 languages. With 115,000 industries, three major soccer teams, 34 universities and 3 airports, Sao Paulo is the picture of a prosperous city. The city's history goes back 450 years, when it was first settled by the Portuguese. Today it has a youthful character, however, with 50 percent of its population under 18 years old.

Blessed with one of the largest land areas and richest resource bases of any of the cities in the Third World, Sao Paulo has developed a strong economic base, despite mismanagement by corrupt politicians over the decades. Many kinds of houses and apartments with a multitude of architectural designs are scattered across the rolling hills. The rich emotions, family relationships, and flamboyance of the *Paulistas* contribute to this city's better lifestyle.

Poverty is far less apparent than in other world-class cities throughout the Latin and Asian worlds. Only one and a half million live in the *favelas*—a mere 17 percent compared with 19–67 percent in the Asian cities. But this figure hides the reality of an estimated 500,000 Brazilians moving annually to Sao Paulo and the three million living in *corticos*.

Corticos are decaying apartment buildings in the center of the city that are unsafe. Few stay in the corticos for more than four years. Battered by the psychological stress of living and working in an oppressive urban situation, most move to the favelas on the periphery of the city. There are also about 700,000 abandoned children roaming the streets of Sao Paulo.

The favelas of Sao Paulo are the consequence of many social, economic, and political ills of society. They are the "last stop" for many who have been in transit. Forty-one percent have been downwardly mobile prior to their entrance into the favelas. Here live the hard workers beside the thieves, the rural migrants beside the city veterans, the established family beside the abandoned youth. They are the most heterogeneous places in the city. Only five percent of favelados in Sao Paulo have claim to their land. They all have this in common: they have come to conquer, and they have met defeat. Only 12 percent have stayed for less than a year. Whereas a mere 3 percent of the favelados earn minimum salaries, among the working class of the city, 40 percent have achieved this mark. According to city authorities in 1976, 98 percent of the shacks had no sewage facility, 80 percent had no plumbing, and 66 percent had no electricity.[4]

PAULISTANOS LIVING IN THE FAVELAS

	Residents in Favela	% of population
1968	41,600	0.8
1972-73	71,840	1.2
1974	117,394	1.6
1977	390,000	5
1982	600,000	7
1987	1,500,000	17
2000	1,500,000 (and 3,000,000 in corticos)	19.8 (31)

Favelas are some of the most violent squatter areas in the world. They contain youth gangs known as *marginales* (those marginalized by society), or as the gangs prefer, *boys of the night*. The secretary of social promotion for Sao Paulo estimates 2.4 million marginales—30 percent of the young population.

4. Rio de Janeiro

Seven hours away from Sao Paulo, the skyline of Rio de Janeiro thrusts high into the air. Hotels dot the beaches. Hidden in the midst of the wealth, the tourism, and the beauty are the crowded favelas of the city. If one is going to be poor, it is smart to be poor in the most beautiful city in the world.

Survivors from the war in 1900, *Guerra de Canudos,* became squatters on a hill in Rio de Janeiro named *Morro de Favela.* From this came the Brazilian word for squatter—favelado. In

1948, the first census recorded 105 favelas, with 138,837 inhabitants or 7 percent of the city's population. Favelas were growing at 7 percent per year (1940 to 1960), in contrast with an overall city growth of 3.3 percent per year. By 1974, there were 283 favelas in Rio de Janeiro. Today, there are more than 500—over 30 percent of the city.

Many of the migrants to this city come from the semi-desert areas of the northeast of Brazil, areas where the climatic conditions and feudal social structures have resulted in extreme poverty.

The general consensus on the Removal of Favelas program that took place between 1962 and 1974 is that it failed. Court victories of two prominent favelas, Rocinha and Vidigal, reinforced the impression among the *carioca* (inhabitants of Rio) that favelas are here to stay. Waves of power generated in favelas from time to time have ushered in legal, political and economic favors for the favelados.

Notes:

1. Extensive references to sources of statistics are available in a manuscript copy of this book at Fuller Theological Seminary library, Pasadena, CA 91182, USA. Figures are from between 1980-85. Also the Urban Leadership Cities Database, P.O. Box 20-524, Glen Eden, Auckland, New Zealand.

2. United Nations Human Settlements Program, 2003, *The Challenge of the Slums*, p 267.

3. Paredes, Tito, ed., *PROMIES Directorio Evangelico: Lima, Callao y Balnearios,* Concilio Nacional Evangelico del Peru, 1986.

4. Kowarick, Lucio, "A Espoliacao Urbana," *Paz y Terra,* Sao Paulo, 1979.

Chapter Seven

From Latin Growth to Asian Need

There are more churches in Sao Paulo and Rio de Janeiro than in other cities of Latin America or Asia. In Sao Paulo, 15,000 churches have been counted, with a greater movement among the poor than in any other city. Many favelas have three or four churches. It is estimated that two thirds of the above churches, or 10,000, are in the 1,086 favelas in Sao Paulo. The majority of these are Pentecostal, particularly Assemblies of God.

Evangelical churches in Brazil are also growing. Of the 150 million people in Brazil, 24 million are evangelicals. Some churches are attempting social work programs in the favelas. This response has not yet resulted in significant church planting. There has recently been a significant movement by evangelicals to reach out and establish homes for street children. There are now about seventy evangelical homes for this purpose. Antioch Mission, one of the first Brazilian sending missions, has developed a ministry to drug addicts as well as to street children.

The church among the poor has largely grown through spiritual power encounters. In Brazil, there are many public confrontations with the next major religious grouping after the evangelicals—the spiritists.

A pastor in a favela

The stocky pastor motioned us away from the bullet holes in the window. We sat down, and he told us the story of a congregation of 200 that had formed in one of the most violent slums in the world.

Gangs of bandits that functioned out of the community at times came right into the church building for their gang wars. Once a gang returned a loudspeaker system stolen from the church, fearing that they would receive God's judgment if they kept goods stolen from him.

Another time, a woman walked up the aisle, knife in hand. She slashed at the pastor across the pulpit, missed, and fell to the ground under the protective power of the Spirit of God.

The pastor's hands shook as he talked. Three years of stress to establish this church were taking their toll. He worked during the days to support himself, and preached and worshiped every night.

We left him in the middle of the road at the entrance to the favela—an unschooled man with the intellect of a professor. A missionary for the slums of Asia?

We founded a new mission to send such men to Asia.

Movement in Latin America; silence in Asia

The reasons for such a movement among the poor in Latin America and such an absence of any movement among the poor in Asia are still unclear. In Latin America, there has been a dynamic of church planting in rural areas. Then, as migration has occurred, pastors have moved with their people to the favelas and pueblos jovenes of the cities. This pattern in Asia, however, has not resulted in churches among the urban poor. Some possible reasons might be:

1. A greater dependence in Asia on foreign money, resulting in pastors who move to the city to obtain middle-class positions.

2. The basic movement in Latin America has been Pentecostal rather than mainline evangelical. The concept of the empowerment of the Spirit is linked to ministry among the poor.

Mainline evangelicals have tended to be more a book culture among the middle classes.

3. Pentecostal reluctance to require a lot of time in seminaries and Bible schools seems to encourage the development of pioneering leaders. In Asia, a Bible-school approach to training leaders unintentionally results in training poorer rural pastors for middle-class status in the cities.

4. The middle classes in Latin America have been linked with the Spanish and Portuguese, who have been closed to the gospel outside of the Catholic tradition. The poor in Latin America, on the other hand, come from the more oppressed indigenous cultures that resent Spanish culture, even though they may be attracted by the cultural flow in many ways. This is in contrast to the Asian scene, where a positive attitude towards Western culture by the upper and middle classes have meant a responsiveness at these levels to the gospel, which is associated with the West. The poor in Asia, however, see their poverty linked with the oppression of Christian colonialists.

Sending the Latin poor to Asia

It is possible that God will raise up some apostles from among the middle-class church of Asia to bridge the gulf to their own squatter communities. Perhaps he will call some rich to live among the poor. On the other hand, why not co-opt some of these trained Latin Americans—perhaps several hundred—to catalyze this? They have the faith.

In fifteen years, Pastor Waldemar of Brazil, while developing the project *Servos Entre Os Pobres* under his mission Katros, has recruited 350 missionaries for this task. The Brazilian church does not have all of the finances needed to get them there, nor to enable them to survive. By faith, they wait on God, and press ahead into other Latin countries, for God will overcome this barrier. Other missions in Brazil arrange for their missionaries to spend time in Western nations en route to the field as a way to raise money.

Brazilian culture breeds resilience. The character of a missionary was woven into the history of the people. In their strengths—relationship, worship, and spiritual dynamism—they may also find their weaknesses. Excessive dependence on Brazilian culture, arrogance towards artistically-poor cultures, and a worldview leaving little room for loner-types are difficulties that have been experienced on the field.

A new missions movement

Someone had drawn a city on the blackboard with a favela on either side—a picture of one of the world's richest mega-cities, Sao Paulo, with its fifteen million people and multiplex of cities, and skyscrapers pointing up into the skies.

As I was preaching to this group with a determination to "push through" until a new mission movement had emerged, the Spirit of God descended! I preached the burden of my heart; preached of the needs of the poor of Asia; of the needs of an Asian church that is unable to reach the poor by herself; of the contrast between the 5,200 churches at that time in Sao Paulo and the 132 in the city of Calcutta—two cities of equal size.

God had prepared this people as he is preparing people throughout Brazil. Of the thirty people who came forward to give their lives for ministry in the favelas, twenty have the intention of going overseas. I looked out to see a sea of smiling faces—men and women with commitment and experience.

The next week, this group gathered again, eager to learn and excited about the commitment they were entering into. For 18 months, their mission had been developing a ministry to the street children. Now they were entering a new phase—ministry among the favelados. We talked of the theology and practice of planting a church among the poor. Already there were contacts in three favelas through the ministry to the street children. Team leaders were assigned to evaluate some favelas and prepare to get teams into them.

A church and economic base

That day a new phase had begun—a phase of training not only missionaries from Brazil but missionaries for the poor. In Sao Paulo and Rio de Janeiro, the greatest movements among the urban poor of any place in Asia and Latin America exist—over three thousand churches in the favelas, usually led by favelados who have gifts of pastoring and have chosen voluntarily to remain in the favelas and love the poor.

For every missionary, thirty people need to tithe. Can churches be taught a new pattern of giving? Can pastors intent on building empires release this money from Brazil to the greater needs in nations now unknown to them?

We do not expect significant church planting to take place among the Asian squatter areas by people from the affluent West—affluence makes it too hard to live among the poor. Western mission to the poor tends to be defined as development. Traditional Western theology and structures do not meet the needs of the poor. I say this, despite having set up two missions from Western nations to accomplish this goal, and having an extensive background in community development.

Foreigners, be they Western or Latin, are an important catalyst for the national Asian churches. But they are only a catalyst. We must model in such a way that indigenous ministries, indigenous leadership, and indigenous missions emerge. The aim is not mission. This is too small. Nor is it church growth. This is too limited. *The aim is the discipling of the peoples—indigenous, discipling movements among the squatters in a city.* These will not emerge from highly financed mission programs. Missions that would catalyze these must be sending workers who choose lifestyles of voluntary poverty among the poor.

God is calling for Latin missions with commitments to lifestyles of non-destitute and incarnational poverty—and years of voluntary singleness for many—to catalyze indigenous movements of churches among the unreached squatters of Asia.

How much could God do?

At the 1989 Lausanne II Congress in Manila, a gathering of many of the world's evangelical leaders, there was a major strategic focus on the urban poor. Mission strategists had just brought together lists of strategic goals for the year AD 2000, and they were requested to revise these goals, placing a primary emphasis on the urban poor.

The target proposed was threefold: a vital, ministering church, culturally and geographically accessible to every urban poor person; a movement of churches of the poor in every major city; and transformation of slums and squatter areas. God will do what we ask.

As you read, please bow and pray for:

1. Two incarnational workers in every squatter area.

2. A church in every squatter area.

3. A movement among the poor in each mega-city.

4. Transformation of slums and squatter areas in some cities.

5. Incarnational workers from among the poor who can affect economic and social structures and political options.

6. Mission leaders to make the squatters a priority.

7. A major thrust from Latin America and Filipino churches to other Asian squatter areas.

8. 50,000 cross-cultural workers in the slums raising up indigenous leaders movements of 10,000 in each city.

Chapter Eight

Pilgrimage Among the Poor

Let me describe a personal pilgrimage. It has resulted in the establishment of the Urban Leadership Foundation and several other missions and religious orders. It is now being worked out through the building of a network of many missions towards the urban poor in the Encarnação Alliance.

The Jesus of the poor

When I first entered the slums, I found an integration of all I had known about the life of following Jesus—a sense of the presence of his Spirit, preaching, humility, loving, and caring. And I knew that I had found a key to understanding the heart of the one who chose to be poor among the poor.

Living in the slums also brought me to the central purpose that links Jesus' works together—a passion for knowing God. Out of all of this came the first draft of *The Lifestyle and Values*, which has defined the core values of the various missions that since have been established.

During those early years, we defined our central purpose as *knowing and following Christ*. From this and for this all other purposes flow.

Purpose one: following Christ

We desire individually and corporately to develop intimacy with Christ and to walk in his footsteps. This means imitating his character and attitudes as we seek to live out his principles of self-denial, sacrifice, and service in the context of the twentieth century slums of the world's great cities.

The desire to follow Christ results in a certain lifestyle, both among the poor and when relating to the middle class.

1. Identification

Following Jesus' pattern, who "though he was rich, yet for your sake he became poor, so that by his poverty you might become rich" (2 Corinthians 8:9), we commit ourselves to live and work among the urban poor, to live as nearly as possible to their standard of living, while maintaining reasonable health and recognizing emotional, physical, cultural, and family limitations. We intend always to master the language and culture of the people among whom we minister.

2. Non-destitute poverty

The Master not only chose poverty in birth, life, and death, he also calls his servants to such a lifestyle. We recognize our basic needs for food and clothing (1 Timothy 6:6-8, Matthew 6:25-33), which may include tools of our trade or children's toys. We recognize the just need, inferred from the Scriptures for each family to own its own home, although some, like the Master, may choose a mobile, apostolic life with nowhere to lay one's head (Luke 9:58). In putting our treasure in heaven, we covet the unsearchable riches of Christ.

We desire to possess nothing that cannot be shared with those around us. Regarding what we have, we hold it not as our own but rather as lent to us for a season. We will seek to exclude from both our personal and communal lives the cares of the world, the delight in riches, and the desire for other things (Mark 4:19). We will avoid the abundance of communal properties or wealth. Buildings, administration, and ministry shall be developed in the simplest manner consistent with good health and with efficient, well-pleasing work.

3. Inner simplicity

Renouncing possessions is an outworking of an inner simplifying of our lives which leads to the openness, gentleness, spontaneity, and serenity that marked the Master. In renouncing possessions we seek to simplify our external lives in order to simplify more clearly our inner lives and focus on knowing our Lord.

Along with outward poverty, we desire an inner humility; along with servant works, we seek the spirit of a true servant. In caring little for this world where we are strangers and pilgrims, we set our hearts on that spiritual home where our treasure is being saved up, and on that glory which we shall share with our Lord, provided we suffer with him.

We encourage middle-class Christians to such simplicity of lifestyle. For some it means earning less, and using their time for the kingdom. For others it means to earn much, consume little, hoard nothing, give generously, and celebrate living. Such lifestyles are infinitely varied. We refuse to judge others in such areas.

Jesus the apostle

During the long hours in prayer and the obedience of entering the slums in Manila in those early days, a new knowledge of the presence of God and a release of power came. Surprisingly, God, in his sovereign will, did not permit me to remain in the slums of Manila.

God had his hand in this apparent blockage to ministry among the poor and used it. His was a broader vision than mine. Out of the pain of leaving the poor came the urge to create a book that has changed lives, calling men and women to live among the poor. *Companion to the Poor* was the formulation of a new evangelical theology for living and working incarnationally among the destitute.[1] At that time, such a ministry was not easily accomplished within accepted evangelical beliefs. God has since brought about a growing evangelical commitment to core biblical truths affirming such ministries. Indeed, such a theology is now becoming popular under the theme of the kingdom of God.

As I worked on that book, I had a growing sense of God speaking, commanding the mobilization of the church in my own nation of New Zealand—an apostolic movement of missionary entrepreneurs to the poor of Asia's slums. Servants to Asia's Urban Poor was born.

It was developed around the document that I partially quoted above, *The Lifestyle and Values.* These values had grown out of reflection on the older historical orders, and a realization that core values are far more important than structure in ministry. A second booklet, *A Strategy to Reach the Poor of the World's Mega-Cities,* dealt with the wider vision.[2]

I went back and studied the lives of the great pioneers of earlier centuries, particularly Assisi, Xavier, and Wesley. The notable thing about their movements, in contrast with modern mission societies, was a primary emphasis on knowing God. This has been a central value in Catholic orders working among the poor. (I am not here affirming their doctrines—only looking at the effectiveness of their structure.) For example, although famous for her social work, Mother Teresa's workers spend only five hours per day in work; most of the day is spent in prayer and in the Word.

This primacy of spiritual discipline, of seeking God, is absent in most Protestant missions whose aims are the work for God, rather than to know God.

Purpose two: knowing Christ

In our minds, knowing God includes the traditional evangelical understanding of knowing God in obedience, through time in prayer and the Word, together with the Franciscan perspective that knowing God is to be found through loving the poor, and the Old Testament perspective that righteousness involves social justice. The result is some lifestyle commitments and spiritual disciplines.

We seek to know our Lord more intimately through:

- Obedience and devotion.
- Simplicity of possessions and renunciation of wealth (Luke 14:33).
- Incarnation and service among the poor of the slums (Matthew 25:34–40).
- Preaching the gospel to the poor (Luke 4:18).
- Seeking justice for the poor (Jeremiah 22:16).
- Commitment to community.

1. Spiritual disciplines

We believe our whole lifestyle should become a true walking in the Spirit. We hold to the importance of Spirit-directed self-discipline in the cultivation of spirituality, through regular meditation, study of the Word, worship, prayer, and fasting. We recognize that without steadfastness in these disciplines our lives will be inadequate to cope with the stresses of living among the poor. Our first work is intercession, from which springs our ministry.

2. A lifestyle of celebration

Our lives are to be a sign of joy among the people. The center of our lifestyle is the daily celebration of our Lord's death and resurrection. Wherever we go, we seek to lead others into this celebration of the resurrected Lord, bringing the hope of Christ into slums without hope, the joy of Christ into slums of despair.

3. Joy in suffering

We rejoice, too, in suffering, knowing that suffering produces character (Romans 5:3-5; James 1:2:4).

4. Sabbath and jubilee rest

Celebration, rest, and joy were built into the Scriptures in the concepts of the jubilee and Sabbaths. Knowing that joy flags under overwork, we will zealously keep free one day per week for rest outside of the slum areas. We will season our year with weeks for celebration and festivity, rest, and retreat. The seventh year should be a year for rest, reflection, and recommitment.

5. Self-examination

We will read and review our lives at least monthly, rewriting our values and lifestyle yearly, in consultation with a spiritual adviser.

Only after these objectives came the work goal of the missions: establishing multiplying fellowships. Growing from the center of evangelical and charismatic Christianity, and based on four years in the slums of Manila, the ministry values that enable this to happen emerged. I had enough experiences with the dramatic intervention of the Holy Spirit in ministry among the poor to realize that he is the one who founds churches, missions, and movements. During these years, I had also grappled with the social and economic factors associated with poverty.

Purpose three: establishing multiplying fellowships

We desire to help in the establishing of multiplying movements of disciples congregated into indigenous fellowships and churches which minister according to the gifting and power of the Spirit. With the Bible as our rule for faith and practice, we affirm the following values. These are not rules but shared emphases.

1. Evangelism and disciple-making

Our primary commitment as communities is to go and preach the gospel (Mark 16:15), and to go and make disciples of all nations (Matthew 28:18–20). We recognize that this central thrust occurs in the midst of a wide diversity of ministry, gifts, and calling. While our Master was preaching, he also went about doing good (Acts 10:38),

healing the sick and delivering from demons (Matthew 4:
24), declaring the gospel by both word and deed.

2. Service to the urban poor

While acknowledging the love of Jesus for all men, we
choose to focus our love and discipling among the urban
poor of the Third World's great cities, seeking to follow
Jesus' approach of preaching the gospel to the poor (Luke
4:18).

We will only minister extensively among the rich and middle
class if the poor are significantly helped as a result, and
upon consensus of the mission team.

3. The power of the Holy Spirit

We choose to work in the power of the Holy Spirit, seeking
to lead others into the fullness of the Spirit, and into the
exercise of spiritual gifts and the expression of spiritual
fruit. We look to him as leader and administrator, the one
who opens new communities, who ministers, who reveals
God's will, who heals and delivers. We expect him to work
miraculously on our behalf.

4. Peacemaking, justice ,and development

We seek to live in harmony with all men, but in seeking
peace will be involved in reflecting the just nature of the
God we seek, into the structures of society, in such a way
as to speak out for, to defend, and to uplift the poor among
whom we work. We will act in such areas by being as wise
as serpents and harmless as doves, seeking to effect
change by bringing repentance and reconciliation, though
this may at times involve non-violent confrontations.

In establishing poor people's churches we will seek to avoid
social dislocation by reaching whole communities. We
seek also to establish technically skilled and economically
independent church leadership. We commit ourselves to
encouraging middle-class and rich Christians to give to the
poor, as Paul did (2 Corinthians 8:3–15), in order that some
level of equality be attained.

We seek to uplift the economy of the poor by working where possible to get the skills to produce, the means of production, and control of production into the hands of the poor. This involves introducing appropriate technology, cooperatives, cottage industries (in preference to mass production), and profit sharing. Our intended model is that of holistic ministry, and small rather than large-scale projects.

We are committed to biblical justice and equity and therefore renounce the abuses of both capitalism and Marxism. We renounce the greed of the profit motive, the exploitation and dehumanization of humanity, and the exhausting of irreplaceable natural resources by capitalism. We renounce the use of force, violence, the class struggle, and bitterness inherent in Marxism. While for specific goals we may find ourselves aligned with various political groups, we are committed to none but the politics of the kingdom of God.

Jesus, lover of the whole world

God kept speaking of other cities through visions, moving me to walk through them and intercede for them. (Every major advance in ministry seems to have come to me this way. I am not saying that others should expect this, or that young Christians, with little discernment, should spend their time seeking this. I only affirm that this has been my experience.) I began walking the streets of other cities, and decided to write this book. His call had changed from reaching the poor to reaching and transforming the cities, including both the poor and those who create their poverty.

In the process, I took the core of a second team to Bangkok, to survey and prepare for entrance into that city. This team is now established, and the New Zealand mission is looking towards another South Asian city. It has also developed an Australian base.

The call was obviously wider than what we had envisaged, and the Lord spoke to me to move on and develop the broader mission, rather than maintaining my leadership of the New Zealand work. God has gone on blessing that work. The workers on the field have continued to follow *The Lifestyle and Values*, for the foundations were well laid, with enough workers to give a group dynamic that has been lasting. And God's promises at its outset have provided a covenant with him for its continued growth.

A large part of the success of these teams may be attributed to their patterns of decision-making in a team context. These contain the seeds of mutually laying down our lives for others.

The Body of Christ

One of my main callings in life has been to build teams, and my experience in the slums led to a firm conviction that unless a team structure was built solidly into this mission, workers would not survive the stresses. So one of the values became fellowship of commitment.

God gave a good initial team from New Zealand. Pete Falconer and his wife Libby sacrificed many years of their lives for the establishing of the home base. Colin Harrington brought to the work experience in team leadership from his previous years in Indonesia. Several workers emerged from the Spreydon Baptist Church.

1. Fellowship of commitment

We choose to work, together in communities of four to
twelve brothers and sisters, working in pairs or family units,
and coming together at least once every two weeks for
a time of training, of fun, or of ministry to one another, a
communal feast, a time of confession, and for celebration of
the death and resurrection of our Lord.

While guarding freedom of conscience and spirit-directed individual initiative, we choose a partial sharing of income, possessions, and ministry goals.

2. Decision-making in teams

We commit ourselves to submission to one another. Each of us has God-given and communally confirmed leadership roles. We commit ourselves to obedience to our brothers and sisters in these areas.

In all questions of importance, as far as possible, decisions should be made by consensus. If a community leader senses a profound lack of agreement on an important issue, let him reserve judgment and in order to go forward, make a provisional decision, ready to return to it later, for standing still is disobedience for brothers and sisters advancing toward Christ. Those with responsibility for leadership must exercise authority but with humility. If a grave crisis arises in which there is a division of opinion, we will decide only after at least a day of prayer, humbling, and fasting.

Something old, something new

I began to think about a dual-level missionary order, a concept as old as the Franciscans and before. How could we call some to live among the poor, and yet at the same time involve others who loved the poor, but for one reason or another could not pay the price of dwelling among the poor?

Those of the first order are workers living right in among the poor. Those of the second order are people who are giving their lives to serve the poor, while not living among them. We established the next mission, structuring Servants Among the Poor (now Servant-Partners) as a religious order with vows of non-destitute poverty that would send North Americans.

The idea for Servants Among the Poor had come to me one night, when I had a vision of twenty people in the slums of Mexico, praying for the sick and preaching. Five weeks later, twenty people were gathered there. Then came several months of beautiful fellowship with Drs. Tom and Betty-Sue Brewster developing the organization. Tom initially gave leadership but passed away when I was in Calcutta. I had to return to the States to restructure Servants and to find ongoing leadership.

Workers on every continent have come out of all of this. Betty-Sue Brewster now teaches a course on "Incarnational Mission and the World's Urban Poor" at Fuller Theological Seminary in Pasadena, California, along with several language-learning courses. A group of people began a training program by living among the poor in downtown Los Angeles. Their community is known as Cambria Community.

At the same time, Paul Miller, a brilliant and deeply-loved friend, formed Urban Leadership Foundation (formerly Servants International Resources) on my behalf. This was set up so that I could do research and would have an ongoing ministry organization from which to spawn indigenous works. Through this foundation, along with gifts from my New Zealand base, I supported myself while a missionary to the United States. I did not want to use money given for the work, lest I be charged with coming to the States to make a fortune!

This kind of cautiousness grows out of considering the Apostle Paul's examples of raising and using finances. We built the work on several financial values.

Responsible faith

Jesus taught us not to be anxious about daily necessities, for he will provide if we seek his kingdom (Matthew 6:25-34). We choose to live in this spirit of carefree trust and joy. We expect that as we minister spiritually to others, God will provide for us physically in return (1 Corinthians 9:10-12).

We also recognize that in a twentieth century international context this requires responsible financial structuring by the sending churches and mission agencies through whom much of God's provisions are channeled. In general we trust God alone for our needs, while responsibly and graciously making our needs known to others where appropriate. In order to enter new areas, many will, at times, like Paul, work in secular careers to support themselves.

Finding Jesus in Latin America

The next work was birthed in the tenth city to which God had directed me to intercede. On a hillside near Sao Paulo, in an evening of prayer, it seemed good to ask God to capture the dynamism of the emerging Brazilian mission thrust for the poor of Asia. Under Pastor Waldemar who had planted many poor people's churches, and been central to the formation of another mission, *Servos Entre Os Pobres* emerged, and is now a project of the mission *Kairos* which he directs. This mission now has teams among the poor in thirteen Latin, Asian, and African cities.

During the same night of prayer, God also spoke to me about a wonderful Brazilian wife, Ieda, who would be my companion on this journey in him. For many years God had left me single. In an apostolic ministry among the poor, singleness is a gift that may be greatly used. Taking a long look at the history of celibacy in the church, we have encouraged both this and sacrifice in marriage.

Gifts of singleness, sacrifice in marriage

We recognize the importance of family life in the Scriptures, yet, for the sake of the gospel, with an eye single to his glory, and seeking a life of undivided devotion to him, many of us will choose to remain single for some years, being under no compulsion but having our desires under control and not seeking marriage. Christ is our true companion and comfort, who does not weaken human affection but enables us to love more richly with his love all with whom we come in contact.

Some couples, for love of the poor, may remain childless for a period of time. Yet others will be willing to be separated from loved ones and children for periods of time. We count on the Lord's promise to repay a hundred fold for all such sacrifice and remember always the gift to us that God the Father made of his Son. Couples with children will need to trust God wisely for the well-being of their children.

We recognize these states as gifts from God and look with confidence to him to give the grace needed for this life. In thus accepting the demands of such a life we must ever be on guard against the temptation to self-centeredness, coldness, or a lack of sympathy with the interests of others.

A call to the global Christian community

Our role in each country has been to walk with Jesus, to speak his Word. As his Word creates life, we draw together those called into training cores, find and build a cohesive board, and appoint an ongoing leader.

But the task is far bigger than we can accomplish by setting up new missions. The call of Jesus, the warrior King, now leads us to call, on his behalf, other missions into the battle for the poor. There are missionaries whom we have trained and who have been sent by other agencies with different structures. Invariably, they have been prevented from fulfilling their calling to the poor by the structures themselves. For this reason, I have begged mission leaders to set up alternative orders within their own missions. This was the reason behind writing chapter two of this book.

God is doing this. At Lausanne II in Manila, a gathering of the world's evangelical leaders, God made the urban poor one of the central themes of the congress, despite the fact the organizers did not plan to feature them significantly on the program. The grandiose and possibly God-given plans of a related congress, "Global Consultation on World Evangelization by AD 2000 and Beyond," do not even mention the urban poor except as part of development and aid programs. But the resulting AD 2000 movement accepted the urban poor as a central component to the development of this movement.

Particularly, at Lausanne II, God spoke through the song of a well-known Filipino song writer, Gary Granada. Gary is a personal friend, and we lived side by side in the slum of Tatalon. In the beautiful poetry of the Philippines and to the lilt of a guitar, his song told of a little squatter home, and asked the question whether it really was a home. The impact on such a grand Congress was to focus its heart towards the poor.

At the same time, missions such as the Overseas Missionary Fellowship (OMF) are encouraging workers to minister in the slums. Worldwide Evangelization Crusade (WEC) leaders have talked of it, and will talk of it again. Youth With a Mission (YWAM) has targeted the slums and attempted some works in them. YWAM is increasing its commitment to language and culture learning and to recruit long-term workers committed to church-planting.

Jesus, the integrator of mega-cities

Over a period of time, it has become apparent that the cries of the poor will never be answered unless we undertake battle on behalf of the cities that create their poverty. The next phase in following Jesus is a call to the cities, to pastor the pastors among the poor, to intercede, and to prophesy against those powers that hold the poor enslaved.

Jesus is king over cities, and over principalities and powers, whether they be manifest in economic structures, modernization, political oppression, or government bureaucracy. His name must be declared to those subject to the powers in each of these contexts.

But the primary focus of accomplishing this task cannot be upon Western missions but upon Third World missions. With or without the help of the West, they are going to reach the poor. This is the new direction of mission history.

Consider the 60 mega-cities with over five million people, each containing an average of 500 slums. By the year 2010, if the number of slums doubles as expected (along with prostitution areas, and drug gangs and prisons), and if we plan on two workers living in each area, we will need to see 120,000 workers in place and ministering if the poor of the world are to be reached. Missions from Third World countries to Third World countries will be the catalysts of multiple indigenous ministries.

Thus Urban Leadership Foundation has developed as a networking and training agency in many of these cities. Urban Leadership Foundation is committed to mobilizing and building networks among existing missions and churches by:

1. Catalyzing movements of churches among the poor.

2. Establishing movements of disciples among the elite who can transform the poverty.

3. Bringing spiritual and structural renewal into urban churches so they can reach the poor.

4. Encouraging missions from Third World cities to the poor of other cities.

Jesus, the downwardly mobile

Our personal call from Jesus was to return to the grassroots level in one of the poorest cities of South Asia—Calcutta. We returned with a team of workers to do battle for that city and people. Prophets for a time are found among the leaders of the nations. Then they are found, unknown, among the poor.

Because we initiated the work in Calcutta through much suffering, our board has requested that we return to a central city, and from here continue in the broader process of mobilizing the mega-missions and churches to the poor, and facilitating the

129

movement of Latin Americans into Asia, Asians into Russia, and Africans into Europe. We have chosen to do this from our base in New Zealand.

Let us press on together in this great task of bringing Jesus to the poor! Before he comes!

Notes

1. Grigg, Viv, *Companion to the Poor*, Monrovia, California: MARC, 1990.
2. This booklet and others are available from Urban Leadership Foundation.

PART 2

CHURCH-PLANTING MODELS

Chapter Nine

Enter! The Man of Peace

We need a prince who becomes a pauper,
if he would govern like a king.

Nothing matches the thrill of entering a community, seeking to bring the kingdom of God to it, and extending the kingdom of God over it. It takes all our physical, emotional, spiritual, and mental energies. No other lifestyle is so demanding. No other lifestyle can be both less rewarded on this earth and so greatly rewarded in the heavenly places.

This lifestyle begins in compassion, leads to intercession, advances through living out the incarnation, and is based on the long, hard obedience of a disciplined and sacrificial life.

Friends of the bottle

He became my best friend. He was a soft man at heart, with a great understanding of life, but the pain of his wife's death had never left him. He was an alcoholic.

Pastor Jun and I had compassion on him and spent many hours with him, talking over life, God, and freedom from the power of the bottle. It reduced him to continual inebriation. He died calling for Pastor Jun and me. He died in the knowledge of God's love. He died an alcoholic.

He was the first of the four to go. There were four of them, four friends in the demon grip of alcoholism. We took compassion on all of them, and they became our friends. One came from a rich family but now lived in the slums. When I last visited, he was the only one of the four still alive. Each of the others died painful deaths.

"I'm the only one left," he said. "I know God has his hand on my life, but I cannot break the power. I am sending my wife and children every Sunday to the church."

Compassion means much love, a little response, and great pain. Compassion is the heart of ministry. It is the source of identification. It is the wellspring of proclamation. Its multiplication is the heart of church growth. It is the motivation for seeking justice.

Compassion leads us into intercession. But there is a price to pay for the power that moves the hand of God and establishes the kingdom in the heavenlies. The price is incarnation among the poor.

For richer churches, this ministry of intercession means collective commitment to a simple, sacrificial lifestyle, coupled with a growing experience of the power and gifts of the Spirit. If, because of history or doctrine or lethargy, a church is unable to pay such a price, it should not even begin to consider this kind of a call to serve the poor.

In closed societies, where public proclamation of the gospel is impossible, there is a place for aid programs in this entrance phase as a means of establishing rapport with the people. The danger is that workers may come to perceive these programs as the primary entrance point of the kingdom. The kingdom breaks open new territory through proclamation—not through aid programs.

Entrance through a Brazilian man of peace

It was early on Christmas Day. I wandered up the small stream along the rows of plywood homes—a favela in Brazil. Since it was Jesus' birthday, I wanted to give him a gift. Perhaps he could lead me to someone among these poor—someone with an open heart. At the end of the stream, I crossed a hill of middle-class homes. There before me, stretching out to the airport, lay a favela waking lazily in the Christmas morning sun.

As I found the track down the hill a favelado laboring upwards shouted a greeting. Down among the houses a group of people were chatting. I stopped and inquired about the favela in my halting Portuguese, and told them I had come to preach the gospel

Farther down the track, the valley opened out and here was another favela—a quieter one. Somehow it looked peaceful. The homes seemed sturdier.

On the afternoon of my birthday, I came back to talk with some people there. The first person I spoke with was a drunkard. I left him quickly, remembering Jesus instructions to find the "man of peace."

A tall man with a beard was standing by the road.

"Now, I have observed that bearded people tend to be more sensitive and wise," I thought, stroking my own beard. I stopped and talked with him. He and his wife had lived in the favela for eight years. Most of the favelados came from the northeast.

We talked for an hour. He showed me the Catholic Bible he and his family read each day. We opened it to Mark and there was the passage about preaching the kingdom of God . . .

This was my point of entrance.

There is no single model for entry to a community. The Apostle Paul gained entrance to cities through a combination of family connections, speaking in public places, taking advantage of the patronage of Jewish leaders, or through the conversion of the Roman officials who dealt with him. Sometimes he went to his own ethnic group, the Jews, or to his occupational group, the tentmakers.

Jesus gave us some useful principles, however:

And whatever town or village you enter, find out who is worthy in it, and stay with him until you depart. As you enter the house, salute it. And if the house is worthy, let your peace come upon it; but if it is not worthy, let your peace return to you. And if any one will not receive you or listen to your words, shake off the dust from your feet as you leave that house or town. (Matthew 10:11–14)

Incarnation: becoming one of the poor

Jesus' effectiveness in evangelism was partly because of his dependence on the poor: "Freely you have received, freely give. Do not take along any gold, or silver, or copper in your belts; take no bag for the journey, or extra tunic, or sandals or a staff; for the worker is worth his keep" (Matthew 10:8–10 NIV).

What does it mean to depend on those to whom you go to minister? The specific instructions here are not to be reproduced, but the principles may be. In the biblical instance, the disciples were on an evangelistic trip. Our situation is different. Particularly for those who are looking at church planting in another culture, we have initially to consider a more stationary model than did the apostolic twelve. Unlike them, we have to learn a new language and a new culture.

Permit me to suggest how this biblical pattern might work out for us today. We need to live among the people at their level—not independent of them—despite our resources. As a typical single missionary among squatters in Manila, I once listed the following in my house:

EQUIPMENT FOR A SINGLE MISSIONARY

- small one-cup water heater
- 220v/6v adaptor
- a good cassette recorder for language study with a small AM/FM radio which replaces expensive newspapers
- chess set
- string
- watch with date, alarm (replaces calendar, alarm clock)
- potted plants
- toiletries

- small container for coins for phone
- frying pan
- sandals
- shoes
- coconut husk for cleaning
- plastic bags
- stapler
- stamps/envelopes
- small two-burner and gas tank (as cheap as kerosene or wood and twice as efficient)
- good rug
- two small pots
- anti-bacterial soap
- 3 sets knife, fork, spoon, plate, glass (for two guests)
- dustpan
- hard broom
- yearly planner
- iron
- chairs (can be made there)
- tray for dishes
- 3 pillows
- 3 sleeping mats
- can opener
- scoop for water
- tea towel
- pot scrubbers
- hangers
- writing equipment

- Bible and reading material
- 3 sets clothing (wash one set each day)
- formal dress
- 3–4 Christian music tapes
- small Philips screw driver, cutters, hammer, chisel
- umbrella
- language/music tapes
- mouth organ
- small broom
- large knife
- egg slicer
- two buckets
- washing basin
- water jug
- chopping board
- 3 blankets
- 3 mosquito nets
- electric power cord
- light socket
- medium size fan
- desk (can be made there)
- typewriter
- fly spray
- 40 gallon drum for water
- Vitamin B capsules
- small traveling bag
- scissors
- 2 towels
- 3" mirror
- songbook and guitar

Acceptable roles

Drs. Tom and Betty-Sue Brewster, who were instrumental in initiating the USA-based Servants Among the Poor (now

Servant-Partners), have popularized five roles that are fitting for new workers moving into an area: learner, servant, friend, storyteller, and intercessor.[1] As we play these acceptable and non-threatening roles, relationships and cultural understanding can develop that lead to effective ministry.

The humble person can move into many situations and earn people's trust. Likewise, the person who enjoys their humanity and loves life can move into many situations and earn peoples' love.

Effective missionaries are those who are wise enough to earn an acceptable status in the community so that their voice will be heard, and who can learn to accept with grace their ascribed status—a status that is often given by the people because of class, race, color, or role. They know that as guests they are often honored more highly than they truly deserve.

We cannot identify with "macho" sins of drinking, gambling, and immorality, but we can humble ourselves to accept tasks that define masculinity or femininity in that culture—tasks such as building houses, fetching water, cooking, or raising children.

Winning hearts

Ministry to children is frequently the entrance point to a community. It should not, however, become a strategy for long-term church planting. A wiser, more lasting strategy is to minister to the needs of children by concentrating time and energy on their parents. "And if anyone gives even a cup of cold water to one of these little ones because he is my disciple, I tell you the truth, he will certainly not lose his reward" (Matthew 10:42 NIV).

In most societies, women come to the Lord first. Perhaps the reason for this is that women in most poor societies have only one major relational question to answer when they convert—what will be the effect on my husband and children?

For men, the issues are far more complex. They must consider carefully the impact of conversion on their relationships with other men in the community, particularly in the face of the accusation that they are no longer men, or no longer part of the society. A man's conversion will involve relatives, friends, job security, status, and self-identity.

Male church planters must be careful not to give all their time and attention to the first female converts but rather through them reach the men of the community. It is not caring for women to bring them into the church without their men folk. The church planter must always aim to reach enough men for the kingdom so that a stable eldership may emerge from them.

Perhaps the saddest ministry lesson I have learned took place when I returned to an early fellowship and saw what had happened to the marriages of the first converts. I sat up one night counseling one who is engaged to a man with another wife, and another whose husband, a non-believer, is now a drug addict, and another whose marriage was birthed in immorality—all because we failed to push through to reaching enough single marriageable men.

Notes

1. Brewster, E. Thomas and Elizabeth S. Brewster, *Language Learning IS Communication—IS Ministry!,* Pasadena, California: Lingua House, 1987.

Chapter Ten

Patterns of Proclamation

These twelve Jesus sent out, with the following instructions: "Do not go among the Gentiles, or enter any town of the Samaritans. Go rather to the lost sheep of Israel. As you go, preach this message: 'The kingdom of heaven is near.'"
(Matthew 10:5-8 NIV)

Before he comes, go quickly!

Presence leads to proclamation. Jesus preached and taught with brilliance and wisdom, speaking the very words of God. He knew what was inside the people he met. God revealed to him the inner life of a woman at a well, of a woman who touched his garment, of a man who climbed a tree to see him. He spoke to their needs with the power of a word from God—a word of revelation, a word of knowledge, a word of wisdom. Proclamation of the word of God had power because it accompanied the exercise of spiritual gifts.

The impact of the kingdom comes from the proclaimed Word, which is the power of God for salvation (Romans 1:16) as it is taken by the Spirit to meet revealed needs.

A slow approach to evangelism emphasizes building initial acceptance and friendship in the community. This slow approach is the only viable one during the first few years when a worker is learning language and culture. It may begin on the first day, as the worker lives among the people and prays for their needs.

Then follows the formation of small Bible study groups, either with families or even with groups of alcoholics. These studies often last only for three weeks because the broken social structure makes it difficult to develop a disciplined pattern. Each group meeting has to be celebrated as a special occasion. A pattern of forming groups, then reforming them, with new approaches each time, seems to work well.

Through these, people become converted. Social activities, such as an outing at the park, birthday parties, and then worship, can gradually be developed, drawing together people from several Bible studies.

The church planter needs to keep weekly records of who is in what group, where new contacts are forming, where new groups of people are opening up, and how to link these together, one with another. There is a need, as well, to keep records from the outset about each contact and convert. These records may be kept either in a loose-leaf notebook or on small cards in a file. "Know well the condition of your flock and give attention to your herds" (Proverbs 27:23).

The second approach to evangelism is like a "fast break" in the sport of basketball. It is the approach of the evangelist or the wandering apostle. It involves entering a community with a team, and for a series of successive nights, proclaiming the gospel until a significant group has been saved and can form a church. We expect that many missionaries, after their mastery of language and culture, can exercise such a mobile ministry.

Probably a combination of both approaches is most effective. This would call for building a network of relationships and then bringing in an evangelistic team for a period of active public proclamation.

Put it up quickly

"If you don't get the building up within three days, the materials will be stolen," he told me.

While he was building the little wooden churches, his team—wife, son and daughter—moved through the favela and started Bible studies with mothers and children. In the evenings, using a loudspeaker, they would call the people to come and hear. Then the gospel would be preached.

In each place, fifty to a hundred people would be converted. He would go to the local minister's fraternal, find a pastor who wanted to move to the city, and invite him to come and pastor this newly-planted church. This pastor would sleep in the squatter church until he found a home in the community.

Twenty-five churches were formed through this evangelist, his family, and his incarnational pastors.

Opposition

Just as Jesus was thrown out of his synagogue when he declared his mission to the poor, so workers among the poor face opposition, persecution, and violence. If we walk in Jesus, if his power and glory are manifest through us, we must expect the opposition he experienced.

Entrance into a slum is a political act—one that rich landowners and politicians may perceive as being against their interests if they exploit the poor. The people themselves, bound by centuries of darkness and bitterness, will oppose the light. Demonic powers are present. Jesus warns us of all these.

A pastor of courage

Pastor Jun Paragas and his wife, Milleth, are a remarkable couple in Tatalon, Manila. One of the marks of their lives is their perseverance under opposition.

Upon their first entrance into the slum, some twenty years ago, they quickly discovered the dark gossip and backbiting of some in the community. They expressed love in various ways to these. At times rocks were thrown on their roof by those they were seeking to reach.

For periods of time, love succeeded in winning over some hearts. Then several Catholic leaders in the community would seek to duplicate each aspect of the work, to talk against it, and to keep people away from the fellowship (just as the devout Jews troubled the Apostle Paul).

When there were errors of judgment or sin in the church, the whole community would turn against Pastor Jun and Milleth. When there were new expressions of love for people, the mood would change. At one point, when they were absent for a few months, the community turned against them with much darkness, taking down the tent that was used for a place to meet.

As in the case of the Apostle Paul or of any pastor, at times there has also been opposition from the people within the very church they have spent years of their lives serving. One of the early converts moving into leadership opposed Pastor Jun at one point. Now the relationship has healed. Others have become disgruntled. Dealing with one member's sin led to a round of criticism. Another time, there was dispute over the role of pastor. Again, a spirit of forgiveness and humility brought healing.

Outside agencies seeking to help the work have brought no end of criticisms. They have sought to help, or control, and then have moved on.

But the call to a pastor is to remain firm, to stand unbending, and to hold on to the territory that God has given. Sometimes faltering, often discouraged, and at times making mistakes and having to redeem them, this couple has remained until the church has begun to mature in Christ.

Chapter Eleven

Works of the Spirit of God

"March!" He said,
so I marched
to the beat of a different drum,
walking a long obedience,
hearing the Beloved One
as He called, "To the poor! Quickly!
a glass of juice,
a touch on the head of this child,
a laugh with this prostitute,
as sadly she tells of her trade
and her desire to walk away.

"And the faces, dead—yet alive—, the children, all
spindly and pain, cleanse them, heal them, raise them,"
His cry came again and again.

"With what?" I screamed back,
across the noise of the fight,
the lonely hours of wrestling
not with prayer (so spiritual)
but with administration,
and letters to workers,
all night.
"My spirit is dry—
no laborers here—
and so poorly do I know You,
Your power seems so far away.
What can I give? How can I pray . . . ?"

Then He came. Oh! He came,

surrounding with love,
away with the pain.
His peace flooding over my spirit,
my body enwrapped once again
in Him who sustains the universe.

I lifted my feet,
on that long obedience into Him,
who is found among the needy;
laid my hands
on the spindly bent legs of a hungry girl
and prayed, in His power, for her healing,
gave money to a blind man singing,
wept with my old drunkard unsaved.

And He came,
and I knew Him once again,
who is beyond thinking—
King of my heart.
Leader in battle.
Savior of megacities.
Lover of the migrant poor.

Do you know him? Do you know his presence and peace that passes all understanding, as he comes again and again to overflow us with his love?

Evangelism with power

Jesus came preaching and teaching the kingdom, healing the sick, and casting out demons. Three of these four activities are mentioned repeatedly in various patterns throughout the gospels. He sent his disciples out to do the same. Evangelism was always, for Jesus, set in the context of healing the sick and delivering people from the demonic.

I have walked among the poor, dazed, knowing the impotence of my life, as I face such a mass of destitute, darkened half-faces. Then, by his presence and power, he touches them, one by one. He is the transformer, and as I walk in his glory among them, he brings them hope.

Forgive me if this seems mystical, or strange. It should not, for this is the normative life of a disciple cleansed by the washing of the water of the Word.

Do you know those times of refreshing, sensing his presence—sweet, like a perfume? There is no effective ministry among the poor without this knowledge of his presence. An anointing of the Spirit and dependence upon his power is the starting point for ministry to the poor (Isaiah 61:1).

The entrance point into communities is through this power. The breakthrough of the kingdom comes with preaching, teaching, healing and deliverance. It may also be accompanied by development projects or aid, but it is the Spirit that gives life, and then enables such projects to bear good fruit.

Of over a hundred churches planted among the poor, I have seen only two that came into being through the giving of aid. By itself, aid does not break open new territory for the kingdom of God, although it may create a desire for teaching because the people see Christ's love demonstrated. It may be the godly response in many emergency and destitute situations, but we must be careful. The motivation to give aid can be either from God's Spirit or from human planning.

The Spirit and a lady

We had spent time talking about how to form a worshipping, celebrating fellowship in the red-light district of Ermita in Manila. Now we were actually out on the streets, sitting in a restaurant with five of this artist's friends—prostitutes. Only we didn't call them that, for each was hurting inside about the past.

Her outgoing warmth had drawn them to her. While they shared laughter and jokes, the conversation would often dip down into issues of seriousness.

"I don't want to live this life, but what else can I do. I had nothing left, when I left my boyfriend. I had to live. I want to get out but there are no jobs. I have to pay my rent. My family don't know what I am doing. They think I have a good job. It is too late now. I tried to get free but it doesn't work."

"Only the power of God can give you meaning and freedom."

Five steps are essential in ministry to the squatters.

1. Compassion (as in the person of Christ)

2. Incarnation (presence)

3. Intercession (prayer)

4. Proclamation

5. Power

Power is so important that it requires some extended comments. I do not know of a single church among the poor in any of the cities I have studied that has not been planted in the midst of signs of healing, deliverance, and miracles.

Anointed with authority

"And he called to him his twelve disciples and gave them authority over unclean spirits, to cast them out, and to heal every disease and every infirmity" (Matthew 10:1-2).

How do we recognize those who have this empowering with authority, this anointing with power from God in their ministries? We find it in love. Paul makes this clear by placing 1 Corinthians 13, his renowned chapter on love, between two chapters about spiritual gifts.

But do we look for some sign such as speaking in tongues? The Bible does not indicate that this is a necessary sign. While affirming that it is a useful and positive gift if used wisely, privately or publicly with an interpreter, Paul clearly states that not all speak in tongues (1 Corinthians 12:30).

Luke 4:18 shows us some things that are more readily observable in those who have been anointed by God. Each is evidence of love. Each occurs in a context of love. Anointing of the Spirit is shown in a compulsion to preach. Anointing is shown in healing and deliverance. Anointing is shown in involvement with the poor. Anointing is shown in seeking justice.

When I refer to the anointing of God, I am not talking of receiving the Spirit, nor even of receiving spiritual gifts. I believe that all receive the Spirit at conversion (Romans 8:9). When he comes, he comes bearing gifts. I am talking about empowering—of the release of the power of the Spirit and his gifts that comes when we walk in love and fellowship.

The apostles were to be the anointed ones. In Matthew 10:1, they experienced his anointing when he laid his hands upon them. Similarly, God gives us special authority, gifts, or empowering for certain tasks. He does this through delegation by elders (1 Timothy 4:14), just as the elders of Timothy's church released Timothy into ministry with a prophecy and laid their hands upon him.

The disciples were told to wait for a deeper, more lasting experience of the Holy Spirit. "For John baptized with water," Jesus said, "but in a few days you will be baptized with the Holy Spirit" (Acts 1:5 NIV).

Some have built on this verse a doctrine of "tarrying" or waiting. This is a specific event in the history of the church, however, and not a doctrinal statement. There is enough evidence in the Bible and in the church to believe that before God anoints us for a task, he often wants us to seek him through a time of fasting, prayer, and waiting. Perhaps there are issues of purification that he wants us to work through, or perhaps there are factors of intensity of desire that he wants to know about.

Hindrances to the anointing of God

All Christians receive the Spirit at conversion. Some experience a great overflowing (or immersion or baptism) of the Spirit when they are converted. For others it seems never to have occurred. He may be in us, but there are blockages that have never been dealt with so that he can freely use us.

Sin will block the work of the Spirit. Daily we need to have God cleanse and search us. For some, emotional scars from the past may be blocking the link between our emotions and the Spirit. When these hurts, often unknown to us, are revealed by the Holy Spirit and healed through prayer, we may have a new freedom to hear the Spirit and to walk in him. Sometimes, demonic factors from the past may not have been dealt with at conversion.

The Spirit and growth

He had been a violent son of a violent father. He had a hunger for God, and his conversion had led to changes. It was real. But one night he would be at a prayer meeting and the next night he would be drunk. His involvement in street fighting raised tricky pastoral questions in the church. How could we discipline a believer like this? Until . . .

One night, I had been preaching on the power of God to heal. There was an atmosphere of faith, so we asked the Spirit to come and minister. He came as we waited and fell on this violent son. Trembling under the Spirit's power, he saw picture after picture of the traumas of childhood, the source of the violence—and God healing each hurt, each wound. Then he prayed, one by one, for the sick in the room and watched God's power anoint them.

From that day, God took a violent man and turned him
into a pastor. His father was also saved. Spirits were dealt
with. People began to study the Bible. He began to preach.
Today he is a pastor in training in a jail ministry.

No amount of counseling or Bible study could deal with
such deep wounds. They needed the power of the Spirit of God.
There can be little effective ministry among the poor without this
power.

Many are hindered from a fullness of the power of the Spirit
by doctrinal barriers that block their minds from relating to a God
who is present and doing miraculous things. Others have never
seen the Holy Spirit at work, so they lack models, and hence
cannot discern between his works and those of other spirits,
withdrawing into a fearful rejection of any spiritual phenomena
whatsoever.

There is also an ebb and flow in this area of the anointing of
God. Sometimes Jesus had to go out for a night of prayer. Later
we find the power of the Lord with him to heal. Jesus himself
tells us that the wind blows where it wills, and we cannot tell
where it comes from nor where it is going. So it is with the Spirit
(John 3:8). The work of the Spirit is too diverse to be placed in
theological boxes. What is important is the reality of his anointing
for ministry.

Confrontations of power

John Wimber has popularized this concept using Alan
Tippett's phrase—*power encounter*.[1] It has come to mean the
symbolic confrontations between the power of the Holy Spirit and
the powers of the demonic that take place as the gospel is breaking
into a community.

Power encounters between the kingdom of God and the
kingdom of darkness are particularly evident when we are on the
pioneering edge of mission. They are more so among the urban

poor, where even secular sociology and anthropology demonstrate a higher incidence of demon possession.

The act of entering a squatter area is in itself a profound encounter between the two kingdoms. It is a declaration of victory over the spirits that dominate such areas. When a person enters a squatter area to live and minister, it is normal for significant spiritual phenomena to occur.

Entrance phenomena vary widely. When new workers enter a community, I have seen members of their families become emotionally and mentally unstable. Other times there have been dramatic occult phenomena—violent fevers and sicknesses, or demons beginning to become afraid and stirring up trouble in a multitude of homes in the community on the same day. Sometimes the demons cry out, telling the people that the workers have come to cause them trouble, naming workers and their home countries before workers have had the chance to introduce themselves.

The kingdom of God invades with power. As it does, we experience the first fruits of the "powers of the age to come" (Hebrews 6:5). We have a taste of the power of that coming kingdom here in the present. It is not yet a banquet. We will feast at a banquet on the day when the rulers of this world are destroyed and the King of Kings is manifest in all his glory.

Sometimes we are surprised by these signs of the future. We find ourselves experiencing the miraculous in many different ways. Often it is in prophetic words about the future, or in healing and deliverance from the powers of this age. Again, it may be in direct revelations from God of specific unknown situations ("words of knowledge").

A Shepherd in the mist

It was Christmas in Calcutta. We were celebrating. I had given lights to this bustee family. As Hindu neighbors came to see the lights, we would tell them a little of the Christmas story.

I asked a 78-year-old man: "How do you know God? I mean really know God?" I knew that there were many nominal Christians who have never really known God, and I wanted to discover more about this man's faith.

"Let me tell you a story," he said. "Eighteen years ago, I was climbing a mountain with my baby daughter in my arms. Some mist came, and in the mist I became trapped, unable to move up or down.

"Suddenly in the mist a big man appeared, leaning on a staff. He helped me put my foot on the next step and then the next until we arrived at the top of the mountain where the rest of my family was watting. I reached into my pocket to give him two rupees for his help, but when I looked up, suddenly . . . he was gone!"

"From that time," he said, "I have known the Shepherd."

God had reached into the slums and revealed himself. But nobody in the 18 years since had come to tell more about how to follow that Shepherd!

The Spirit and justice for the poor

In the last phrase of Luke 4:18, we find Jesus speaking of bringing in an age of justice, the age of the kingdom—a time when equality will reign, when the poor will be uplifted and the rich brought low.

He had been cursed by a tribal enemy. As he died, he had a conversation with Jesus, who told him to go back to the living, for it was not his time yet. He must go and minister to the poor.

He began to pray for the sick. The lame, deaf, and blind were healed. Once, he raised a man from the dead. During a rebellion, the leaders of both sides would come to him, for he had become known as a holy man.

He encouraged the police not to fire, not to use real bullets. He encouraged negotiations. He helped develop trade unions to deal with the fundamental cause of the rebellion—the loss of the people's ecological environment through open-caste copper mining.

The man who knows the Spirit will often be the man whom God chooses to effect justice.

I believe that from among movements of men and women who will live among the poor, God will call some who, feeling the pain of the poor, are able to speak prophetically to those in authority. In India, only a holy man could speak in such a way, and holy men live as poor men. Incarnation among the poor is a prerequisite for this kind of prophetic role to the rich.

Notes

1. Wimber, John, *Power Evangelism,* San Franciso: Harper and Row, 1993.

Chapter Twelve

Biblical Theology for Poor People's Churches

What is the goal of life? According to the Westminster Catechism, "the chief end of man is to enjoy God and glorify him forever." Romans 8:29 tells us we were predestined to be conformed to the image (likeness) of his Son. One aspect of this goal of the Christian life is summed up in the old phrase, *imitatio Cristo*—the imitation of Christ.

If we accept this as the goal of the Christian life, what then is the goal of Christian ministry?

Jesus commands us to make disciples of all nations. That means developing people who are walking behind him, learning from him, and seeking to become like him. Colossians 1:28–29 tells us that Paul's goal is to "present everyone mature in Christ." For this he toiled, "laboring with all the energy which [God] mightily inspires within me."

Ephesians 5:27 makes it clear that God desires this maturity (or as some translations put it, perfection), not alone for individuals, but for the church, "without stain or wrinkle or any other blemish, but holy and blameless" (NIV). For we move to maturity in Christ as we move to unity and maturity with our brothers: "We will in all things grow up in him who is the head, that is, Christ. From him the whole body, joined and held together by every supporting ligament, grows and . . . does its work" (Ephesians 4:15–16 NIV).

The aim of the Christian life is perfection and maturity in Christlikeness. The aim of Christian ministry is the perfection and maturity of the church in spiritual unity with Christ.

What then is the aim of Christian missions? We are to "go and make disciples of all nations" (Matthew 28:18). The aim is not only to put missionaries on the field. The aim is not only to establish churches. The aim is not just to produce mature churches or growing churches. The aim is *to disciple the peoples.* The goal is to form movements—movements of mature churches among the peoples.

The church—declaration of Christ

It is the church that is the body of Christ, not just individuals. Individual compassion, incarnation, intercession, and proclamation are insufficient. We must press on until the church is established in any city. The apostle among the poor may incarnate Christ initially, but it is the emerging church or churches that are in a fuller sense the incarnation of Christ—his body. The apostle may proclaim, but it is the church that daily manifests to principalities and powers the resurrected Lord and the defeat of Satan on the cross (Ephesians 3:10).

But what is meant by "church"? It is generally perceived as the worshipping people of God gathered together under the preached word, each exercising his or her spiritual gifts in ministry, under a defined leadership of elders, pastors, and/or deacons, in a variety of structured relationships.

The structural components of this have become known in a school of thought called "church growth" theory. Based on an American world-view of structures and sociological pragmatism, it has developed some helpful concepts and research. Its basic conceptualization revolves around evangelism, discipleship, and the structure of the church.

But the commission of Jesus, as we have seen it, is for holistic and relational discipling. From this, and from the centrality of his preaching of the kingdom, church growth concepts unwittingly have been largely divorced. Jesus' commitment was not to evangelistic or pastoral structures, although he used these. His commitment was to love people. His commitment was to extend the kingdom. His commitment was holistic.

Over the last decade among evangelicals there has been a growing understanding of the role of the kingdom of God in our theology. First, we moved from "great commission missions" to a more holistic perspective on mission. Then came a new understanding of the kingdom of God as a broader theological concept that under girds the various components of mission and ministry. This broad concept of the kingdom has also made possible an integration of charismatic thinking into mainline evangelical perspectives.

CHURCH GROWTH MISSION
Its Generally Perceived Emphases

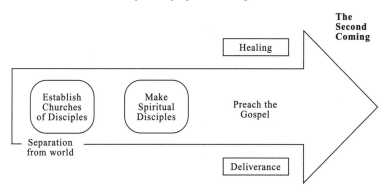

Mission is redemption of people in sociological contexts.

The Second Coming

Healing

Establish Churches of Disciples

Make Spiritual Disciples

Preach the Gospel

Separation from world

Deliverance

Focus: Ministry to world of sinful people

157

KINGDOM MISSION
A Broader Historical and Holistic View

Kingdom Mission is redemption of people resulting in societal change and healing for creation

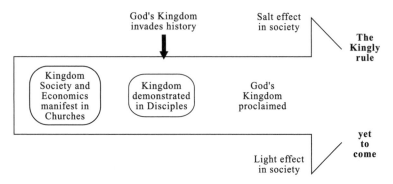

Focus: Poor and needy of a fallen world

HOLISTIC KINGDOM MISSION
Its Focus and Socio-Economic Impact

Kingdom Mission is redemption of people resulting in societal change and healing for creation

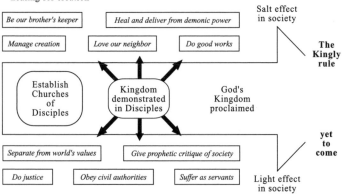

Focus: Poor and needy of a fallen world

These theological trends are timely, for they have at last provided evangelicals with a theology that can grapple with issues of poverty and the poor, urbanization, and injustice, while not denying the centrality of proclamation.

The kingdom—basis for a squatter theology

What is the kingdom of God? To understand effectively the nature of the church in the slums, we need to look beyond structural church growth studies to a holistic kingdom of God concept.

Jesus came preaching the kingdom of God. Thirty years later we find Paul in Rome, again preaching the kingdom of God. It is the central theme of the gospels, and gives us a more holistic perspective than one that focuses only on the growth of the church.

Church growth is an insufficient goal for which to give our lives. The kingdom of God is an objective that sets us free for a variety of ministries. The kingdom encompasses all of life. Church growth theory encompasses only a small part.

Traditional evangelical mission has focused on preaching the gospel, making disciples, and establishing them in churches. Kingdom-style mission sees these as central elements in a holistic pattern of ministry that encompasses every area of life.

Is the kingdom separate from, involved in, or set over the slums?

Based on a theological understanding of the relationship of kingdom with culture, we may ask practical issues about church-planting among the poor.

For example, should we establish the kingdom in the slums by gathering believers *separated from* the community (as in Anabaptist, Baptist, Holiness, and Pentecostal concepts of a kingdom that is *against* culture)? Or should the believers identify themselves *in* the slums in fellowships that seek to infiltrate all areas of life (according to the Anglican, Lutheran, Wesleyan transformational model)? Or, rather, should they be considered as *over* the slums (as in the identificational-dominance Calvinist model)?

No single, traditional, Western model of the kingdom or church suffices. A new synthesis that is specifically useful for ministry in the slums is needed. Such a model may well find components in each of the above.

From the Anabaptist, or separational paradigm, we find components of incarnation among the poor, based in theologies of Jesus as the model for our life.

From Reformed teaching, there are aspects of moderate kingdom theology—in contrast with dogmatic Calvinism—that enable us to deal with issues of injustice within the city.

From Pentecostal theology we learn the practice of ministering in the power of the Spirit to the poor.

From Lutheran, Anglican, and Wesleyan church structures, we learn the importance of authoritarian leadership structures for ministry to the poor.

Point of focus among the poor

A theology of the kingdom also predicts the style of ministry that should be central in working among the poor. There are many possible Christian or Christian-influenced responses to the plight of the slums. Which is most strategic? The answer depends on the strength and resources of the church, and the issues of oppression and poverty that are present in any given situation.

1. Economic determinism

If the cause of the poverty of the slums is seen as an economic lack, we will probably end up with a Christianized development agency. Compassion for the victims of oppression most frequently results in an economic response. This was true for Jesus, and it is true for us. We give aid. Linking our compassion with an analysis of the economic structures of our society results in Christian developmental responses to the poor. This is a kingdom response and a good one.

2. Sociological determinism

On the other hand, if we perceive that the poverty of the poor is caused by cultural and social factors, our tendency, over a period of time, will be to opt for more community organizational solutions.

Current theories in this area fall into the broad category of *empowering the poor*—enabling them to fulfill their destiny by learning about their own dignity and strength, and then, step by step, gaining their rights. These can be good kingdom responses. Often they have been emphasized by liberal and liberationist theologies, which with inadequate biblical roots are open to capture by Marxist philosophy. This is not a reason for evangelicals and Pentecostals to ignore the issues. Nor is it a reason to copy their categories.

3. Political determinism

Many go further than this, seeing the poverty of the poor as being caused by political systems and the misuse of power. Depending on where you start ideologically, you may perceive it as the result of exploitative capitalism and class struggle, of multinational rape of the nation, or of the abuse of power inherent in Marxism. These we have discussed previously under the rubric of marginality and social dualism.

To recognize oppression as the basic cause of poverty implies the need of a corresponding Christian response. To see the effects of oppression among the poor requires a kingdom response. The Scriptures are very forceful on the issue of living justly and effecting justice for the poor.

4. A Jesus-style ministry

The logical starting point for a Christian is to go to his Master, who is truth, manifested truth, and hence probably has the best answer to the issues. How did Jesus respond to the poverty of the city?

First, he was involved in dealing with it. He incarnated himself in it. He became one of the oppressed poor.

Second, he saw spiritual transformation as primary.

Third, he had a longer-term view than we do. He looked for the primacy of the kingdom—not of economic, social, or political development. Economic development, for Jesus, was a result of proclamation and subsequent submission to the King. In his eyes, repentance and discipleship were more significant than an approach based on political change.

At the same time, he made it clear that the kingdom at times impinged on economics, politics, and sociology. His kingdom was spiritual, but it involved new societies, new patterns of economics, and had a political philosophy of servanthood. Leadership development was central to his activities. But it was a leadership development whose cutting edge remained in spiritual ministry.

For this reason, it seems appropriate to focus on evangelism, followed by discipling and forming new social groups of converts. This has become known as church planting.

If our desire is spiritual confrontation with principalities and powers, we must also focus on church planting, because the lack of churches in the slums means an inadequate ethical base from which to seek political change. If it is in our hearts to effect justice for the poor, we focus on church planting because significant movements among the poor have a habit of effecting social and political change.

Interestingly, whatever views are determinative, some sociological conclusions are general to each of the four options above. Whether the organizations are economic, political, or religious, the key to change among the poor is multiplication of small organizations. Economically it is the multiplication of small cooperative ventures. Politically it is movements of small cells of totally committed cadres. Spiritually it is the multiplication of small churches or fellowships knit together in a web-like movement. Each of these empowers the poor, enabling them to begin to take their own destiny into their own hands.

Chapter Thirteen

Group Structures for Squatter Churches

In John 17, Jesus reflects in prayer about the work he had accomplished on earth. It is his final prayer, and final words usually contain central convictions. He prays for those whom God the Father has given from the world. He does not now pray for the world, but for this group of twelve.

Here he defines the goals of group discipling. He has manifested the Father. He has taught the Word in such a way that the disciples have obeyed. He has protected them, leaving them in the world, but sanctifying them in it. He has sent them forth and has modeled for them how they should minister. He prays for their spiritual unity.

These men are central elements in his ministry. Through these men he sees the world. He has formed a new sociological paradigm—a new small-group structure and a new pattern for birthing a movement. Based on these building blocks we can develop patterns for forming churches.

Three structures for the poor

I have found that there are three patterns of church structure that serve the urban poor:

1. Multiplication of squatter churches

The pattern prevalent in the ministry of Latin American churches among the poor is a multiplication in geographically-defined squatter areas and slums through an incarnational, small-group-movement approach. This model I have defined for missionaries in a number of writings.

These local slum congregations speak the heart language of the people, have local eldership, but are linked to other slum churches or vertically dependent on a middle-class church. They enable the slum dweller to feel at home in a slum culture, but have some ties to the outside middle-class city structures.

Many slum residents, while connected to the city, rarely venture into that city. A squatter may be a city-dweller in his or her own mind, but he or she is not necessarily identified with the structures of the middle-class city. The kind of church we have referred to in the preceding paragraphs is the only one that is likely to be appropriate for such a squatter.

Some traditions talk of a return to the New Testament church patterns. In the slums, however, first century patterns are inappropriate. There are no villas for house churches to meet in, so a local church building must be built (frequently known in Latin America as a *templo,* or "temple"). In Third World slum areas, there are no godly Jewish converts with stable families and depth in the Scriptures who can immediately step forward to lead new congregations. In the slums, heavy dependence upon the pastor for leadership may continue for some years. There is no concept of a synagogue to clarify what a church should look like, causing the poor to import middle-class Western or Catholic styles of church.

2. A gang-structured discipling web

A gang-like discipling movement works among specialized groups such as addicts, alcoholics etc. It may have a structure similar to a drug gang, but it is built around the authority of discipling relationships that emanate from a strong, central, intensive, discipling, charismatic figure.

Alcoholics Anonymous, jail ministries, and work among drug addicts, such as those of Jackie Pullinger or Teen Challenge, are among the current models of these city-wide ministries among the poor. They are not churches, yet churches may result in the squatter areas from such effective discipling.

3. A central-city, front-led superchurch

In some urban areas, there are great inner-city, charismatic celebrations held in the trade language of the city (in Asia, this is often English). The squatter can be linked to a middle-class city structure through these large-scale celebrations, yet at the same time attend smaller cell groups among other squatter and slum people that are holistic and incarnational. The middle-class fellowship has sufficient income to underwrite an indigenous pattern of supporting these smaller churches among the poor.

A woman transformed!

She had served as an assistant to the wife of a deposed dictator and was used to getting things done. Now she had just completed the foundation for a new church in the slums.

She had been touched by God in a big, upper-middle class, charismatic fellowship that met in a shopping mall—at times there had been 4,000 attending. The leaders had sent her to this garbage dump as she responded to God's call. Every day she traveled an hour and a half to reach the people who lived at the dump. Hers was one of five new outreaches to the poor from this particular fellowship.

This approach, however, cannot even be considered where the poor speak a different language from that of the rich and middle class. John Maust makes an interesting observation:

My informal investigations turned up only two Quechua-language evangelical congregations in all of Lima. More

Quechua churches seem a pressing need, considering the influx of thousands of people who grew up speaking one of the Quechua dialects as their mother tongue. Statistics say that 30 percent of the 18 million Peruvians speak only Quechua. These people will never go to a superchurch. And if they did, they couldn't invite their neighbors, who probably will never be able to afford the bus fare. Incarnation in this situation is our only option.[1]

Four seasons of growth

Just as there are normal patterns of personal spiritual growth, church growth of poor peoples' churches also follows regular patterns. Some steps must precede others. Some areas need to grow before others can develop. 2 Corinthians 3:18 tells us: "And we, who with unveiled faces all reflect the Lord's glory, are being transformed into his likeness with ever-increasing glory, which comes from the Lord, who is the Spirit" (NIV).

The chart on page 170 came from Gene Tabor and the Philippine leadership of REACH, a chart whose initial framework is known as the FOCUS Chart. Based on experience among the poor, this chart illustrates four distinct phases in the development of the life of a disciple and of fellowships of disciples as they move step-by-step to maturity.

Whereas most methods are most useful in the culture where they originate, the principles in the FOCUS chart's analysis of ministry appear to be universal. Starting with these principles, we can determine methodologies in each culture or sub-culture. The principles are based on processes a group of believers goes through when the Holy Spirit is working in a healthy manner in them. Beware, however—the processes are not the Holy Spirit. They are only the evidence of his indefinable and infinitely varied work.

The idea of a growth-oriented theology is implied in 1 John 2:12-14, where John talks of three phases of growth and defines some qualities of believers at each phase. From these, we may derive some ideas of what to focus on at any given season of growth.

> I write to you, dear children, because your sins have been forgiven on account of his name. I write to you, fathers, because you have known him who is from the beginning. I write to you, young men, because you have overcome the evil one. I write to you, dear children, because you have known the Father. I write to you, fathers, because you have known him who is from the beginning. I write to you, young men, because you are strong, and the word of God lives in you, and you have overcome the evil one.

1 JOHN 2:12–14

Children	Young Men	Fathers
• Know Father	• Strong	• Spiritual children
• Sins forgiven	• Word abides in them	• Companionship with Father
	• Overcome evil one	

We can define the characteristics of each phase described by John. The knowledge of God mentioned for both children and fathers in the Greek text is the same word. In practice, however, we realize that John is talking to children who have first experienced knowing God, and to fathers with a deep intimate relationship with God. We may also infer that the spiritual fathers have spiritual children.

While John defines three phases of the Christian life, in practice we have found there are four distinct phases, as the development of spiritual fathers is not a simple process. Before these four phases, we should remember that there is a "zero phase"—evangelism.

By looking at the characteristics above, we find a single word that defines a focus of ministry at each of four phases. (Notice, however, that this is a merely a focus—we do all things at all phases, but we concentrate on some at certain times). Many American books on disciple-making define discipleship by specifying goals for each phase. In Asia, and among the poor, this is a threatening and counter-productive approach, because it runs against the holistic cultural values of traditional societies. This chart is useful in Asia because of its focus on an atmosphere for ministry rather than on goals for ministry at each phase.

THE FOUR SEASONS OF GROWTH

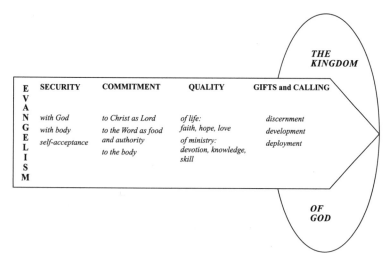

First season: security

Forgiveness of sins and knowledge of the Father indicate a focus on assurance and security. For those with difficulties in their relationships with their human fathers, there has to be healing if they are to love God. Some have difficulty in relating to others. They need a warm, loving group with lots of fun and fellowship, where fears are put to rest and new skills in relating can be learned.

During this phase, a leader will concentrate on teaching those aspects of the nature of God that lead to security—forgiveness, love, faithfulness. What are known as the basics of Christian growth are also important—how to become familiar with the Bible, how to have a daily quiet time, how to read the Bible, how to pray.

Togetherness and a sense of family and friendship are factors in all these activities, including many fun activities such as outings, sports, and meals together. It is also a time of fruitfulness for a new Christian, for he or she has many friends who may not believe in Jesus Christ. An older Christian also needs to be present, for while the new Christian can stir interest, he or she may not know how fully to communicate the gospel.

Charismatic worship is useful at this stage because it creates an environment where the presence of a loving Father God is seen and felt and preached through word and song.

Healing of major past hurts is also an aspect of growth at this time. The Scriptures say little about the psychology that is popular in present evangelicalism concerning inner healing. The central element in the Scriptures is forgiveness for those who oppress, and confession to those we have offended. Healthy patterns of confession and forgiveness need to be built into a fellowship as a basis for the continuing work of the Holy Spirit.

Self-acceptance is important during this phase. People tend to accept themselves on the basis of good looks, achievements, or status. God has a different basis of acceptance—his forgiveness on the cross and his fatherhood. If these areas do not become strong during the early Christian life, there is insufficient basis to handle later pressures of ministry.

Second season: commitment

Young people are strong. It is the younger generations who participate in sports and go to war. There is a level of commitment in youth that develops and can be encouraged.

Commitment to each other at this phase differs from that in the first phase. For people from broken families, a commitment to the family of God is a major undertaking. The first phase of growth in the family of God is one of fun and fellowship. Commitment to the Body during this second phase is a commitment that is tested. After realizing the failings of other members, after perhaps having some conflict with another member, then each new Christian faces the challenge of continuing to love. There needs to be a regular evaluation of the issues of forgiveness and restitution in group relationships—usually at the communion table.

I have used a phrase—"Commitments 1,2,3"—as a basis for building core teams during this period of ministry. Commitment to the Lord comes first, to the Body second, and to ministry third. If there are relational problems within the team, they will take priority over the external ministry of the team. The external ministry will always be there—there will always be needs, and the Lord promises that we will bear fruit. But relational problems are an immediate block to his working in and through us.

There are also issues of commitment to the Lordship of Christ. The discipler has to help people evaluate that Lordship in each area of their lives step by step. Will Christ be Lord in the areas of finances, family, marriage, missions, reputation, and honesty? Any of these things may come under testing during this phase of growth.

This is a time also of battle—of spiritual warfare. Young Christians need a commitment to the Word of God as the weapon of war. The Word also is their food and authority for life. Many may have an academic acceptance of the Word of God as authority. But discipling involves more than that—it involves helping new believers to turn to the Word for practical instruction on matters of family, finances, relationships, and so on. There needs to be training, as well, in the proclamation of the gospel, and in spiritual warfare.

During this phase there may be many long, late-night talks with older, mature Christians as the younger Christian works through issues. Small groups are a good setting for this. Too-close individual discipling relationships with a high-powered older Christian may be threatening. But during this second phase, long talks are inevitable and probably necessary as the new Christian works through many issues.

Training seminars are very effective during this phase of growth. Over a period of time, believers will have evangelized those who are responsive among their friends. The non-responsive will have drawn away from them, leaving them thus to find their friends increasingly in the church. This is healthy. But as they grow in commitment to the Great Commission they need help to start re-establishing relationships with non-Christians, and training in how to share their faith effectively.

It is good to encourage new believers to form evangelistic teams during this phase. Towards the end of this period one senses that fruit is about to come. It is the sign that someone has truly become not just a follower-disciple, but a faithful, tested disciple of Christ.

Third season: quality

The discipler encourages the fruit of character and ministry to emerge through teamwork and by bringing the new believer into

GROUP STRUCTURE FOR EACH SEASON OF GROWTH
(in a relatively responsive context)

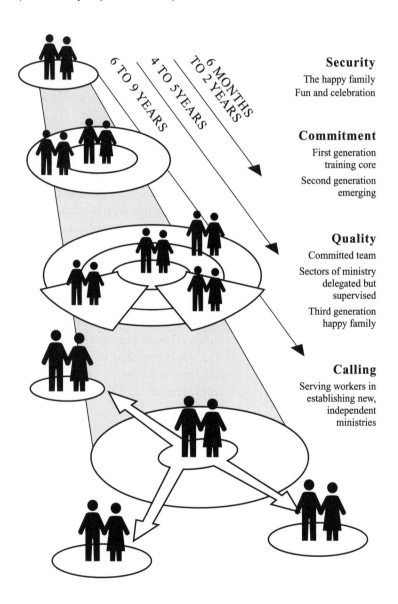

Security

The happy family
Fun and celebration

6 TO 9 YEARS

4 TO 5 YEARS

6 MONTHS TO 2 YEARS

Commitment

First generation
training core

Second generation
emerging

Quality

Committed team

Sectors of ministry
delegated but
supervised

Third generation
happy family

Calling

Serving workers in
establishing new,
independent
ministries

a close relationship and the home life of the discipler. Working through the Beatitudes is a good pedagogical tool for relating the Word of God to character issues during this phase.

This is also a period where deeper levels of commitment, skills, and a heart for ministry can be developed. Supervised ministry experiences are needed, with increasing levels of responsibility, and other occasions where the leader works with the growing Christian.

All believers should be developed through this phase into a maturity in Christ. They should be given basic ministry skills for leading another to Christ, holding a small Bible study, and personal discipling.

Fourth season: gifts and calling

Finally comes a phase where intimate knowledge of God and his calling makes it possible for specific gifts to be discerned and developed. Now the person may be deployed in a place of ministry where his or her gifts will be fully utilized. Some are called to develop as leaders, and energy must be concentrated on their lives. Others need help finding their place in the Body so they are fulfilled in their gifts and roles.

During this phase, greater degrees of freedom occur as leaders spin off into new ministries of their own. Others are better gifted to remain working as co-laborers with the ministry leader.

Integration

The usefulness of such a chart is that we may enter any group, discern at what level of growth they are, and minister to them at the appropriate level.

The first and last phases are ones with a great deal of freedom and variety for the people involved. The middle two phases, on the other hand, are phases of tightly committed training, where the ministry leader expects high levels of commitment and exercises a significant level of direction and authority.

The time frame for each phase varies with the individuals, experiences, and cultures. Generally, the first phase may take from six months to two years, the second from one to two years, the third will normally be completed by the fifth year of growth of a new convert.

Discussion with many ministry leaders indicates that it takes eight to nine years to train a spiritual father or mother. Indeed, in this final phase, not all are called to be spiritual fathers or mothers. There are many other gifts that need developing. The length of time to produce a spiritual father or mother is apparently independent of the structure of training they go through, be it in a Bible college, or through a lay leadership movement—it still takes about the same length of time.

The charismatic dimensions of deliverance from the demonic, the exercise of spiritual gifts, and the healing of emotional wounds are an important element in the provision of security in the first phase. They are generally overemphasized in charismatic circles, however, simply because the new believer's character problems often limits the extent to which the Spirit can use a person. At the end of the third phase, one sees extensive impact of the Spirit and fruitfulness in ministry, and it is here that the development of spiritual gifts enters a deeper realization.

Many young Christians seek the exercise of dramatic gifts and are disappointed because they seem unsuccessful. It would be far better to give themselves to growing in knowledge of the Word and of the Lord. In time, fruit will develop from a life of abiding in Christ, and gifts will become evident. Similarly, many fundamentalist evangelistic and discipling programs put pressure on people to produce fruit in evangelism. While evangelistic skills need to be learned, the Scriptures teach that fruit is the result of abiding in Christ, in his Word, and in prayer. It is not the result of increased pressure and techniques (John 15:5-7).

Security precedes fatherhood

He was a new missionary who had never dealt with the issues of security during his early training. The trauma of his parents' death, experienced as a teenager, had severely damaged his ability to understand fatherhood.

He was now trying to function as a ministry leader (phase four), and the lack of security was crippling his capacity to be a spiritual father. The flock was reacting to this lack. He would try to compensate by developing new programs. But because he lacked the fatherly concern needed to execute them, the programs failed.

He would spend hours staring into space or walking alone, seeking release from the emotions he felt. Guilt increased. Eventually his ministry was paralyzed. Then God began to minister his fatherhood to those early hurts.

Each season is a prerequisite to the next.

A word of warning is called for here. The four seasons chart is human wisdom based on the experience of application of the Scriptures to Christian growth. It is a focus for that growth's different phases, but it is not the infallible word of God.

Place of personal discipling

Many Western discipleship models emphasize personal or one-to-one discipling. This works well among individualistically-oriented peoples, but not in most of the world. A discipler's task is to create the environment of growth at each point—not to do everything alone. The group dynamic is crucial. Personal discipling patterns need to be there, but should not be overly emphasized, particularly in group-oriented cultures.

The discipler needs to form a healthy relationship with the young Christian and to be available at critical times, but he or she should not become overly intensive in discipling, as this can be very intimidating for anyone. The members of Christ's body, his church, minister to each other. The discipler's task is to create the environment where this can happen.

Apostolic "thrust" and pastoral concerns

In the early phases of its development, the church will tend to manifest more of an evangelistic, apostolic style. In later stages, more pastoral issues will come to the forefront. Correspondingly, in earlier phases we would expect more power encounters. In later phases we would expect to see more emphasis on economic and social development. An overemphasis on power evangelism may lock young churches into a pattern of continual turnover of new converts without long-term pastoral care. The church planter's task requires maintaining a fine balance between these poles.

THE FOUR SEASON OF GROWTH
In the Context of the Poor and Needy

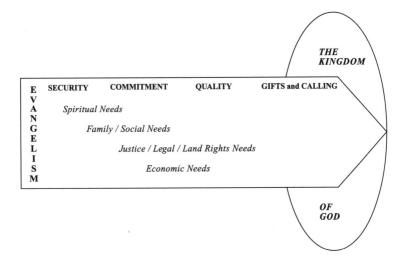

Holistic poor peoples' churches

God's intentions are for maturity in us as individuals, in churches and in the world. Paul sought to present every individual "mature in Christ" (Colossians 1:28–29). We are to develop the church to be "without spot or blemish" (Ephesians 5:27). We are to pray and work for the world so that "thy kingdom [may] come" (Matthew 6:10). The gospel deals with all these areas, for "all things hold together in Him" (Colossians 1:17). The gospel embraces all of life and creation.

Thus we may re-diagram the four seasons chart (p. 178) to consider these four areas at each of the four seasons.

Physical need and spiritual growth

The four seasons of growth follow a pattern observed by psychologists in the levels of development in children as well as in cultures. In 1954, Maslow discerned a pattern which defined the primary needs of mankind at a survival level.[2] If these are met, then people pay attention to needs at a security level. If most of these are met, people then have enough energy to pay attention to their needs for a sense of achievement. The highest level Maslow defines is self-actualization, a term that Christians have some difficulty relating to because of its linkage to New Age thinking. Perhaps we would define it as a level of maturity, of total dependence upon God.

In Israel's exodus from Egypt, the Lord's task was to change the character of a stubborn, stiff-necked, slave-mentality people. Our task among the poor is not dissimilar to the process followed by Israel during the exodus.

Similarly, when Jesus began his ministry, he found some secure, achievement-oriented businessmen, some government officials, and a few revolutionaries. He structured a context where these four levels of need could be met for team members. In doing this, he gave leadership to a movement that spread mainly among those who were lacking at the levels of security and survival. His core team members were not destitute. They were not failures.

Survival

Our primary level of need is to survive. If we are unable to meet basic needs for food, clothing, and housing, our whole psyche concentrates on finding solutions to this problem.

For example, the Nazis succeeded in cutting down the food level of people in concentration camps to 700 or 800 calories a day (men normally need 3,000 and women need 2,400). There were no riots and no sexual problems between men and women. All their attention was focused on getting the next meal. It is the same with the destitute poor.

God, in the desert, met the survival and security needs of the Israelites so they no longer had to focus all their attention on these issues. So too, Jesus provided for the twelve who traveled with him through the support he generated from his ministry,

John Wesley was saddened by his inability to reach the poorest of the poor. William Booth took up the challenge, developed an economic base, and began to see fruit from evangelization and discipling.

Security

Ruth Benedict, an early anthropologist once studying an island tribe, asked the question, "Why were the island children so insecure?" The answer appeared to be related to a lack of identity. Children were cared for by a multitude of older people. They did not know which of the adult women was their biological mother. The result—an unmet security need and a static society. Because all of their energy was focused on meeting this security need, there was no achievement. Security always comes before achievement.

Among the poor, we must work to enable the potential leaders of the fellowship to arrive at economic self-sufficiency (meeting survival needs). We must develop healthy group dynamics for the family of God so that their security needs are taken care of.

A movement among the poor must develop a clear structure with various levels of leadership and fellowship. The nature of the structure may vary, but consistency and clarity are critical. To a certain degree, the people must know what to expect. This is why many non-incarnational Western missions end up with a modest rate of church growth, even though they do not develop indigenous patterns. The structures they produce, while not easy for the national people to work within, are stable, and hence produce some degree of security.

One structural pattern, for example, that tends to recur among peasant cultures, and hence among slum churches, is the choir. In Brazil, where choirs abound, one sometimes even sees dueling choirs in the same church—the ladies' choir outdoing the youth choir, or the guest choir serenading the local church choir. These choirs provide a secure context of growth for new believers.

Why is there a need for such security? People cannot move to a place of subjection to Christ as Lord of all if they are not first secure in their relationship with God. How do you trust him if you are not sure he is faithful? How do you trust him to provide until you have experienced his provident sovereignty?

If these first two levels are met, people have enough psychological energy to develop at the next level.

Achievement

Jesus met his disciples' survival and security needs. Then, to meet their achievement needs he gave them the truth and sent them out to minister. We need to encourage new churches to develop financial structures that free leaders from financial restraints in order to devote themselves to ministry.

John Wesley never would have succeeded in his ministry if he had not received a regular stipend from the church. This met his survival needs. Working from this base, he could freely give himself to high levels of achievement.

Maturity

Culture in any society normally has been advanced by the leisure class. In the same way, theological and new ministry concepts generally come from those who have the time for meditation, creative study, and thinking. The people who engage in these activities are not dependent on achievement for their self-identity or self-esteem. They achieve not to meet needs, but instead for the joy of achieving. People at this level constantly seek to create and to understand. While they may relate well to others, they are not controlled by emotional needs in relationships.

The overall leadership of movements among the poor will probably come not from the poor themselves, because few are able to develop their gifts to this level, but from the educated elite who have had time to attain the required level of maturity. To be effective, these leaders must choose lifestyles of voluntary poverty.

The four categories of growth that we have mentioned parallel those of the four seasons chart, but add the important factor of meeting survival needs as a basic step for enabling the poor to grow to full maturity in Christ.

From fighter to leader

He was one of the first to come to know the Lord in the community. He hungered after God, eager to learn all he could be taught. At first he oscillated back and forth between his old drinking friends and the newly-discovered prayer meetings. He did not want to lose friendships.

The pastor remained patient with him, talking with him about the testimony involved, and helping him to apologize to the other believers whenever he got drunk. One morning, after a drunken night, he talked long with the pastor and made a decision to stop drinking.

His hunger for God and the Word remained. He began preaching around the barrio, and many were affected by his new testimony. One night some old enemies turned up outside his house. He tried to talk to them with grace, but the enmity ran hard. They drew knives. He and his father ran into the house and returned with their machetes. They chased the men.

There was much counseling. Again there was public repentance. In the counseling it became obvious that the fight had occurred under the influence of evil spirits. Prayers were offered in the house and for the new Christian. His father gave his heart to the Lord.

His desire for the Lord continued to grow. The pastor remained patient. The new convert started some new Bible studies. People started coming to the Lord.

One day, under the ministry of the Holy Spirit, the Lord showed him many past scenes and brought balm into each one. The fighter was being transformed. With a new-found anointing from God, the Bible studies grew. But sadly so did the tension between the new believer and the pastor who had so nurtured him.

The last time we talked, he himself had become a pastor. Now he worked in unity with his former pastor. The story is not finished, for God is not yet finished.

Notes

1. Maust, John, *Cities of Change,* Latin American Mission, 1984.

2. Maslow, Abraham, *Motivation and Personality,* New York: Harper and Row, 1987.

Chapter Fourteen

Pastoring the Poor

Pacing holiness for new converts

There is much sin among new converts. The pastor must exercise strong discipline over them, while at the same time being "tender like a nursing mother taking care of her children" (1 Thessalonians 2:7). There needs to be a sensitive oscillating between judgment and mercy.

Because of these patterns of sin, the first generation of converts often will not survive, just as the first generation in the Exodus did not survive. They lacked models who walked in obedience to God. Their children in the faith, seeing how their parents are handled, learn alternative models from the leader. They watch as the first converts go through their tragic backslidings. Because the younger generation learns these lessons, it frequently forms the long–term nucleus of the ministry.

As leaders emerge in the new congregation, it is normative for them to come into confrontation with the authoritarian leader. This is partly because the poor often fear immediate authorities. Partly it is because of the overly authoritarian styles of leaders—styles that may be necessary during the birth of a church.

Skillful training is needed to help the church planter move from a tightly-knit training model to a model of collegiality with other leaders while still maintaining final authority. Part of the solution to this problem is a good structure that provides levels of autonomy as new leaders emerge, yet offers clear lines of authority. Another part of the solution is a concept of ministry that helps churches grow by freeing people into ministry.

The centrality of the home

The home is the center of ministry in many cases of effective church planting among the poor. Where ministry is focused around the home there is a strong transferal of life patterns, of character, of values, and of the Word.

Jackie Pullinger in Hong Kong has had no room of her own for many years as she has had many needy people coming to live with her. Again, the transferal of life and values, coupled with a dynamic public worship time, has brought forth fruit in hundreds of lives.

Practical hints for pastors

1. Build momentum

It is important to reach enough people to establish and maintain social momentum. As a means of doing this, keep constant charts and records. Stay on the edge of relationships. By that I mean, know where you are with every relationship in the community or church, and keep them constantly in prayer so you will be sensitive to the next step. Constantly be developing new groups.

2. Break down social barriers

Draw the people together in social activities before calling them together in the religious activities. McGavran's big theme is that the barriers are social, not religious. Seek out people in each segment of the community. Allow time for community-wide discussion of major moves.

3. Celebrate

If you use a fast approach with evangelism, the phases of group dynamics move immediately from an initial mass of converted people to regular worship. In a non-receptive culture where the growth is slower, and a slow approach to evangelism is used, there is apt to be movement from the development of Bible studies to some form of integrating people socially.

At first, this is generally not best developed as worship, but more as social and relational activities. This should be the case until new believers develop some degree of security with each other. These activities, however, should definitely include some elements of worship, such as singing and Bible reading, along with outings, birthday parties, camps, and so on.

The third phase is to integrate the newly forming relationships into a worshipping congregation. Chuck Hufstetler, a church planter in Manila who taught me a great deal, used to talk of *contacts, converts, cells, congregation,* and *celebration.*

The culture of poverty indicates small churches will most probably emerge among the poor, due to lack of management skills. Thus, worship patterns should be developed primarily for this size of congregation. Make the management decisions on most issues in such a way that they can be reproduced. Set patterns of worship. Make large gatherings occasions for people in traditional societies to enjoy event-oriented and relationship-oriented celebrations, rather than performance-oriented celebrations as can often happen in Western worship.

4. Maintain a good public reputation

It is good to aim to become the social and spiritual leader of a community. Work, therefore, for a good name in the community by avoiding confrontation as much as possible, and by working with people of good will in those areas where collaboration is possible.

The squatter area will be reached when the leaders of the community are reached. It is a good idea, as you reach out to the poorer people, constantly to be drawing the natural leaders of the community into your confidence and discussions on issues. This will establish trust and lay a foundation for their conversion.

Leaders will generally wait until others make commitments before they themselves take a stand—particularly elected officials, who have vested interests in their position in the community. Do not waste a lot of time on appointed officials except to maintain good relationships. Look instead for the natural leaders, those to whom the people go for advice in emergencies.

Establishing a legal structure

It is ideal to enter a community with legal documents for the emergence of a church in order. This is not difficult if the new congregation is a healthy daughter of another church. The eldership of a mother church provides the initial legitimizing authority and appoints the church planter. Ideally, the mother church evaluates with the church planter those whom he or she draws into the team, while leaving sufficient freedom for the church planter to recruit and build that team.

As a church planting team develops, the "parent" elders should release appropriate aspects of this authority, but remain as an outside reference and advisory board. This is important since there are continual changes in roles and power relationships between members of a church planting team as the ministry unfolds. There are often disputes that are the result of learning how to work together with other highly motivated and often strong-willed pioneers. The leader's authority is often challenged, and a good outside board can sometimes help resolve such conflicts.

Maintaining integrity before the public requires bookkeeping and legal papers. If these are submitted initially through the mother church, it gives the pioneers freedom to concentrate on ministry. If there is no mother church, the papers should be obtained at the outset of the work, and books and an accounting system set up as in any small business.

When a diaconate and eldership begin to emerge, it is essential that they take over formal responsibilities from the pioneering team and the pastor for the legal and accounting aspects of the fellowship. The sooner this happens, the better. Yet we are commanded also to "not be hasty in the laying on of hands" (1 Timothy 5:22).

Inadequate legal structure

One of the mistakes in my first years of ministry among the poor was that I did not initiate the legalization of our first church. Partly, this was because the extra paperwork would have consumed more than the church's income. We did not have a clear daughter relationship with what is now the mother church, because there were doctrinal changes and ministry strategy changes necessary to work with the poor. They were not understood at that time by the churches. The result was inadequate bookkeeping. This was rectified.

The next thing that happened was that foreign missionaries arrived. Because of a lack of clear legal definitions, they took over several areas of church life. After some time they moved on. Since doctrine and strategy had been demonstrated, the church became a daughter church of the middle-class church, still without legalizing any structure in the slum.

Then another mission came in to assist in development. It essentially took over responsibility for the church. The pastor found himself in a difficult role—having no legal status, yet still the pastor of the church he had pioneered through all this time. It was ultimately recommended that the church be legalized independently of the outside development program.

It is always wise to incorporate before too many people are involved in a church-planting venture.

Pastoral issues

1. The family

Modernization and urbanization produce changes in family structures. There are also changes in role structure, in decision-making patterns, in socialization of the young, and in ways of relating to complex, non-family organizations.

For example, a family back in the rural area may have been a complete productive unit, working the land. In the city, adults work in organizations outside the family. Meanwhile, children attend schools with other children from a wide variety of backgrounds—not just the village context. While the home was originally a homogenous unit that was functionally comprehensive, the home and workplace now become divorced, often with both husband and wife working outside the home and facing changed roles.

The church and the church planter must address the question, How do you facilitate this adaptation?

The pastor can help greatly. Such help will involve assistance in the assumption of roles outside family, in developing new patterns of socialization and social control, in enabling competency to meet external social and work requirements and choices, and in helping families define loyalties in this new context.[1]

2. Psychological problems

The marginalized poor often seem to be so deprived that they are only half people, devastated by twin catastrophes—rapid social change, with its breakdown in family structures, and poverty itself.

There are many resulting issues of oppression, desertion, sexual molestation, and guilt that affect almost all squatters deeply. The primary processes of healing are not psychotherapy or counseling, which often have poor linkages to the Scriptures and a misplaced lack of focus on the role of the church, the Spirit, and worship. The primary process is the church—ministering together and to each other weekly in the presence of the Spirit of God, gathered around the Word of God.

The poor are not healed instantaneously. For many, there will be no healing, but only a place of acceptance in the midst of others with great unhealed areas. The weekly altar call in most poor people's churches is a place of healing, week by week, that little by little advances the healing process through the years.

Some aspects of healing are also cultural, for the poor in the slums have largely lost their cultural roots. Karl Schmidt tells of a simple proverb used for aiding the migrant poor in the South Pacific:

Love your own culture;
Regain it where lost;
Enrich it where possible.[2]

Social and cultural factors in church life are a great healer.

3. An oppressed people

The poor have been oppressed for centuries, first as rural peasants and now in the city. The result is a deep pain in their spirits. There is bitterness and resentment in their hearts, but all is submerged behind a smiling, graceful exterior. Central to the worldview change involved in becoming a Christian is a new pattern of response to oppression.

Marxists affirm the bitterness-oppression struggle, increasing its intensity. This brings no healing, only darkness. Christians, however, overcome evil with good, hatred with love, bitterness with forgiveness. The result is healing in the inner spirit and a growing ability to handle conflicts in such a way that healthy consensus between opposing parties may be attained.

In my experience, an understanding of forgiveness is the central teaching priority in discipling the poor. It is built from stories in the Old Testament that tell of the sovereignty of God in dealing with oppressed peoples. An experience of God's forgiveness equips the poor convert to cope with the reality of oppression—even when it continues while standing up for rights and dignity.

Envy, envy—cockroaches in the heart!

It is ten years later in Tatalon, a squatter community, now with 48,000 people in upgraded two-story and three-story homes.

Before me are a sea of faces—faces I have loved from the days when they were marked by sin. Today I see ten years of the work of the Spirit of God. There is a maturity there now, a softness, a graciousness one to the other. But not all sins disappear overnight.

I preach again of the dark world of the inner soul, the world full of envy, jealousy, bitterness—those cockroaches that come out from the heart. And the people laugh and smile. They know, they identify. This is their life. And they feel my words are spoken as one of them because I sat for years in their midst, hearing, feeling the inner darkness of those centuries of oppression from which they are emerging.

And once again this week, brothers are reconciled and light replaces darkness in the scarred souls of the maturing poor.

Exercising discipline

As a Baptist, I ask why most Baptist churches do not grow among the poor. The major reason seems to be that the democratic authority structure of Baptist churches is inappropriate to the situation of the poor. The poor prefer forceful authoritarian leaders who love them, yet exercise strong discipline over them. This is particularly true among squatters, where a broken social structure must be combatted with discipline in church life.

Churches and movements tend to be initiated around stalwart charismatic leaders who create strong patterns of doing things and delegate authority to others.

Paul's leadership defense in 2 Corinthians 10–12 is an excellent model. He raised up his own churches, not laboring where others had labored, and the realm of his authority was clearly demarcated. He rejected those who came into his churches from other types of Christianity, for they had a different spirit that was divisive. He rejected false apostles and identified their characteristics—ministering for financial gain, speaking with misleading rhetoric, acting deceitfully, critiquing the apostolic authority of the original founder, seeking position.

These same characteristics are seen today. In a sense, seminaries are set up to produce those who minister for financial gain—their graduates expect to be paid for their services. The characteristics of a false apostle are also found among those who would use the poor to make a name for themselves, or a living. This is easy to do through involvement in giving aid. I know of men who like to tell stories of the poor without ever having spent a night among them. Read the stories of Nobili or Assisi. In their time, church leaders loved power, took control of effective ministries to the poor, and eliminated the pioneering source of effectiveness. It is well for pastors among the poor to guard their flocks tenderly and to be cautious of those bearing gifts.

Paul, in contrast, suffered with his people as he birthed his congregations—he held them in his heart. This was the basis of his authority. He did not seek reconciliation with false apostles. To seek such reconciliation may hinder a movement's growth. The pastor in the slums, or the one who would see a movement developed, must be careful to delegate only to those whose loyalty and faithfulness to his authority are integral to their obedience to the Lord.

What of the attrition rate?

Attrition means death in battle. When related to churches it refers to those who are converted and then fall away. Proverbs tells us to "know well the condition of your flocks." Jesus reports to the Father at the end of his ministry that "not one of them is missing except the son of perdition." There is a divine responsibility to protect the flock as it grows.

A number of factors in the development of poor people's churches cause a high attrition rate. The first appears immediately at conversion as the new Christian faces the changes from an old lifestyle. The primary difficulty here is for the convert to enter the kingdom and church without losing relationships with worldly associates—for example, a drinking man and his drinking friends. If the group dynamics are not healthy, or the ability of the pastor to discipline with grace is not great, many will be lost.

This applies at each phase. Planting churches is an art. Failure to develop the right atmosphere, the right focus on structure, or the right teaching at each phase will lose people. So will a failure to exercise appropriate leadership styles at each stage of development. But there are special problems within the broken social structure of the urban poor.

Jealousy causes loss

It was a church I had helped found. An early convert talked to me of the natural jealousies of the poor: "Now we are faithful to the Lord. My life has changed, thanks to you. But we have been separated from the church. It is because of jealousy—so much talk."

Another told me of frustration with physical facilities: "The church building is so small we can't even stand to sing. So I went to the church out on the highway."

Yet another with strong evangelistic and leadership gifts: "The church should be evangelizing among the people. It will never grow in this area. So I went to the big church in the city center."

A woman shared her insecurities: "The leader told me I should be a teacher, but I am not gifted to teach, so I do not go . . . ."

All of the above are expressions of the fragility of relationships among the poor; of how easily security can be damaged; of the complexity of factors needed to keep the flock together. They require gentle, patient and firm leadership. The pastor and his wife in this church had stood firm through all these testings, and God had honored their ministry.

Economic factors and church growth

1. Redemption and lift

This phrase refers to the fact that as people are redeemed they automatically move upwards economically and socially. As a consequence, they lose touch with their non-Christian friends. Many squatter communities, however, are relatively stable. The poor do not move out of the community as their situation improves. Rather, the community is upgraded, legalized, and becomes part of the middle-class city in many cases. There are exceptions to this, such as in Sao Paulo, where favelas are limited to land under control of the politicians, and cheap housing is available. In Sao Paulo, as people move up, they move out.

Redemption and lift does not necessarily isolate the church from the people. Indeed McGavran's analysis of this issue did not focus on it as a negative phenomenon, but on the speed and manner of its occurrence and on its impact on relationships with the non-Christian community.

2. Support of pastors

In Latin American countries, it is normal for the squatter pastor to be self-supporting, working in a demanding job during the day and in the ministry at night. In other cultures, such as in Manila, squatter ministries are often linked to a middle-class congregation or denomination or to a foreign organization.

It is not clear whether this is a result of cultural or economic factors. It may be due to the emphasis placed upon dependent relationships between rich and poor, or to Westernized patterns of the church still dominant within the Philippine culture. This Westernization is evident in the pattern of Filipino seminary training that moves the poor into a middle-class status, often supported from overseas. On the other hand, it may be a factor determined by the availability of jobs and the possibilities of employment.

3. Emotional and physical disability

Oppression of the poor, while creating an environment for them to be rich in faith, also limits their development and the development of the church. Among the poor, new believers or church leaders are often sickly or die young because of bad water, the constant presence of garbage, or relocation because of disputes over land. In this situation, of what value is spiritual ministry? These reasons alone are sufficient for us to turn to the fight against poverty as a major aspect of our desire to see the church grow among the poor.

4. Breaking the property barrier

Weld and McGavran talk of keys to the cities.[3] They challenge the church planter to resolve the barrier of property. In some situations, it is better not to set up church buildings, as they are costly and may create barriers. They may also focus the attention, time, and energy of new converts on the wrong issues. Often when we talk of developing a cell–structured church, we understand that a building would not be helpful. This is true particularly in movements among professionals in Western cities.

Among the poor, however, house churches often do not grow but tend to die because people become disappointed at worshipping in unsatisfactory conditions. Bible studies and family devotional patterns tend to have a longer life. House churches, Bible studies and family devotions are a beginning, but since it is hard to find a home that is big enough for a church, the people should buy a lot and erect a simple building or rent a warehouse.

Usually squatter pastors erect churches with their own hands, helped by their flock. There is enough evidence from the cities I have visited to indicate that the rapid erection of a simple building using the materials of the people is a critical factor in the growth of the church, rather than a hindrance to its growth. It is also cheaper to get land for this when the squatter area is just beginning than after the church and community are fully formed.

This is an area where foreign funding is non-destructive and can be used for great effect in the initial phases of buying land. Foreign money can provide for part of the cost of the initial building in numerous squatter areas throughout a city.

5. Securing land

It is also important to be seeking justice for the poor. The central element in this is usually land rights, a subject that needs to be covered thoroughly in a separate book. Suffice it to say that half the people of the world do not have rights to the land on which they live. And that the obtaining of those rights brings about a dramatic change almost overnight in their ethics and spiritual receptivity. The issue of land rights is perhaps one of the most critical theological issues of our day. It most certainly is a central issue in planting churches among the poor.

I was sitting with a development worker discussing the lack of Bengali churches in Calcutta.

In passing, he mentioned that perhaps the reason for a lack of churches in the bustees of India is the lack of available land—not necessarily land for churches, but land for burial. Hindus, who cremate their dead, do not want burial grounds near their homes. In discussions he had with a group ready for baptism, this had become their primary question.

Notes

1. Sassman, Marvin B., "Family Systems in the Seventies: Analyses, Policies and Programs," *Annals,* No. 396, 1971, pp. 40–56.

2. Harre, John, *Living in Town: Problems and Priorities in Urban Planning in the South Pacific,* Suva, Fiji: South Pacific, Social Sciences Foundation and School of Social and Economic Development, University of the South Pacific, 1973, pp. 93–101.

3. Weld, Wayne and Donald McGavran, *Principles of Church Growth,* William Carey Library, 1974.

Chapter Fifteen

An Inside Perspective on Squatter Churches

In order to bring God's kingdom into the lives of millions of slum dwellers, we must gain an insider's perspective into the culture of the poor. This gives a basis for predicting the kind of churches we should expect in the slums. Anthropological wisdom is a basis for effective love of the poor.

Peasants in cities

Early anthropologists studied and contrasted primitive and civilized peoples in an evolutionary context. As the deficiencies of an evolutionary view with its implied superiority complex became obvious, Robert Redfield developed a neo-evolutionary "folk-urban continuum" in 1947. From a survey of numerous ethnographic studies, he demonstrated the differences in culture between idealized "folk" societies and urban societies.

An ideal type of folk or primitive society may be developed by comparison of numerous studies. These may be contrasted with the literate or semi-literate, the industrialized or semi-industrialized modern city . . . Where cities have arisen, the country people dependent on cities have developed economic and political relationships as well as relationships of status . . .we call [this] peasantry.[1]

In 1954, Redfield and Singer expanded this concept into a three-part typification which we may label *tribal peasant* and *urban,* and developed theories on the processes of change that occur between these societies.[2] Mary Douglas further categorized the traits of these three "ideal" types.[3] Generally, the evolutionary and neo-evolutionary theories of cultures have been rejected, but the models have remained useful, both as historical analyses of urban development and of non-historical patterns of migration.

Anthropologists have traditionally chosen peasant and tribal cultures to study where most of the people in the group (with some deviance) share an integrated system of beliefs, values, and learned behavior. In turn, this belief and value system is integrated with the various subsystems of their lives—political, social, religious, economic, etc.

Generally, this integration does not take place in the urban context. Instead, we see a series of intersecting cultures and institutions that pull and tug the new urban dweller. To describe this, Redfield and Singer developed a number of theories about cultural change. The focus of their anthropological study, however, was on the borders between clashing cultures rather than on an integrated culture. It was the study of cultures in transition. The chart on the next two pages summarizes various categorizations.

Church and culture

We must consider the relationship between church and culture. Our understanding of the Scriptures will determine the kinds of churches we are able to develop and how we deal with the city. There are essentially three approaches when considering the relationship of church to culture:

1. The church as separate from and opposed to culture (Fundamentalist, Pentecostal, Anabaptist);

2. The church identifying with culture (State churches); or

3. The church transforming culture (Reformed perspectives).[5]

All three perspectives come from the Scriptures, and we need

THREE POLAR TYPES OF SOCIETY[4]

	TRIBAL	PEASANT/ MULTI-GROUP	URBAN INDUSTRIAL
TECHNOLOGY	Hunter-gardner Subsistence/ generalist	Beginning of agriculture Crafts, artisans	High tech/complex Specialization, muliplex roles Agro-business
SOCIAL STRUCTURE	Strong group, kinship Clan, tribe, lineage	Strong group Multiple groups	Strong individualism Groups are functional aggregates Short-term contractual relationships
Family	Extended	Varies widely	Nuclear (old, sick excluded)
Dominant Diads	Father-son	Parent-child Patron-worker	Husband-wife Friend-friend
Mobility		Peasants not mobile	Social/geographic mobility
Integration	Organization of larger units along ethnic, family lines	Hostility/rivalry and hierarchy between groups Lowest group oppressed and emulates elite	Heterogeneity and relativism
ECONOMY	Subsistence	Market	Commercial
Land	Shared, group owned	Tenants on Lord's land	Individual ownership
Energy	Human, animal, tools	Human, animal	Fuel-powered machines
Goods	Few-group use	Many by artisians	Vast number-for money
POLITICAL STRUCTURE	Mono-cultural Independent clan groups	Town/peasant, city-state Structured like tribe	Nationalism and interdependent states
Dominant Institution		Feudal Lord-servant Patron-client	Corporation

	TRIBAL	PEASANT/ MULTI-GROUP	URBAN INDUSTRIAL
Leadership	Tribal council	Dominant ruling group. Feudal bi-level structure. Each group has leadership.	"Big men," dynamic leader. Networks, voluntary association. Bureaucratic institution.
Power	Weak	Very great (lords)	Divided among specialists
Control (law)	Shame when norms violated.	Shame, gossip, civil law.	Freedom Civil/ criminal law
Decision-making	Mutual responsibility. Group decision making.	Peasants-limited rights. Lords-full freedom.	Individual and personal
Communication	Up and down. Oral societies.	Downwards and horizontal within group	Literate and postliterate. Mass media, public.
RELIGIOUS WORLD-VIEW	Animistic. Uniform. Small traditions.	Animism + National Religion. Great tradition (integrates local).	Many religions. Secular. Pluralistic.
Importance	Permeates all life	Important	Unimportant
Perception of church	High church/rituals dominant	Bastion of right in midst of evil and godless group	Collection of individuals in chaotic world. Big leaders with strong sense right/wrong.
World	Good	Evil, but our little culture is good	Chaotic, not evil
Truth	Eternal	Belongs to our group	Intensely personal
God	High concept		
Sacred	Tradition	Group (group rituals)	Secularism
Sin	Violation of cosmic order	Violation of group norms	Violation of self (self-fulfillment stressed.)
Ancestors	Nurtured, placated	Respected	Forgotten

wisdom to know which to pursue at any given time. This question is complex because the Scriptures have a dual perspective on the world. It was created by God and hence good. But the world was also linked to man's fall, and hence cursed and under the power of the evil one.

History also plays a role in forcing the church to take positions. Under oppressive regimes, where the church has no opportunity to exercise responsibility for society, one would expect a "church against culture" view to prevail. In an open democracy, such as in some Western countries, there could be expected to be a strong "church transforming culture" perspective—this being a permissible role for the church in society. In societies where church-goers make up over 20 percent of the population and wield great power, more identification between the church, the power

THREE MAJOR CHRISTIAN VIEWS OF CULTURE

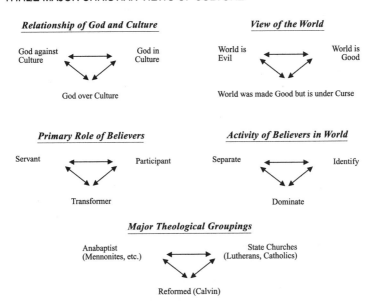

Relationship of God and Culture

God against Culture ⟷ God in Culture

God over Culture

View of the World

World is Evil ⟷ World is Good

World was made Good but is under Curse

Primary Role of Believers

Servant ⟷ Participant

Transformer

Activity of Believers in World

Separate ⟷ Identify

Dominate

Major Theological Groupings

Anabaptist (Mennonites, etc.) ⟷ State Churches (Lutherans, Catholics)

Reformed (Calvin)

structures, and the culture of the nation is likely, and we would expect to see forms of state churches emerge.

An identificational model of theology is not the same as an identificational lifestyle with the poor. In practice, those who are more separatist tend to identify with the victims and outcasts of society, whereas an identificational theological model leads to an uncritical acceptance of cultural norms and an upper and middle-class life.

The church in a transitional culture

In a cultural change model, the people of the slums are described as a sociological group of people in transition from peasant (or in some cases from tribal) society to urban society. Each of the characteristics in the chart titled "Three Polar Types of Society" may be examined to consider the likely patterns of conversion, growth, and the sociology of the church in this transitional phase.

To answer the question of the form of the church in the slums, we must be careful not to presume that the implanting of our past theological heritage (molded by our history) will be relevant. True, I am making an impassioned plea to middle-class readers of this book, asking them to bring transformational theology into ministry among the poor. But at the same time, the following analysis will demonstrate that the majority of indigenous churches among squatters will be separationist because of the nature of the cultural milieu.

Churches are likely to be against culture and essentially irrelevant to the needs around them. Other factors cause us to expect that they will develop culturally into what are commonly recognized as Pentecostal styles. For those of us from other traditions—for whom the issues are theological—this fact may be a staggering blow. It will require rethinking our relationships with brothers and sisters with whom we formerly disagreed—culturally as well as theologically. For the sake of the poor, we may have to develop new theological, cultural, and structural perspectives. Is our love sufficient to face such dramatic changes and their implications?

While the church among the poor may emerge this way, its situation highlights the need for middle-class evangelicals with a good understanding of the kingdom to give themselves to the task of strengthening these churches. An understanding of a kingdom qualifies them as those best fitted to help the church of the poor move from culturally-determined views to new perspectives formed from the Word of God, bringing transformation to their cultures of poverty and injustice.

I hold strongly that God is deeply concerned with transformation, transformation not only of individuals but of societies, as the kingdom breaks through the kingdoms of this world. He is the God who so loved the *world*.

Squatter church characteristics

Let us compare some of Redfield's 1947 descriptions of folk culture (included in the "Three Polar Types of Society" chart on pages 201 and 202) with some of Peter Berger's 1974 definitions of the nature of modern (urban) man.[6] At the intersection between these two views, we will consider implications for developing churches at the interface of peasant and urban cultures. (Their concepts will appear in italics).

Those who come from *small, isolated, non-literate, homogeneous societies with strong group solidarity* (Redfield's primary description of folk society) usually seek that same pattern in the city. They may not find it—except perhaps in the church! This tendency would lead believers to develop a church that continues the ideal of the old *extended familial relationships*. In practice, most urban squatter churches that I have evaluated do this. They consist of three extended families and friends. Growth tends to stop at this point as the energy needed to maintain the relationships of such a group preclude further outreach.

New believers would expect *strong group solidarity* and *sense of belonging*. Based on this, we would expect churches that are *isolationist* and *separatist*, except for evangelistic forays into a perceived hostile environment. Anyone who knows the church among the poor of Latin America will readily identify these elements.

The culture of their past causes peasants in the city to develop churches that are strongly *traditional and patterned, personal, yet spontaneous*. The Western urbanite perceives this as disorganized, because the group's activities, while following fixed traditions, are infinitely flexible to accommodate relationships with each new person entering the meeting. There is a great deal of spontaneous communication that continues through the performance of the expected worship rituals. Used to flowing with the culturally determined goals of a small village clan, slum dwellers do not pursue a high development of critical thinking.

The result is that patterns and traditions brought into the slums by the missionary or local pastor are quickly adopted. They are perceived to be as important as the reasons behind those patterns. In the village, the purpose of certain activities was never questioned. Tradition was the answer. In the city, the question is still not asked, even though activities imported from an overseas church may not appear to relate to the people's needs. The church may be planted by the outside change agent or by a thoughtful slum leader, but initial customs tend to fix the rights and duties of each person in an essentially non-changing context.

There is no *division of labor* in a folk society. The only division of labor is between males and females. Every man is able, to a greater or lesser extent, to fulfill each of the roles of the society. *Decision-making* is by *consensus*, and the Christian peasant in the slum expects to be involved in all activities of the church decision-making and in the processes of forming consensus. He expects this without having any concept of serious division of labor.

The only exception to this equality is reserved perhaps for the pastor, who is perceived more as the *patron* from another class, in status even if not economically. Pastors trained in Bible schools that are based on a Western model have understood this without informing their culturally mystified missionary professors. Peasant and pastor thus maintain roles that provide some form of stability and relationship, related back to the older traditional society. To the missionary or church growth expert, this is seen as inertia, lack of growth, or failure to delegate.

Thought processes are *personal, associational,* and *symbolic.* The world is perceived as personal. This is in contrast to the impersonal perception of Western man. Based on this, we would expect greater impact in preaching and teaching the parables of Jesus or the personal and symbolic stories of the Old Testament patriarchs than through *critically analyzed, theoretical breakdowns* of complex conceptual biblical themes and implicit, generalized, abstract systems.

In the peasant or tribal context there is no *habit of experiment,* nor reflection for intellectual ends. Thus we would expect that the people of the slum church would be cautious and conservative in initiating any new thing.

Entering the city, however, puts the migrant in contact with a new *problem-solving inventiveness.* Change in one area of life predisposes the migrant to change in other areas.[7] Abstract systematic thinking begins to infuse the thinking of a migrant family over two and three generations, particularly as the children attend school and enter the business world of the middle-class city. Orderliness, clear categories, taxonomies, mechanistic causality, separation of means and ends—all characteristics of the *homeless mind* (Berger's term for Western man's mindset)—begins to influence decision-making patterns and planning strategies. The people are open to learning these new ways of thinking step by step, for they see them in operation around them every day.

Since peasants usually come from a *sacred society,* the peasant in the city searches for the sacred. It is my observation that after five years, this seeking declines rapidly. As the *secularity of the city,* coupled with its implicit assumption of maximizing oneself (having a good time or achieving desired status or financial goals), a reliance on the old sacred traditions and the perception of the sacredness of all things break down.

In folk society, *magic* is commonly practiced—much of which is made up of rites and rituals that have no effect at all. It is to be expected that this would carry over culturally into the church. We would expect to see a mixture of the central biblical realities—preaching and teaching as well as healing and deliverance. But along with these comes a tendency towards adopting set ways of praying for the sick—good Protestant, Evangelical, or Pentecostal rituals that should guarantee effectiveness. Fortunately, God is ever full of mercy and grace and not bound by these ritualistic expectations.

In folk societies, *festivals are integrating points of structure of the society.* This is difficult for a Protestant to grasp, having rejected traditions, rituals, artwork, and festivals along with Catholic saints and the rosary. I believe that festivals are a significant biblical theme, accentuated by Jesus, and of great relevance in slum churches.

The economics of urban church life is perhaps the area of greatest contrast to the economics of the rural church. In folk societies, *tools and means of production are communally shared,* as they would be in a healthy slum church where *koinonia* is well developed. People produce what they consume in peasant societies so that the society is independent economically. This is not the case in the slums, however, where new patterns of savings have to be taught for people to survive.

Modern Urban Personality

Berger, in developing the concept of an urban worldview, defines the two components of modernity as technological production and bureaucratic organization. He claims that the following patterns develop in the urban situation:

a. *Componentiality,* or the breakdown of something into basic or atomic interchangeable parts that can be manipulated;

b. *Interdependence of components* and their sequences and consequences, producing a formula approach to events (The same events are seen as producing the same results); and

c. *Separation of means and ends.*

These characteristics, according to Berger, bring about a mechanistic view of the world and of social organization. The consequences in social organization, as seen in the factory and bureaucracy, are a mechanistic approach and an engineering mentality. They result in human control and manipulation of both nature and the social order—actions that are difficult to reconcile with the biblical concept of managing creation and being our brother's keeper, a role not of dominance but of equality.

According to Berger, we find standardization and reproducibility of thought patterns in the urban world-view. Tasks are broken down into subtasks in a linear fashion. Measurability, production, and profit orientation are seen in speech patterns, emerging vocabulary, and new relationships.

My experience indicates that the above outcomes described by Berger, while evident in urban middle classes, are not evident in the slums. They occasionally intrude but are not significant in the culture of the urban poor. He describes other personality characteristics, however, that do emerge among slum dwellers.

Berger describes the urban personality using terms like *componentialization of self* in public (anonymous self roles) and in private (personal self), *alienation between components, emotional management, multi-relationalism* (a sense of "Everything's happening to me at once"), *dissociation* ("It's not my problem"), and *meaninglessness and anomaly* ("I see no order"). Berger's assessment of the urban personality emphasizes negative perspectives. Perhaps he gleaned it primarily from the milieu of psychological studies in the city—psychologists tend to focus on problems. Or perhaps he drew on the earlier negativism of the Chicago school that Oscar Lewis battled.

Why should these characteristics occur in the slums and not the ones listed earlier? These latter personality traits develop mainly because of the breakdown in the closely-knit rural family, not from modernization. Loss is felt not as the migrant family moves into the technology and industrialization of the city, but as they lose personal, face-to-face relationships. Even in the slums, where such relationships are still prized and more obvious than in the middle-class areas, they have to give way to multi-relationalism. Often the immensity of problems and needs the migrant passes every day in the slum leads to a dissociation from those problems.

Many families in the slums live in isolation from each other, afraid of all relationships outside of their rural clan. They have a public self that they bring to the church, but unless the church contains a number of people from those old clan relationships, they will be hesitant to reveal their private selves. To break down these walls, the successful church in the slums must develop patterns that match the old community relationships as much as possible. One key to success in this is the migrant's sense of long-term loyalty. Another is the sense of "in-groupness."

These factors do not lead to a continual expansion of the church beyond about 70-120 members. The church planter needs to establish a series of tightly-knit groups (churches) of this size rather than to follow church growth ambitions for bigger and better churches.

Interestingly, what many might call "lack of management skills" among the peasants in the city may be viewed positively as the persistence of effective "folk culture" traits of relating and decision-making. The new skills of urban life described by Berger are not better than the old in coping with life in the city, so we are wise not to make value judgments about the ability of those in the slums to manage. Modern management skills are largely inappropriate in coping with the culture of the slums.

It will be frustrating for the Christian worker to enter the slums expecting to impart such management skills without studying the long transitional periods required to move from one pattern of thought process to another. It is doubtful whether this transition can be made in a generation—except perhaps by a small handful out of each ten thousand migrants.

Notes

1. Redfield, Robert and Milton Singer, The Folk Society," *Classic Essays on the Culture of Cities,* New York: Meredith, 1969.

2. Redfield, Robert and Milton Singer, "The Cultural Role of Cities," *Classic Essays on the Culture of Cities.*

3. Douglas, Mary, *Natural Symbols,* Harmondsworth: Penguin Books, 1996.

4. These were developed largely by Wayne Dye under the tutelage of Paul Hiebert, and are expanded in Hiebert and Meneses, *Incarnational Ministry,* Baker, 1995

5. Based on Webber, Robert E, *The Secular Saint,* Zondervan, 1981.

6. Berger, Peter, Brigitte Berger and Hansfried Kellner, *Homeless Mind: Modernization and Consciousness,* Vintage Books, 1974.

7. Rogers, Everett M., *Diffusion of Innovations,* Free Press, 1995.

Chapter Sixteen

Squatter Culture and the Church

Oscar Lewis developed his theory of a "culture of poverty" in reaction to Redfield's study of transitions. He studied groups of poor, migrant peoples within the city who had enough cultural integration to define some generalized characteristics. These he claimed to be universal to groups of poor in other cities. Much of Lewis' theory was not new, having been generated by Lampman[1] and Harrington in their studies on American poverty.[2]

Understanding the culture of poverty

Lewis' theory is not truly about a culture in the classical sense of the word. Rather it is an excellent analysis of a subculture from a synchronic view—at one point in time—set in a much wider diachronic (historic) perspective—the continuum of change from folk to urban contexts. There are many criticisms of this theory, but it is not my purpose here to analyze these. Instead, I want to apply Lewis' theory to the greater task of establishing the church among the poor.

Lewis lists over seventy characteristics of the culture of poverty, first differentiating it from poverty itself, which is generally seen as economic deprivation. He views the culture of poverty as a subculture within itself:

With its own structure and rationale, a way of life handed on from generation to generation along family lines . . .it is a culture in the traditional anthropological sense in that it provides human beings with a design for living, with a ready-made set of solutions for human problems, and so serves a significant adaptive function.[3]

There are many groups of poor people that do not fit into this culture of poverty, because in Lewis' theory it is distinctly related to the emergence of a two-level economic system in capitalist cities. Poor rural or tribal peoples, some poor, low-caste urban Indians who are integrated into the wider society, and poor Jews in Eastern Europe who are highly educated and organized are examples of poor people who are not described by Lewis' concept.

The culture of poverty is both an adaptation by the poor to the contextual culture and a reaction to their marginal positions in a class-stratified, highly individualized, capitalistic society. Thus, the behavior and values of the poor are not determined by their situation but are a culturally learned response.

Limitations of Lewis' theory

There has been a great deal of criticism of Lewis' theory. Nevertheless, while it may not be the most useful tool for those whose focus is the transformation of poverty, it is perhaps the most powerful tool we have for anticipating what the church in the slums should look like, and for analyzing what it does indeed look like.

Lewis' theory is also significant because it moved the emphasis away from the individual alone to the individual in context. It has also shifted the focus from the study of problem families among the poor to a more positive study of effective coping behavior in the environmental context and culture of the slum.

Disengagement from the larger society

"The people . . . make little use of banks, hospitals, department stores, or museums . . . . There is a hatred of the police, mistrust of the government and of those in high positions, and a cynicism that extends to the church."[4]

Lewis writes of fear, suspicion, apathy, and discrimination among the poor. He points out that the relationships of the poor to police, army, and public welfare officials reinforce these attitudes. A new missionary told me how she had explained to a squatter child that he could trust the police. She then walked out of the community to find a policeman at the corner taking bribes from passing traffic violators.

It would seem that Oscar Lewis has accurately expressed reality, but not entirely so. I have observed that in Manila, for example, as a part of their delight in the freedom of the city, Philippine squatters frequent the museums, department stores, and hospitals of a world that is different than theirs. I think it is safer simply to assume a predominance of the characteristics mentioned by Lewis in the midst of a wide spectrum of attitudes towards the institutions of the city.

The pastor needs to become what Gulick called a "culture broker."[5] Or, Santos' economic term, redefined as a "cultural middleman" may be applicable also.[6] Daily the pastor has to help the people relate to the institutions of the city, and do battle against fear, suspicion and apathy. At the same time, the pastor has to fight corruption within the city's institutions in order to serve the people.

The pastor or change agent in the slums is a link between the culture of poverty and the industrialized sector. Despite the brutality of the police and the corruption of government officials, the pastor is in a position to foster trust and sound relationships between the poor and those in power who can assist them. Pastors also have moral power, which at times may be brought into play to compel corrupt officials to provide assistance.

In Latin America or in the Philippines, by an incarnational lifestyle among the poor, the Christian worker can deal a death blow to the prevailing distrust of the church.

The attitudes of distrust and fear are also tempered by the dominant attitude in the city towards the poor. In Brazil, two decades of military oppression of the favelados have resulted in a general public perception of the favelas as places of great evil, violence, and fear, breeding mistrust and fear among the favelados. This is in contrast with a city like Lima, where the pueblos jovenes are perceived favorably.

An alternative economic system

People in a culture of poverty produce little wealth and receive little in return. Chronic unemployment and under-employment, low wages, lack of property, lack of savings, absence of food reserves in the home and chronic shortage of cash imprison the family and the individual in a vicious circle.

Thus, for lack of cash, the slum householder makes frequent purchases of small quantities of food at higher prices. The slum economy turns inward, showing a high incidence of pawning of personal goods, borrowing at usurious rates of interest, informal credit arrangements among neighbors, and use of secondhand clothing and furniture.[7]

The economics of church life are going to reflect these characteristics with frequent cash shortages and different expectations between members and the church about the repayment of loans. A credit cooperative approach has been found to be successful by a number of groups.

Equipment for the church usually is bought in fits and starts. Most pastors' build churches themselves with help from members. Often, they are completed years after worship is begun. Obtaining secondhand equipment from middle-class churches is a realistic way to speed the process.

Low level of organization

Since residents come from highly structured rural societies and enter highly organized and complex urban societies, slums exhibit a severe breakdown of organization. There is a lot of socializing but only within the nuclear or extended family. Yet there may be a strong *esprit de corps* because of enforced isolation. This *esprit de corps* of many slums is a plus factor for the outsider who becomes an insider, since it forms a natural parish.

On the other hand, the disorganization and breakdown of family life in a squatter area implies that a church there will lack strong organization. Where there are no extra resources to manage from day to day, people do not develop skills of management. Since building and maintaining a church larger than about seventy people requires management skills, most squatter churches will stay small.

Wider issues of community organization, beginning with small things such as obtaining water or garbage clearance, need to become an important part of building the community. They provide a way of identification with the people in their needs.

Disengagement in marriage values

People talk of middle-class moral values but on the whole do not live by them. Common-law marriage avoids expense and gives both man and woman freedom in a context where futures are uncertain. It gives the woman a stronger claim on her children and rights to her own property.[8]

Marriage values of the imported European culture are often in conflict with the submerged values of a far older culture. By becoming involved with the people, the church planter can assist in marriages, providing support and counseling without charging the costly fees they normally would have to pay. Indeed, marriage values are often one of the first issues after conversion.

There are many complexities concerning who is the rightful husband and father of which children. The church planter needs to be discerning about how to apply the Scriptures, encouraging people to remain in the state in which they were called (usually married to a second or third husband or wife with children from each), or to seek reconciliation and restitution. The culture has its own morality by which biblical principles may be applied to various situations. The church planter needs to teach from the Bible, and then have the people themselves determine the ethical courses of action.

The role of men is the key to the transformation of these families. Strong leadership and good biblical teaching of men concerning their family life is critical for family development and the long-term establishment of a church.

Shortened childhood

The family in the culture of poverty does not cherish childhood as a prolonged and protected stage in the life cycle. Initiation into sex comes early. With the instability of marriage by consensus, the family tends to be mother-centered and tied more closely to the mother's extended family. The female head of the house is prone to exercise authoritarian rule. In spite of much verbal emphasis on family solidarity, sibling rivalry for the limited supply of goods and maternal affection is intense. There is little privacy.[9]

Protection of children is a difficult problem in these families. As they grow up, many lose the emotional capacity to respond because of the traumatic experiences they have had to pass through. Often, people are seen only as a way to acquire things. The solution to such problems is not for the church planter to get deeper and deeper into counseling but to develop a strong and healthy church structure where the members minister to each other.

Psychological characteristics

The individual who grows up in this culture has a strong feeling of fatalism, helplessness, dependence, and inferiority . . . Other traits include a high incidence of weak ego structure, orality, and confusion of sexual identification, all reflecting maternal deprivation; a strong present-time orientation with relatively little disposition to defer gratification and plan for the future, and a high tolerance for psychological pathology of all kinds. There is widespread belief in male superiority and among the men a strong preoccupation with *machismo,* their masculinity.[10]

The extent of wounds in people's lives mean that the emotional components of worship and the Lord's Supper are critical contexts for healing to occur. As healing is occurring by the power of the Holy Spirit, there is often weeping and other emotional responses. The dynamics of worship in the slum must provide a freedom for this to occur if the people are to be set free.

The extent of these emotional needs means that they will not be healed over a short period of time. The pastoral structure needs to be developed in such a way that long-term progress is assured, but short-term patience with failure lays a foundation of grace. Feelings of fatalism and helplessness dissipate under the regular inspiration of the preached Word and as brothers and sisters in a healthy church help one another grow.

The weak ego structure among slum dwellers means that the church planter in the slums must constantly deal with disputes between members. There is often the need for church discipline in cases of immorality. The *machismo* that Lewis mentions is only an obvious characteristic in a few places. On the whole, men have to be encouraged to take responsibility and begin to redeem their lost sense of dignity and leadership.

Conclusion

My father-in-law recounts his first contact with Christianity in Brazil, when fundamentalists came to preach the good news and a few people converted. These converts seemed to become isolated from the rest of the town.

"A couple of years later, the Assemblies of God entered the town," he remembers. "With their noise and their open worship and their miracles—things very Brazilian—the whole town knew what was going on."

A prototype emerged that was not only identifiable but also desirable to the people.

Despite the theoretical and tentative nature of Lewis' work, its core rings true to the experience of workers among the poor. Lewis' culture of poverty provides a useful set of characteristics that enables us to reflect upon effective patterns of ministry among the poor—patterns that are desirable to the people.

Notes

1. Lampman, Robert V., *Poverty: Four Approaches, Four Solutions,* Eugene, Oregon: University of Oregon Press, 1966.

2. Harrington, Michael, *The Other America: Poverty in the United States,* Penguin, 1965.

3. Lewis, Oscar, "The Culture of Poverty," *Scientific American,* Vol. 215, No. 4: 3-9, October 1966.

4. Ibid.

5. Gulick, J., "Urban Anthropology," *Handbook of Social and Cultural Anthropology,* J. Honigman, ed., Rand McNally, 1973, pp. 979-1029.

6. Santos, Milton, *The Shared Space* (tr from Portuguese by Chris Gerry), Methuen: London and New York, 1979.

7. Lewis, "The Culture of Poverty."

8. Santos, *The Shared Space.*

9. Lewis, "The Culture of Poverty."

10. Ibid.

Chapter Seventeen

From Churches to Movements

The aim is not missions.
Nor is it the planting of churches.
The aim is not multiplication of churches.
The aim is to multiply fellowships
  in such harmony with the soul of a people
  that movements of disciples are established
  who know this movement is Christ's answer
  to the cries of this peoples' heart.

The 4,000 men and women whom Saint Francis of Assisi gathered in ten years constituted a movement like the one described above. So did John Wesley's urban poor churches, which multiplied to scores, with seventy-five thousand new believers in his lifetime. From 1955-1970, the Conservative Baptists in the Philippines grew from zero to 1,500 members. These are patterns of reproductive believers and churches—i.e. movements. A movement is defined by Gerlach and Hein as:

> People who are organized for, ideologically motivated by, and committed to, a purpose which implements some form of personal or social change; who are actively involved in the recruitment of others; and whose influence is spreading in opposition to the established order within which it originated.[1]

They list factors that are crucial in movements:

1.   A cell-like structure involving various personal, structural, and ideological ties.

2. Face-to-face recruitment by committed individuals, using their own pre-existing significant social relationships.

3. Personal commitment generated by an act or experience which separates a convert from the established order, identifies him with a new set of values, and commits him to changed patterns of behavior.

4. An ideology which codifies values and goals, provides a conceptual framework for changes, defining opposition, and forms a basis for conceptual unification of a segmented network of groups.

5. Real or perceived opposition from that segment of the established order within which the movement has arisen.[2]

Movements grow from communication of a positive and convinced faith. They tend to be absolutist in their beliefs, to have a strong *esprit de corps,* and tend to reject other groups because of it.

Clearly, movements involve multiplying groups of people who catch simple ideas and make the ideas their own. Often they will be sparked by a charismatic or prophetic leader. This leader's continued leadership after the initial phases may or may not be crucial, as the ideas and multiplying structure soon have dynamism of their own.

Eric Hoffer, in *The True Believer,* describes three kinds of leaders needed to develop a movement—the *man or woman of words* who is a philosopher, seeing, conceptualizing, and formulating values; the *fanatic* who takes these ideas, whittles them down (with distortions) to what is reproducible and realistic (to the horror of the philosopher); and the *institutionalizer,* who takes the growing numbers of people and formalizes the structure, eventually killing the very core that provided the impetus for growth.[3]

Someone coined the progression: *man, mission, movement, machine,* and finally, *monument* to capture this same progression from vision to movement to organization.

The Bible teaches that the church is initiated by apostles and prophets, expanded by evangelists, and consolidated by pastors and teachers.

Movements are based on voluntary lay leadership and the key deployment of supported workers to develop these lay workers.

A wise mission leader once reflected that healthy lay movements will not continue unless the very top leadership has opportunity and resources to be formed in theological, philosophical, and strategic thinking.

The rate of multiplication of cells and individuals in a movement is determined both by the number of conversions and by the number of leaders or leadership groups developed at each level. The extent of long-term multiplication is determined also by the extent of cultural indigeneity, good structures, and viable reproducing patterns. When movements speak to the soul of the people, they have a power of multiplication far greater than the simple multiplying power of good structures and patterns.

There are no fixed approaches to planting churches and none to ensure that churches will multiply. But there are a few principles that appear essential. There are many ways to integrate these principles. For example, when Madame Imelda Marcos sent the marines to take the squatters' land in one community, the Christians stood in solidarity with the poor, even as the blood of the dead spilled out on the ground. Out of this came the nucleus of a new church. No textbook could have predicted this method. But the principle of incarnational leadership among the poor, sharing in their struggles while preaching to them the gospel of God's grace, is evident.

Multiplication of churches, in a similar manner, depends on the integration of a number of principles. It also requires some fixed patterns, but in such a way that there is opportunity for creativity.

Integration of educated elite and poor ministries

Movements among the poor, while a strategic first priority, are insufficient to deal with the causes of poverty. Two other levels of ministry must be established in conjunction with such ministries.

1. Movements among the educated elite, involving them in direct ministry in these squatter areas, facilitate the formation of holistic theology and motivate the middle class to transform the structures of the cities. For example, family breakup is prevalent in the favelas. It is predominantly an economic issue. Are there useful roles for a middle class specialist in the field of marriage counseling as believers become established economically?

Similarly, the development of basic management skills is a cross-cultural need. Will a middle-class person with a head for business devote several years to developing core teachings of basic management skills that squatters need to survive? This curriculum could be prepared to be used cross-culturally.

2. A movement among the jet-setting international elite dealing prophetically with the multinational structures of the world, and opposing the unified world economic-political-religious system as it increasingly strangles the poor.

Among these options, it appears to me most strategic to focus first on squatter church movements to which these other ministries can be linked. Let us look, therefore, at the practice of establishing movements of churches in the squatter areas.

Developing a catechism

The theme of the Exodus emerges in a liturgy that is repeated again and again throughout the Old Testament—in story, in song, in poetry, and in worship. Around it is woven the whole gamut of themes of God's redemptive history. It was a pattern that could be repeated and repeated.

Every movement of God has had its own pattern of story-telling, either written, sung, told directly, or repeated in worship liturgies.

From the general principles given in the four seasons chart we are able to develop specific methodologies for each movement. These patterns (methods) are generally not cross-cultural, nor are they effective within different economic classes in society. The principles (which *are* cross-cultural) behind each are embodied in the four seasons chart.

Non-literary devotional patterns

Most poor people cannot read, or at least read well. Thus a pattern of teaching that involves songs and stories is necessary for a movement among them. The use of written Bible studies or books as a basic pattern is not going to be effective among the poor. A simple handbook for pastors is about the limit of usefulness among the poor. In Manila, one group has done work on comics, which many read.

One approach is to develop a series of stories that follow chronologically through the Bible (but over a period, for example, of a year) and cover each of the major areas of need of the new believers at each phase of growth.

These stories need to be linked to dramas and the church year of celebration. The church needs festivals where the stories are told in a media that fits the culture of the poor.

Publications

Despite the literacy limitations of the poor, it is helpful to have some things in writing. This ensures completion of the ministry and of the movement. The following are some models of catechisms used in various contexts:

1. Western university student movements

A series of ten books containing four Bible studies per book on basic topics has been found to be very effective among Western and Westernized students by Campus Crusade for Christ and the Navigators.

2. The Anglican Book of Common Prayer

For centuries, the English church has used the Anglican prayer book. While non-conformists will cry out against ritualism, the reality is that this book from its inception has been the core of maintaining momentum for the dynamism of renewal in the English church. For many people throughout history, it has provided a core from which to develop faith. It has basic patterns of reading, prayer, worship and song, affirms central doctrines and defines yearly festivals. The poor often learn the meaning of things in the rituals themselves rather than in the content of the rituals. Yet as patterns are developed, so life develops alongside the rituals.

3. Bible reading outlines

The Anglican prayer book also provides patterns of reading through the Bible year by year. These are related to the cycles of the calendar. Any movement needs such devotional paradigms and patterns for reading the Scriptures.

4. Brazilian songbooks

One of the keys to church growth among the poor in Brazil is that each movement has its own hymnbook. Brazilians love to sing. Memorized songs form the foundation of a dynamic and emotionally internalized religion for those who cannot read. They also become a symbol among churches of their unity of doctrine.

Brazilian Christians among the poor possess two books: a Bible and the hymnbook of the denomination. It is the hymn book, I suspect, more than the Bible that produces the breadth of understanding of the nature of God on which their faith is molded.

Untrained pastors tend to teach only sections of the Word of God, but the hymnbooks were put together by older leaders working in groups, and they cover the whole gamut of historic Christianity.

5. Converted Rosary

For some families in the Catholic context of Manila, the time for the rosary each evening can be converted, just as people are converted.

6. Group worship patterns

One practice of the Assemblies of God in Brazil is an extension of this principle. It is a simple pattern followed by all the churches. Three nights a week all members attend the church for worship, teaching, or prayer. This is a pattern that is consistent and reproducible. It also accords well with the principle that traditional societies move as groups in their activities.

Summary

A successful movement among the poor, then, will probably have patterns and rituals including:

1. a song book of several hundred songs covering the whole range of doctrine of the church;

2. a regular devotional and Bible reading program expected of each member or family;

3. a consistent pattern of regular meetings, both small and large groups;

4. a basic pattern of teaching that is not literature-based; and

5. a fixed liturgy, whether it is Pentecostal or Lutheran, or ways of praying, reading, singing.

All of these will provide a strong emotional base to the patterns of religion.

A catechism for the four seasons

Another approach we have used many times is to begin with the four seasons chart and ask the emerging leadership of the church for topics and areas of need under each of the four seasons. This results in a blackboard full of fifty to a hundred topics which together form a basic follow-up syllabus. The next step is to come up with biblical stories or other illustrations that are useful to meet these needs.

Such charts are not complete and should not be copied verbatim by another group. They come out of hours and months of discussion. In every subcultural group, this process has to be cultivated and patterns developed that multiply. Some initial structure may be needed. In one case, structure was imported from middle-class student ministry materials. It is essential, however, that leaders think together to develop new patterns that fit the culture of the group.

The seed grows

Many groups want to multiply, duplicating their programs, patterns, and even their churches. It's not difficult to do. Coca-Cola managed to multiply and is now found in every part of the world. All we need is a structure and organizational patterns. It is easy to reproduce religious death anywhere under the name of Jesus. But Jesus doesn't ask us to multiply structures. He asks us to reproduce life—his life in our lives. When this happens, disciples will develop and church structures will multiply.

Life can only come from life.

Life can only produce creatures of its own kind.

Love multiplies. We are to give our lives to others. This will multiply. The Word of God multiplies. Godly character multiplies.

The power of God can be multiplied from one to another. It is intimately connected with dying to ourselves and giving ourselves away to others, with the proclamation of the Word and with godly character. When these things are present, it is healthy to practice patterns, programs, and structures that facilitate their continued multiplication.

The strength of multiplication of a movement is dependent on:

1. the extent to which the cross is at its core, and the values developed from crucified lives;

2. the self-giving and forgiving love at the center of relationships in the movement;

3. the extent of commitment to the Word as the source of food, authority, and revelation;

4. the anointing of the Spirit on the initial core of the work, and the subsequent transmission of patterns of operating in the power of the Spirit;

5. the patterns and structure that emerge to facilitate the multiplication of these core values, relationships and power.

The worth of an individual

Central to multiplication is a sense of the worth of the individual. Jesus told a parable about finding lost sheep. Sheep are found one by one. Movements are based on this kind of self-giving to each individual at points of need.

The love we give to the weakest member on a team determines the values that other team members perceive as important. How one loves the poorest and weakest is what gives entrance to the hearts of leaders in the community (cf. Jesus and Nicodemus in John 3:1-5).

We are to "know well the condition of your flocks, and give attention to your herds" (Proverbs 27:23). This requires constant prayer and listing of names. Church planters often sit down with pen and a napkin (or any other convenient piece of paper), re-diagramming groups of people, listing individuals, so that as different ones are reached, new structures and new groups can be formed to meet their needs. A church planter should have a file card on every new convert and on each key non-Christian contact. This enables constant prayer and pastoral concern.

Jesus saw the world through the eyes of his twelve men. In his final prayer, he concentrated his prayers on them. He saw their worth and believed in their potential and capacity under the power of the Spirit. The multiplication of the ministry is determined largely by the perceived worth of each of the leaders on the leadership team.

Notes

1. Gerlach, L. P. and V. H. Hein, *People, Power, Change: Movements of Social Transformation,* New York: Bobbs-Merrill Co, 1970.

2. Ibid.

3. Hoffer, Eric, *True Believer,* Harper & Row, 1966.

Chapter Eighteen

Leadership for Multiplying Movements

There is a general agreement today that in New Testament times, church structure involved the gathered believers in cells, congregations, and celebrations[1] under the preached Word, and patterns of leadership outlined in Paul's definitions of elders and deacons.

Elders

Eldership and diaconal roles have often been defined in Western churches as primarily administrative or bureaucratic statuses. This has led to stagnant patterns of church life. In apostolic contexts, they are defined in Ephesians 4:11-12 as functions and confirmed statuses, namely, pastor-teachers, evangelists, prophets, and apostles. A healthy movement of churches will develop earned and ascribed roles for each elder and deacon.

Paul, the church planter, appointed elders within a few weeks, months, or years. But he began from a situation of established synagogues from which he could draw people with years of experience, and where many concepts were already thoroughly understood.

In the slums, the situation is entirely different. There are two scenarios. The first is when a significant-sized group of people are reached during the initial evangelistic thrust into a community. Most will be people used to a village-style consensus leadership pattern. Among them, however, some will be people respected by others. Within the first weeks, the church can become self-functioning, with the apostle-evangelist returning on a weekly or fortnightly basis to train this group of leaders.

The second scenario is based on the recognition that squatter areas are places of immorality and broken social structures. It may take five to six years for the first generation to develop qualities that will fit them for eldership. Often, as mentioned earlier, first-generation converts are lost as the pioneer seeks to find patterns and group dynamics to enable them to grow.

In this second situation, much depends on the church planter's or pastor's strong authoritarian leadership over an extended period of time, discipling the flock out of sin into lifestyles of maturity.

Deacons

> It was their first Bible study group. Eight men were sitting outside in the light of the kerosene lamp. One older man had brought his granddaughter to read for him. Each week they each put two pesos into a common fund. Their aim: to purchase Bibles for the group.

From the first Bible study, people should be encouraged in a simple form of giving. This is the beginning of training a church in self-sufficient giving. As commitment grows and giving is encouraged, so the men and women need to be developed to handle the finances of the church. From these emerge deacons.

There are people who obviously have diaconal kinds of gifts rather than eldership gifts. They like handling physical details. They are good at either making or managing money. They are trusted by others.

The initial phases of their growth require appointment by the pastor and accountability to the pastor. In time, they need training in social work, community development, administration, business, or servanthood—these being today's functional equivalents to the roles defined in the Bible. Deacons need to be developed to as high a level as elders and pastors are developed.

Biblical leadership for women

The Scriptures have nearly as much teaching on leadership roles for women as for men. In contrast with their oppressed status in many societies, the roles given them by the Scriptures seek to uplift them. It is clear that there were women deacons like Phoebe (Romans 16:1-2). There are job descriptions for deaconesses (1 Timothy 3:8-13). Women exercise all the spiritual gifts (1 Corinthians 12, 14) and are to use them in leadership, as did Lydia, Euodia, and Syntyche at Philippi (Acts 16:14,15,40; Philippians 4:2-3; Romans 16:1-16), or in praying and prophesying in worship (1 Corinthians 11:5). There are special roles for older women in training younger women, and special attention is given to the woman's leadership role in the family.

There is, however, a limitation on women fulfilling eldership roles in the church (1 Timothy 3:1-7; 2:11-15; Titus 1:5-10) that involve a combination of ruling, teaching, and preaching. The key element identified by Paul is not exercising an authority role over men.

This is a difficult teaching for North Americans to understand because the Scriptures are in conflict with new patterns in North American culture—patterns that have been made law in the United States. It becomes an emotional issue because many women see these new patterns as their way out of oppressed and unjust roles in society. Some see these biblical passages as Paul's reinforcement of oppression.

Unlike some areas of Paul's teaching regarding women, however, the leadership issue is not related in his writings to cultural factors, but to supracultural, universal principles in the Scriptures. It is clear that he uplifts women, as does Jesus, so we cannot reinterpret these passages as an outgrowth of personal or cultural oppression without denying the divine authority behind his writing.

In the squatter context of strong matriarchal family relationships, these teachings and those on the husband-wife relationship are particularly helpful. They give a framework of healthy man-woman relationships and enhance a reintegration of family life. They define new roles for men who, as a result of poverty, have lost respect, position, and authority. And they offer new behavior patterns for women, who have had to develop masculine roles and authority along with their feminine traits, in order to function in the vacuum of desertion by irresponsible husbands.

The biblical instructions about how to deal with widows (1 Timothy 5:3–16) are particularly important in the squatter areas as there are many single mothers and widows. Younger widows are encouraged to remarry. Older widows are encouraged into ministry leadership roles.

The limitation on women is specific to the role of eldership. There is no limitation in evangelism, social work, developmental work or church planting. They will do things differently from men because of their commitment to not exercising authority over men, but this historically has enabled women workers often to be more effective in encouraging the emergence of leadership in new churches.

Natural leaders

Within the slums, natural leadership development is reflected in the upward mobility and development of both economic and political entrepreneurs. Katzin defines an entrepreneur as "an independent, self-employed manager who carries the risk and claims the gain of an enterprise conducted with the object of obtaining money profits."

The economic struggle in the slums tends to produce economic leaders. Christian leadership, through the development of diaconal roles, can facilitate the development of these entrepreneurs by providing a biblical basis for their work. The church can also provide financial mechanisms that afford access to capital and access to expertise.

Similarly, political leadership quickly forms within squatter communities because of the pressures of external politics, particularly in issues such as land rights, water, and sewerage. Christian involvement in community organization can increase the rate of development of these political leaders.

McLelland, in his studies on the socio-psychological factors that form achievement-oriented entrepreneurs, defines them as "people of high status inconsistency. They are upwardly mobile. Their achieved status is higher than their attributed status."[2]

Defining leadership roles

Part of the genius of John Wesley was his provision of leadership roles for the urban poor—roles that they could play at several levels. This gave them status and goals to attain, thereby increasing their motivation towards entrepreneurial activity.

Roger Greenway tells of the progression into leadership of a Mexican pastor. There are clearly defined steps. The young potential pastor begins in a jail ministry, moves on to pioneer a church, then works as an assistant pastor, then goes before other pastors for an exam, and finally is appointed to a church. Each role is dynamic and defined in the folklore of the churches. Each gives the leader a recognized status and growing sense of self-worth.[3]

Incarnational leadership

In his first booklets from which Donald MacGavran later developed his church growth theories, Bishop Pickett provides extensive analyses of the effects of church leaders living among the people and church leaders living outside of a caste to whom they were ministering. His conclusion is clear—living among the people is essential for extensive development and growth of an indigenous church that reflects the soul of the people.[4]

One significant movement in Asia was started by a dynamic friend in Hong Kong, Jackie Pullinger, through a ministry to drug addicts. As these addicts are freed from their addiction, many of them move back to the poorer areas where their families live. Out of this ministry has come a movement of disciples, many linked in small fellowships.

The key? Jackie has for years lived and worked with these people in the destitution of the Walled City of Hong Kong. She has lived among them. She spends most of her time on the streets. After 18 years she still has no room to call her own. A life lived among the poor as one of them is the key.

Leadership from the outside?

Some have said to me, "Don't be too fixed on the idea of incarnation as the key."

To further explore this, I talked and visited with those who had tried various approaches to ministry among the poor from outside slum communities—missionaries and pastors with a heart for the poor, evangelists who visit the slums regularly to preach, and churches that offer aid programs. I discovered that these approaches from the outside have rarely been successful, beyond establishing one or two families long-term in middle-class churches. But there are exceptions.

He was a tall man bending slightly with little pince-nez glasses that masked the intellect and humor behind the long, serious face. On his head sat a blue corduroy hat, covering slightly-graying hair.

"Almost every month we used to start a church in the favelas. I had a good job at the American school managing the grounds, which gave me good money. As we needed more staff, I could get work for the men who are now the pastors of the different churches."

We visited five of the many churches planted by this man. He had stayed in touch with each pastor, giving advice and support and encouragement. A disciple-maker in the slums. I had searched the world for this kind of man!

Another exception to the incarnation "rule" is Roger Greenway's work. Some years ago, Greenway was able to establish significant numbers of slum churches in Mexico, working from outside the slums and sending in workers.[5] The Latin American church as a whole has been marked by Pentecostal growth. Many Pentecostal pastors have little choice other than to work in the slums because of their economic situation, and Greenway worked closely with these pastors.

Is incarnation essential? In Greenway's case and other excellent exceptions to the incarnation rule, success was because of a strategic focus on the slums from the outside. (If we could refocus mission agencies even to this extent, it would be a major achievement!) Yet even when the approach used was that of training and sending workers into the slum, the churches that took root did so when leadership emerged from within the community. Incarnational leadership—although in these cases not that of the missionaries but of the trainees in church planting—was the key to long-term establishment of the church.

For church planting, the leadership of the church in the slums must be incarnate in the community. The missionary, in order to train others in such pastoral work, must set the patterns of identification and model the incarnational lifestyle. As time progresses, the church becomes the incarnate body of Christ in the community, but in the initial years—when new believers, while experiencing dramatic changes, often also slip backwards spiritually—the pastor's life defines who Jesus is in the eyes of the people.

On the other hand, as development work in the slums has been observed, incarnation does not always appear to be indispensable. Even development work, however, is greatly enhanced by workers who engage people from their perspective, rather than work on their behalf. And if developmental work is to be done from a kingdom perspective, where the goal is more than the mere successful implementation of projects, incarnation appears to be necessary.

My conclusions are that non-incarnational roles are appropriate and effective for evangelistic and apostolic leaders who move rapidly from one squatter community to another, generating the momentum of the work. But this role must be linked to incarnational roles for pastoral and administrative leaders.

In Thailand, I visited Buddhist community organizers who have captured this concept of living among the poor to serve them. They are paying a price for enabling the people. Why should Christians pay a lesser price? Incarnation is more effective. It gives the poor a greater sense of dignity. It is more just. It is more loving. Unfortunately, it is not required for development workers.

Short-term church planting

In Manila, a YWAM (Youth With A Mission) training school has established another church-planting model that runs counter to incarnational theory. Every few months, a new short-term team without much language or cultural orientation arrives to live in a house just outside of the slum.

Despite the expected problems related to a lack of indigeneity, their work has been successful. There are problems inherent in short-term missions—problems like cultural ignorance—but there have been enough identification with the poor for the gospel to take root and bear fruit in a church.

The question moves from the necessity to the extent of incarnation. It is an essential one for those who would attempt to establish movements. Linked to it is one of the major issues facing missions in the next decades: how to develop slum church leadership to the extent that multiplying movements are generated.

What will it take to keep a pastor in a slum? Land. If rights can be obtained to a piece of land, the pastor will stay, and in staying will exercise ministry gifts.

One of the recurring factors in a slum community is this: it is rare to find a natural leader who can lead a church to grow beyond more than 70-100 people. There are several apparent reasons. Lack of management skills within the culture of poverty is one. For a church to grow beyond 70 people requires administrative as well as pastoral skills. The extent of pastoral problems and the inability of the poor to provide financially for full-time pastors limit the use of time for broader ministry. Family dynamics tend to limit conversion to three extended families, whose members then get cut off from their religio-cultural ties to other slum dwellers.

Patterns of incarnational leadership

It appears from the available data that the extent of incarnational modeling and pastoral leadership from within the community determines whether the church will be established. My own conclusion is that two levels of leaders are needed: an educated catalyst with a broad perspective and managerial skills, working with a score of squatter leaders who can function as pastors under the first type of leader's broad tutelage.

The catalyst may be a foreigner, or may be one of the converted among the educated rich who chooses to renounce all to minister in Christ's name. About 30 people need to be working in different ways among the poor before such a natural leader will emerge—a leader who is able to do the work, understand the issues, and create the structures that enable a multiplying movement.

The catalyst may also be someone who emerges from among the poor. Such persons will then need outside help in obtaining educational opportunities to extend their breadth of understanding, but in ways that do not separate them from their own people.

Duong Prateep is not a Christian. She is a Buddhist. But she cared for the poor in her slum of Klong Toey in Bangkok. She set up illegal kindergartens for the illegal poor. She entered into conflict negotiations with the government for land rights. Eventually she was awarded the Magsaysay award for her work, and was given status and recognition by her government as a result.

With the money from the award, she was able to study and to learn how to further advance her people. Prateep is a leader of leaders in this, Bangkok's biggest slum.

Middle-class workers

A good man came to live and work in a slum with me—a professional. He stayed three weeks. The transition to heat and cockroaches was too severe. Another came to help with employment generation. He stopped coming after a few weeks. I later found that his mother had made him afraid of tuberculosis (unnecessarily, as there are vaccines). A godly woman came and lived ten days, but emotionally it made her depressed—particularly, day after day, having to cross the courtyard to the small toilet/ bathroom.

Each of the above is now serving the poor very effectively from his or her middle class station in life. Each is following Jesus within the limitations of their class upbringing. They did not fail. For it is not easy for the middle class to go back and live among the poor, and not all are called to serve the poor in this way.

Middle-class people erect many barriers against the poverty from which they have emerged often only a few years before. A fear of a lack of cleanliness in the slums and potential sickness is the major hindrance. Middle-class stories of the violence in the slums abound (although statistically, the slums are far safer than the streets of a New York suburb). If they were to move in among the poor, what would happen to their children's education, and who would be their children's friends?

Perhaps the biggest social pressure is that of the extended family. They perceive involvement with the poor as a drain on family finances, and an insult to the social standing of the family. Lesser problems arise because of the clothing and jewelry the middle class freely buy and wear as part of their own sense of dignity. It comes as no surprise that Perrin should analyze the impact of the middle class workers so severely:

> Many of these young people, so to speak, are branded with a kind of impotence. Many of them come from "comfortable families"—materially and morally (middle-class education)—and for all their zeal and generosity, retain the imprint of a deep indifference, the indifference of people who don't have to fight against life. It is as if, because they "possess the Truth" (!) and a minimum of comfort in their living conditions, they have been established forever in quiet happiness. Their generosity appears as a virtue of perfection—praiseworthy, no doubt—rather than a vital necessity, as it is for someone who has to pull himself and others out of destitution. The outcome seems to me a sort of impotence or spiritual infantilis . . .[6]

The development of Pentecostal (charismatic) super-churches for the rich elite in places like Manila, Bangkok and Kuala Lumpur provides the opportunity of calling the rich to follow Jesus in his renunciation of wealth and in his ministry to the poor. Historically, the leadership of the Catholic orders serving the poor has been from the rich elite who have taken Jesus seriously at this point. Unfortunately, present imported Western theology

LEADERSHIP FOR MOVEMENTS IN THE SQUATTER AREAS

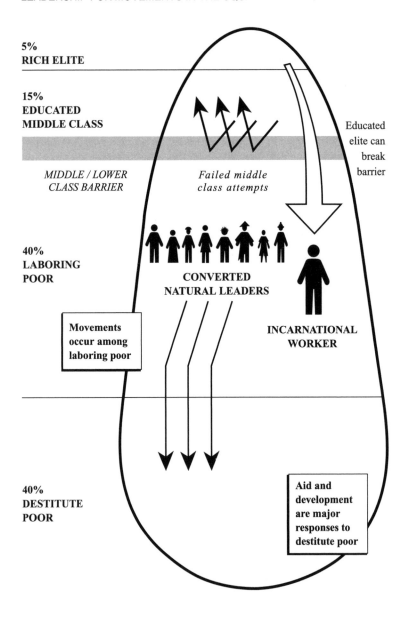

**5%
RICH ELITE**

**15%
EDUCATED
MIDDLE CLASS**

Educated
elite can
break
barrier

*MIDDLE / LOWER
CLASS BARRIER*

*Failed middle
class attempts*

**40%
LABORING
POOR**

**CONVERTED
NATURAL LEADERS**

**Movements
occur among
laboring poor**

**INCARNATIONAL
WORKER**

**40%
DESTITUTE
POOR**

**Aid and
development
are major
responses to
destitute poor**

encourages Protestants to keep their wealth, ignoring the gospel teachings concerning using wealth on behalf of the poor and choosing simple lifestyles, or, for many, renunciation of wealth altogether.

Middle-class leadership is useful in initiating a work, and as a back-up in areas of economic development, legal and medical help, or dealing with political issues. But it appears unwise to invest large amounts of time seeking to develop leadership for squatter churches from this class. Only leaders who live in the community can effectively develop the church.

Similarly, it may be unwise to presume that student movements (the source of many mission workers) will be the key to this task ahead of us. Students may provide some backup, and certainly if they are trained in a poor-focused, holistic theology, they may significantly affect government structures towards justice for the poor. But they should not be the mainstay of our expectations, nor the focus of our time and energy if we are to reach the poor effectively. An exception to this generalization might be an effort to recruit students who are the sons of rich elite families who will find it easier to choose non-destitute poverty while young.

As Christians, we must encourage all people in all levels of society to have a focus of ministry to the poor. This does not imply that all should live among the poor.

We must call all people in all levels of society to lifestyles of simplicity so that others may simply live. This does not imply that all should live among the poor.

We must call all to the patterns of renunciation that we see in Jesus' teaching. This does not imply that all should live among the poor.

But we must also hold out to people the further call of Jesus for many to take up an apostolic lifestyle of identification with the poor in order that the poor people's church might be established.

Training leaders

Without effective training, people reproduce the patterns of the structures and teaching in which they have grown. From generation to generation there tends to be a loss of core values and understanding. Eventually, the shell of a ministry continues to reproduce, but not its heart. All leaders need training in the values, structure, and theology of their movement. But key leaders also need open-ended training, broader than the movement itself, if there is to be continued creativity.

Lay leadership of small cells is the basic level in any movement. Training of elders and deacons is the second, and the leadership gifts of pastor, teacher, prophet, or evangelist develop from this. Out of these leadership gifts develop the apostles.

The best way to train someone is to get the person working. Begin with a responsibility in the Sunday school, youth group, choir, evangelism. Move on from skill to skill, with increasing levels of responsibility.

The trainer's task is to create the environment, define the goals and task, and be available to work through issues at each level. The trainer has to move from giving direct supervision to being a coach, to giving limited freedom, to giving full responsibility. All of this implies an action context rather than a static teaching context.

Bible school or weekend seminars?

Five multiplying churches are sufficient to set up a Bible school in the slums that enrolls twenty people at a time. Church leaders have to be trained in economic self-sufficiency. Often they must be taught to read as well as to be taught in the Scriptures. They must learn patterns of disciple-making and pastoral ministry if the extensive investment of time required for such a school is to be worth their while.

Theological education by extension programs have a seed idea of taking theology to the people. Unfortunately the concept has developed from the top down rather than from the bottom up. Such courses are adaptations of higher-level learning rather than developments of discussions of felt needs by poor pastors.

Latin movements among the poor, however, do not have Bible schools nor theological education by extension programs. Pastors are trained through regular meetings with other pastors every month. This is all that is viable when pastors must work full-time jobs to support themselves. Their patterns of learning are from each other. This is known to educators as a "dynamic reflection model of peer group learning." The question then is how to develop this kind of structure—a structure that a working pastor can afford—in such a way that it gives quality input in key areas.

The training needed is not training to be a paid pastor or Bible school teacher as is taught in Bible schools. The training needs to focus, rather, on an applicational model as change agents in the community. The pastor has to be trained in each level of the four seasons chart and in the integration of these levels. This must be done in such a way as to permit the maximum use of the pastor's gifts. The four seasons chart gives a basis for understanding pastoral skills, the group dynamic skills, the relational skills, the structural components, and the theology that need developing during each phase.

The Encarnação Alliance of Urban Poor Movement Leaders is bringing together training from within the slums of Africa for Brazil, and from Brazil to India in a series of multimedia CD's that include stories from effective workers and practitioners. A comprehensive program of 10 hour modules is being developed at both grassroots leadership and movement leadership levels.

Notes

1. Neighbour, Ralph, *The Shepherd's Guidebook,* Torch Outreach Ministries, Inc., P. O. Box 1988, Houston, TX 77224, 1992.

2. McClelland, D., "Business Drive and National Achievement," *Social Change,* Etzioni and Etzioni, eds,

3. Greenway, Roger, *An Urban Strategy for Latin America,* Baker Book House, 1973.

4. Pickett, J. Wakom, *Christ's Way to India's Heart,* The United Society for Christian Literature, 1938.

5. Greenway, *An Urban Strategy.*

6. Perrin, Henri, *Priest and Worker: The Autobiography of Henri Perrin,* translated by Bernard Wall, New York: Holt, Rinehart, and Winston, 1964.

Chapter Nineteen

Developing Church Planting Teams

There are four phases in planting a church where the development of a leadership team is essential. If the initial thrust into the community is done by a team in training, this will lead to the further development of the pioneering team as well as to the development of an eldership and diaconal team in the emerging church. The church planter, meanwhile, needs to be part of a wider team with other church planters from different areas.

Calling to discipleship

Jesus was our model team leader *par excellence.* He was a warm, personable preacher who drew many to him in those first weeks—some in search of meaning in life, some because they had been healed. Some he chose through prophetic insight—"You are Simon, you shall be called the Rock," or, "From now on you will be catching men," or "Behold, a man without guile."

There were different aspects to Jesus' call. He called people first to himself, then he called them to discipleship (today, we would say "training"). His call was to forsake an economic lifestyle and become part of a new economic body. His call was also to a ministry, to activism, to doing. It was not to a static Bible school or mere instruction.

Out of a broad base of 72 committed disciples (Luke 6:13), in a night of prayer, the Lord revealed to him twelve proven men to be part of his special team. Teams are formed from such prophetic insight, vision, and immediacy with God. Do not recruit people unless God gives them to you, as the Father gave the team to Jesus into his responsibility to keep (John 17).

There is another principle here of developing a broad ministry first. Then you can define the team, the task, and the training with clarity. Build from one ministry to the next. The nucleus of Jesus' disciples came from John's ministry. Paul's team came first from Jerusalem (Barnabas and Silas), then from each of the churches he planted.

Hear God and do the symbolic

Gideon gives us another insight into forming a team or an army. He heard God and obeyed. This obedience became a legend in Israel because it was so symbolic. We need not be afraid of becoming a rallying point nor of proclaiming a cause.

To a large extent, members of a team also select themselves. Those who are faithful remain through the difficult times. Those who are available and can give the time select themselves. Those who are teachable keep seeking to be taught, just as the first disciples of Jesus inquired, "Teacher, where do you live?" Those willing to pay the price survive through adversity, unlike the rich young ruler, who "went away sorrowful." Above all, look for those who love the Lord, for such love is what will cause a man or woman to suffer the indignities of pouring out their souls for others through decades of ministry.

Leroy Eims advises leaders to "keep the team small and hard."[1] A small cadre of committed people is better than a large group of half-committed people. For it is the least committed who determines the team's decisions, not the leader. And how the leader handles the weakest determines how the team members behave to each other. There is also the matter of the span of control—the number of people one leader can effectively handle. For a church planter who also works in a secular job it is about six. For a full-time worker it may be up to twelve.

Building committed discipleship

How did Jesus maintain the commitment of his team? Immediately after selecting his disciples, he took them up to a hillside and defined for them the value system of his ministry in the Sermon on the Mount.

Group time spent in clarifying goals, roles, and the extent and limits of commitment is valuable for building the team's relationships. Am I committed for life? For four years? What are the limits of my love and commitment to my people? Is my commitment to them, or just to my ministry? Jesus laid down his life for his sheep. Will I do the same for my team?

That commitment may mean, at times, laying down our ministry for the sake of our people. It may mean losing our reputation to defend our people.

Second, Jesus led his disciples through a series of experiences. There was total immersion with them in ministry, action and reflection. There was also a time of sitting back and sending them out.

Maintenance of commitment of warriors comes through leadership in battle. "A band of men whom God had touched" (1 Samuel 10:26; 14:52)—these were men who loved a good fight. Nothing keeps a team together as much as seeing the leader involved in spiritual warfare.

They saw him heal with compassion, watched him handle a little orphan girl, saw him pick up an old woman off the street, and bend over and care for an old, dying man. They saw his indignity at the temple of Kali, as the worshippers sacrificed a goat. They caught him at prayer for the city. They saw his sorrow when he could find no church among the poor of the bustees of Calcutta.

They were there when he was washing feet, and as he worked on character issues of pride and envy.

In just the same way, Timothy watched how Paul handled his administrative chores through Silas. Jesus also worked at and expected a deep emotional loyalty. "Simon, Simon, behold, Satan demanded to have you . . . but I have prayed for you," is followed after Peter's denial with the haunting conversation, "Simon . . . do you love me?" (Luke 22:31–32; John 21:15–19)

Paul said the same, without pride, "Be imitators of me, as I am of Christ" (1 Corinthians 11:1). He didn't minister as a professional. He loved people deeply and sought their love in return. Listen to his cry: "Widen your hearts also!" (2 Corinthians 6:13).

Transferring leadership

Towards the end of his ministry, Jesus continued to teach about relationships. In his final prayer it is evident that he believes the kingdom will stand or fall on the unity of his disciple-team.

Finally, after his death and after Pentecost, the team became fully functional. As we transfer leadership, we may expect a loss of some leaders in the team, as there is a reforming of relationships. We can also expect some changes in the exercise of power and authority, and the effective emergence of the newly selected leader.

Since it is the body of Christ that manifests his life, it is always more effective to initiate a church through a team than through an isolated couple. It is difficult, however, to find people willing to relocate into the slums.

To place a large missionary team into a squatter area is also counter-productive in terms of their acculturation and acceptance into the community. Generally it would appear wisest not to place more than two couples into any given community.

Should a team develop during the initial phases of the work, it is important that within a year to eighteen months the majority withdraw, leaving perhaps one couple and a women's worker.

This enables the emerging leadership from the community to grow freely and allows indigenous patterns to emerge.

To develop five churches in different communities is to develop a base sufficient for healthy growth into a movement. A single church can be isolated, with young converts unable to find husbands or wives, and there may be little modeling of alternative approaches. Five churches, on the other hand, balance each other. They also provide a broad enough base for a leadership training program that develops key leaders from each of the churches. Clearly, these squatter areas would ideally be within a bus ride of each other in the city.

In setting up several different missions, I have experimented with different approaches to using foreign teams coming into cities. In ministry among the poor it is essential that the workers be part of a team. It is best if the church planters are located in several different communities with specialized workers assigned to assist them.

Teams in non-Western cultures

Tribal and peasant patterns of team formation and operation are totally different from the Western team concept. This is the major factor when mission societies lose national leadership. The societies often think they are operating efficiently, but have never asked about the cultural concepts of group decision-making.

In tribal societies, members of a team would say, "We decide together." The leader expresses the consensus of the group. We are one in feelings and being. We all carry responsibility for the whole of the operation, even while having divided responsibilities. We help each other in them, deciding by consensus with others. There can be no evaluation of one another, for that would violate our group identity. Always at the end of an activity we affirm that we did well, for always we must affirm the group and each one's role in the group.

In Western societies, the leader adjudicates between individualistic objectives, balancing out those various goals. We are one in that area of our work where there are shared goals. Otherwise, responsibility is divided and delegated by the leader to individual decision-makers. We evaluate, criticize, and judge our performance and each other. We maintain our individuality at all costs. Conflict in establishing the limits of that individuality is accepted as necessary behavior for smooth functioning. Efficiency takes precedence over consensus.

In the West, teams form and reform for various objectives. They are together for a work goal—a cog in a larger machine.

In the non-Western world, groups form as lifelong social commitments. This is often consolidated by marriages where other members of the group are chosen as godparents. Thus it becomes necessary to move a whole group through to the next level of ministry, bending down and picking up the weakest, holding back the fastest, but maintaining group solidarity.

I've often been fascinated watching Bible schools in an Asian context. To the missionaries running them, the goals are being accomplished—namely, they are producing pastors to fill organizational roles in the emerging churches. To the national people, the structures and organization are difficult things to bear, a yoke that doesn't fit well. Meanwhile, within the context of a foreign structure, they are busy creating their own network of relationships—a network that will link them within this imported organization for the rest of their lives, despite its lack of acculturation.

Westerners must learn atmospheric thinking as opposed to structural thinking, relational thinking rather than goal-orientation, and group orientation versus a team-of-individuals-pulling-together orientation.

Leadership and authority

1. Loyalty

Loyalty to the leader and to each other is essential for members of a team. For this reason it is good to grow your own disciples. It is difficult to teach an old dog new tricks, so avoid "old dogs." You can't expect the same degree of loyalty from somebody who has already been discipled. He has other loyalties.

David could have averted civil war by dealing with the disloyalty of Absalom when it first came to his ears. But he thought, *It could not be. Surely my own son would not be disloyal.* We need to be careful to keep relationships open and to expect loyalty from team members.

2. Know the basis and limit of authority

You need also to know the basis of our authority. Are you prophetic? Your authority comes largely from the depth of your knowledge of God in revelation. Are you administrative? Your authority comes from your role in the structure. If you are prophetic, you cannot just assume authority in the administrative realm. Do not usurp authority outside the area which either God or the people have given you.

King David in the desert could have killed his adversary, Saul, God's anointed. He didn't. I can imagine the talk in the Israelite camp after that event. "He said, 'I will not touch the Lord's anointed.'" "He said WHAT?" "Why would he say that?"

And when David became King, no man would lift his hand against him because they knew that God had appointed him. He had not appointed himself. He had not usurped authority.

3. A sea of changing authority

Good church-planting means a continuous emergence of new leaders and roles. Every year there has to be a re-structuring of relationships, of the nature of the team, of roles, etc. As the ministry and vision grow, more people own it. Change of ownership of a vision and a ministry means changes in power relationships. "Who will be the greatest?" is a constant question in the minds of disciples.

Teams need to cope with such change. Know that the basis of your authority will constantly be changing. You need to make sure that a base for authority remains, so that you can affirm that authority when it is under question. But at the same time, you must exercise it humbly, and with gentleness, when needed. Jesus' servant role made him open to disrespect. But he knew and explained his role and authority, "You call me teacher and Lord, and it is true, for so I am."

Personally, I am so dense that I need to have an outside board of three or four people to fall back on in times of dispute, complex issues, or personnel problems.

4. Winning hearts

You must also earn leadership through servanthood, and through being just. People need to be in a situation that makes sense. Leadership is earned through brokenness and confession, through loving speech, and a listening ear.

5. Changing styles

There are also changes in leadership style needed from season to season in ministry. The follow-up phase is one of loose authority. As people enter training and character formation phases, there is a tightening of the authority relationship, but as they move more and more into leadership, it becomes a relationship of co-laborers.

Problems experienced in teams

1. Anti-authoritarianism vs. strong leadership

Western anti-authoritarian values sometimes come into conflict with the necessity of strong leadership to hold Westerners together. James 3:17 tells us of leadership that is without uncertainty, but open to reason. Once decisions are made, there are no changes. This area of the culture needs direct confrontation.

2. Individualism

The best workers, particularly evangelists and prophets, do not always fit into a close team. Work with them off to the side of your team. Don't bend or break them—just love them—and relate their work to the overall ministry of your team primarily on their terms.

3. In-group time vs. ministry outreach time

Keep the team small—but not so small that you as a leader have to carry all the stress. Be careful in the selection of team members. Maintain a balance between your external ministry and your internal, personal ministry to the team. You, as a church planter, need to keep on the cutting edge. Each new person brought in has to be socialized. Hence it is better to form the team all at once, rather than to be constantly including new members.

4. Light and darkness

Non-Christians may not give you a lot of pain in life. But sometimes insiders do. Judas gave Jesus plenty of pain. After a honeymoon period of delight in newfound friends, there often comes among new believers a growing collision of darkness in our personalities. In a team, we cannot run away from each other. That is our choice. The closeness of relationships intensifies unresolved conflicts. Recognize this as being natural. Maintain patterns of confession and prayer. Keep affirming commitments to love. Be patient and forbearing with each other.

Role of the church planter at each phase

As the church planter, you are initially the worker who must do everything, drawing your team into each aspect of the ministry by modeling patterns that are appropriate. You then may delegate aspects of the work. As this occurs, you must keep the laborers laboring, by developing consistent rhythms and patterns of work, by being available when there are bottlenecks or blockages to the ongoing work or personal growth of the worker, and by planned periods of relaxation and team fellowship.

In developing the organization called Servants to Asia's Urban Poor, we established the practice of taking a day out of the slums every two weeks for rest, prayer, and worship, relaxing together and training. This has developed into a pattern of team fellowship meetings every two weeks. I would normally integrate this with a six-week rhythm of more extensive time apart, to maintain team relationships and to give the emotional relaxation and support that enables a continuing commitment to the hard work involved in ministry.

At different phases of the ministry, the Spirit of God seems to bless different aspects of the church planter's gifts. But each leader will find particular blessing in those areas of particular giftedness, and will learn to depend on others for those areas that God has not, in his grace, given special gifts.

The church planter's role has to be at times apostolic. This apostolic gift, it appears, may develop from any of the other leadership gifts. The apostle is one with a mission, who lays foundations upon which others build. He breaks open new territory and establishes new churches or organizations. He may maintain authority over these structures, as Paul did. But he will exercise it with great humility, as also Paul did.

Part of the church planter's role is prophetic. He has to hear from God what God is doing in a community—about the nature of the spiritual battle for a community. Like the Old Testament prophets, he has to call the people to war. In order to enable emerging leaders to function, he needs to seek revelation from God as to their spiritual gifts and ministries, and often through the prophetic word from God he releases them into these gifts, knowing the appropriate times for such ministry.

Clearly, the church planter must sometimes exercise pastoral and evangelistic gifts. An evangelist will plant churches through evangelizing as far and as fast as possible to reach the lost, depending largely on others to give long-term pastoral leadership. A pastor will plant a church by recruiting a team, teaching and pastoring them so they evangelize, and then teaching and pastoring the new converts to maturity. A prophet will see the spiritual battle and God's strategy for an area, calling the church to battle, and as people obey the call, enabling a leader to fight to victory.

In building the initial pioneering team, and later in building an eldership team, the church planter needs to look for people who between them have all of these gifts.

Notes

1. Quoted in a paper on "Teams and Teamwork," by Waldron Scott, Navigators, 1973.

Chapter Twenty

Help! Help! I'm Dying!

The gospel had a daughter—prosperity.
The daughter ate the mother.
—Anonymous.

Poverty invokes a response in the heart of God. Pastoral concern for new believers automatically leads the Christian worker into the complex and perplexing issues of how to resolve economic needs.

Bread for the poor, or bread plus the Bread of Life?

In this chapter I reaffirm my underlying thesis that the church is God's primary agent for social change. As the kingdom enters a community, and afterwards, it brings about economic transformation in the lives of individuals, families and at times, of the community. The causes of squatter poverty are generated by the city. Here too, it is the church of the city that can bring transformation, for the spirit of the city can be transformed by the church.

In Asia, the response to the poor has been inadequate. Churches have given bread to the poor but have kept back from them the Bread of Life. Partially, this is because governments want economic help from Westerners and are happy to allow the entrance of aid programs. They are not interested, however, in missionaries bringing religions that are foreign. Partly it is because of a lack of understanding of the scriptural patterns of incarnational mission on the part of the Western agency—a lack of understanding about the centrality of the church in effecting social change and how the kingdom grows.

Donald McGavran considered this aspect quite extensively in his major work, *Understanding Church Growth*.[1] His work on the issue of serving the poor is outstanding, indicating both a deep social conscience and a brilliant ability to understand the practical issues of poverty. His primary thesis has become known as "Redemption and Lift." I have talked with many affluent pastors who have misused this phrase as a justification for not going among the poor or to derogate church planting and aid among the poor.

Traditional responses

Generally the Western evangelical church has responded to poverty by directly using the gift of mercy to meet perceived economic needs of the destitute. This has been channeled by Western aid organizations either as aid for orphans and those struck by natural disasters, or into an integrated community approach known as *community development.*

This term has developed from a perspective that considers the poverty of the slums to be primarily a micro-economic issue. It tends to focus on economic projects as a means for the economic uplift of families in a community. Occasionally such projects encompass the whole community, in multiple facets. Occasionally they are seen as potential models for wider macro-economic policies.

Community organization

Marxists and more radical social workers have preferred an approach that has come to be known as *community organization.* This perspective has been popularized in Saul Alinsky's models and is common in the Third World, where poverty is seen more as the result of oppression and class dominance or class struggle.[2]

Community organization tends to focus on the process of helping leaders in a community to identify needs, evaluate potential solutions, gather resources and deal with issues of injustice confronting them. It perceives poverty primarily in political terms—in terms of power and in a context of class conflict. There are Christian community organization approaches that avoid some of the ethical failures of those based on Marxist world-views, but take seriously the conflicts and confrontations between various groups in society, often rich versus poor.

As Bob Linthicum formerly of World Vision's Urban Advance points out, community organization is particularly adapted to the city, with its concentrations of political and economic power and of poor and powerless.[3] Community organization tends to be action-oriented and confrontative, as opposed to program or process-oriented community development.

We walked into a slum of 560 houses that lined a concrete path. Then we sat and talked with two 20-year-old men.

"In three months we will be forced off the land," one said. "Already several times they have tried to burn us out."

"Do you have any committee of squatter representatives?" I asked.

"No, everyone does his own thing. Nobody cares for others. If you are rich enough you can move out. If you are poor, there are no plans for you. We have no place to go." The hopelessness of the poor was written on his angry face.

I told them stories of urban poor in other countries—of their battles for land rights, and of their successes.

"You are the first one who has come and talked to us like this. Why do you care?" they asked.

"Because one day I met a king who loved justice and righteousness, and I loved that king."

I told them how the coming king would set up a just government—one where there would be no more poor, no rich. One of them talked of his record as a thief. I told him of the thief on the cross, and of converted murderers I had come to know and love.

> I wanted to stay. I felt sure that a way could be negotiated by bold leadership and prayer to a God who delivered a slave nation.

Evangelism and discipleship in the slum community must involve a servant who will do justice. And that justice will necessarily involve mobilizing the poor to negotiate with authorities. Knowing how to obtain rights is a skill that can be learned. It is a necessary component of a slum worker's equipment. To fail in the political arena is to lose the right to minister to the leadership of the community.

Evangelism is not contradictory to doing justice. It flows easily in a context of working with people at their point of need—the point at which they are being violated. "For I the Lord love justice, I hate robbery and wrong" (Isaiah 61:8).

No easy solutions

The solutions to poverty are not as simple in practice as either of these theoretical approaches or variations allow. The first issue that has to be addressed is an understanding of the nature of the type of poverty itself (its effects). This quickly engenders other questions of cause (see chapter five). We must discover the point of attack where we can best deal with the problem or cause, and the level of society at which action is both feasible and appropriate.

Typical Christian responses of aid and community development, even when done brilliantly, affect only the micro-environment of the squatter area. This is good when related to our commitment to the church among the poor as the central agent of change in the slums. It is inadequate, however, when we consider that the economics of the city have far more effect on squatter poverty.

The primary response of middle-class Christians (while not neglecting other issues) will probably be in the transformation of economic life, political life, government bureaucracy, and other structures of the city that perpetuate slum poverty. It will probably also be necessary to deal with international factors that increasingly loom as dominant forces in worldwide urban poverty.

Three movements to impact squatter poverty

I have spoken of three spiritual movements important in changing squatter poverty. They are necessary to deliver the poor. Without them the poor will not be uplifted. But we should not fool ourselves—they are not sufficient to bring about all the change needed. Only a returning king can accomplish this.

1. Movements of churches among the poor may transform the micro-economic and local political environment. This may be done at the grassroots level in cooperatives, vocational training, small business projects, and organized pressure for land rights.

2. Middle-class professionals, practicing a holistic discipleship and possessing an intimate knowledge of the poor, may effect change in the implementation and governing of the cities at an urban planning level They may be able to assist in matters such as self-help housing, provision of poor people's banking facilities, acting as middlemen to the institutions, combating corruption and initiating medium-sized employment.

3. Christians in the international elite may change the macro-economic systems of international debt, unjust trade, and increasing monopolization by unaccountable multinational corporations.

How the poor escape poverty

It would seem appropriate to explore what natural solutions the poor have found for moving out of poverty. The first observation of interest is that rarely in history have the poor themselves transformed the social system that causes their poverty. This is not their role. They are too busy exploiting every opportunity for survival. Even in revolutions, where the educated elite have been able to use the poor for their own ends, the poor still end up poor. In fact, they often are poorer than before, because of the dislocation of the economic, political, and social structure they have caused.

1. Mutual aid associations

One poor people's solution to poverty is found in the various forms of mutual aid associations. An example of these is a group of street vendors who daily give a small sum into the collective pot, which is given to one trader for that day as a major capital investment in supplementing capital costs of stock. This suggests the possibility of similar cooperative styles of operating within the church fellowship.

2. Eliminating the middleman

As discussed in chapter three, loans among the poor are "flexi-loans" that benefit both the borrower and the lender. The time period and rate of the loans are frequently renegotiated. These loans are often in goods. They often are exploitative.

In establishing the church, one of the first things to do is to free the poor from moneylenders. It is also possible to cut out the middleman from rural areas or the distributor in the city. This way, profits in the businesses of the poor can grow. Again, a credit cooperative is potentially the most viable vehicle.

3. Migration

Historically, the primary means of escaping poverty has been migration. The primary economic uplift in Manila's slums takes place through the export of people to the Middle East as laborers, or to Hong Kong as housemaids, where they earn dollars. The money is sent back to families in Manila's slums each month so that houses can be built.

John Kenneth Galbraith, in a little monograph entitled *Mass Poverty,* demonstrates how this both uplifts the poor in the poorer areas and assists the countries to which they migrate.[4] This is a solution based on the realization that the city's macro-economics is a determinative factor, as far as poverty is concerned, far beyond what any micro-solutions can solve.

The Christian response would perhaps be the development of just employment bureaus for overseas workers. Existing agencies are often exploitive. It is not unusual for a Filipino, for example, to spend hundreds of dollars on papers to obtain visas, job applications, and tickets, only to find the employment agency has pocketed the money. William Booth and other Christians in England clearly saw the employment bureau as one of their primary ways of uplifting the poor.

4. Education

In an urbanizing context, where bureaucracy continues to increase, the entrance level to that bureaucracy is a graduate degree. In cities where there is expanding industrialization, a degree guarantees an income ten times that of an unskilled worker. In a world economy increasingly controlled by information technology, a degree that gives entrance to computers may provide an escape from poverty. But in a decaying economy, where the bureaucracy has increased so that most of income is spent on salaries, and nepotism squeezes out new entrants, a degree may not be an appropriate solution. In Calcutta, for example, hundreds of thousands of educated university graduates have no work.

The normal practice in a poor family is to choose one member—usually an older son—and sacrifice everything to get that member through the educative process. He then provides for the next brother or sister.

The church may have a significant input in this process. This is one area where gifts from rich, foreign churches are positive and non-destructive to the indigeneity of the emerging congregation. The church may also have a significant input in education programs that supplement existing government schooling, enabling the youth of the church to progress to tertiary levels.

Expanding areas of the economy are natural places to seek training, such as computing, engineering and other technical areas. Scholarships should be given on an understanding of being repaid once the person is employed. Sometimes the donor of the scholarship becomes the person's first employer. The repayment can then be used to support another worthy candidate through the same process. This is part of the understood culture of the emerging Third World city.

Middle-class solutions to poverty

"The individual cannot usually break out of this vicious cycle. Neither can the group, for it lacks social energy and political strength to turn its misery into cause. Only the larger society with its help and resources can really make it possible for these people to help themselves."[5]

1. Poor people's banks

One solution that has been looked at in numerous contexts is that of a bank of the poor. One of the primary objectives of the nationalization of fourteen major commercial banks in India in 1969 was to ensure that the requirements of the weaker sections of

MIDDLE-CLASS RESPONSES TO POVERTY

LEVELS OF POVERTY	POTENTIAL RESPONSES
Streetsleepers	Social work relating to existing agencies Direct aid-food, clothing Food for work, housing
Relocation area	Upgrade work operations Food for work or housing Social work relating to existing agencies

Bustees/Slums
(Where housing available, no work)
	Co-op to draw local industries into area
	Co-op into job placement, feasibility studies of jobs
	Direct grants to establish small scale businesses:
	   • food line
	   • clothing line
	   • manufacturing line:
	      electronics
	      welding
	      woodworking
	      chemicals, soaps
	   • avoid handicrafts unless there are existing skills
	A skills training institution nearby
	Food for work
	Overseas job placement agency

Slum-housed (Majority working)	Co-op housing program Credit co-op
Drug addicts, alcoholics	Specialized long-term pastoral communities and rehabilitation centers

society would be adequately met. In keeping with this objective, nationalized banks have been progressively stepping up the flow of credit to priority sectors such as agriculture, small-scale industries, small borrowers, and other weaker sections. The aim was to direct to this sector 40 percent of the total lending by March 1985.

Thus, money has been available to the poor sector but its recovery and utilization has been poor.

P.K. Banerjee gives a strong analysis of an integrated program developed by the Calcutta Metropolitan Development Authority with the nationalized banks. It succeeded in getting loans to the poor in only 33 percent of the targeted industries and provided only 12 percent of the targeted coverage. There were some significant reasons for the failures:

a. Non-deviation from principles of traditional banking;

b. An old obsession for security-tied advances;

c. Bank insistence on furnished guarantees;

d. Non-deviation from individual-approach lending to area-approach lending; and

e. Lack of branches with independent wings for retail banking.[6]

Banerjee discusses a new scheme for retail banking tailored solely to extending financial assistance to the weaker sections of society, with the idea of dispensing with the security and guarantee aspects of the bank loan. Under the scheme, credit is to be considered on the basis of the skill, expertise, and know-how of the borrower. Both disbursement and collections are to be made at the borrower's doorsteps, eliminating the loss of precious time of the small clients at the bank doors again and again. The success of such a scheme depends solely on direct contact and mutual understanding.[7]

The Christian basis for such a model is evident. The practical problems involved would be lessened by its development within the fellowship of the church. Interference from political personnel can be avoided, and corruption lessened.

2. Businesses to lift the poor from poverty

How does one uplift the leadership of a slum church to a level of economic security? We are dealing with a twenty-four hour subsistence economy, without the managerial skills of a money economy. The crucial idea to communicate is that money makes money the more it is used. The poor understand this with their personal money but funds held collectively are often slow in their movement because of traditional decision-making patterns.

We are also dealing with patterns of management skill that are different from that which is known in the city. Why don't people keep records? The poor have a deep aversion to this. To start with they never have sufficient paper. It is used today for records. Tomorrow it is used for other purposes. If the past has been catastrophic and uncontrollable, why record it? Keeping records is not a logical step towards controlling the future. Living on a subsistence wage, one cannot plan beyond twenty four hours. It is illogical to do so anyway, for any money saved will quickly be eaten up by relatives in need or by debt collectors from the past.

We must thus consider two patterns of learning: the nature of learning in a peasant society and the nature of learning in modern society. Peasant society has an amazing characteristic of everybody knowing what everybody else is doing at all times. It is also imitative. Each group is also aware of what similar neighboring groups are doing. Filipinos call it *gaya-gaya,* or the habit of copying what others are doing out of a sense of always wanting to be the same as others. New ideas seem to take off when people in a number of related groups begin something similar and the word spreads.

3. Cooperatives

From the analysis above, the church's basic response to breaking the poverty cycle in the slums is the development of new mechanisms at the border between the upper and lower circuit economies. Among the most effective patterns of economic uplift of the poor, cooperatives of various kinds are significant options for several reasons, both practical and theological. They also are notorious for failure through corruption.

Cooperatives reinforce a number of kingdom values. Sole proprieter businesses may also reflect kingdom values but there are less pressures on the owners to move in the direction of the kingdom and more pressures on them to reflect the values of the world—particularly greed. Cooperatives are at times a logical step for a church that has a common fund for the poor. They require a mutual accountability, which strengthens personal ethics and a sense of social responsibility.

Kagawa[8] of Japan developed the theology and theory of cooperatives extensively two generations ago by building on Raushenbush's works and the Rochdale principles.[9]

In considering a cooperative for a slum church, however, many factors must be taken into account. Cooperatives are not generally successful in a situation of mobility. In other words, the slum would need to have some long-term stability (which is also a necessary condition for the effective development of a slum church). In general, cooperatives also require an extended family context—they are more suited to the group dynamics of peasant cultures. They are not so effective in a buoyant context where there is little poverty.

Bad management of cooperatives is notorious. The management of a cooperative is generally less accountable than that of a company since the boards tend to be more ignorant of management and business skills.

Credit cooperatives or revolving loan schemes provide credit for those who want to produce but have no capital and otherwise would have to borrow money at exorbitant rates. Credit in small quantities and at a reasonable cost will satisfy needs that private banks cannot fulfill. If set up with strong participation of the people, there is strong social pressure to repay loans. Gratitude for being given a loan without the usual red tape or collateral is also an important factor in the success of such schemes.

But good management is needed, including clear book-keeping. There is a thin line between consumer purposes and income-generation purposes. Sometimes a loan has to enable the poor person to survive so that he or she can work for income. Often repayments have to be rescheduled to be more realistic and to fit the family's circumstances.

4. Political confrontation

It is unusual for the poor to rise up in a coordinated manner against those who oppress them. Such confrontation requires organization, planning, strategy, and a middle-class or upper-class mindset. Catholic base communities in Latin America have enabled the poor to understand their situation and the structures of society (*concientizacion*—awareness building), and to use effectively their strength of numbers against the power of those who oppress. It is trained middle-class leadership that enables such confrontations.

Many times this is a viable and perhaps necessary option for evangelical churches. However, I have not found any effective models where such political action and church-planting have been integrated.

William Cook, who has studied these base communities in depth, comments:

The basic difference is that (they) begin as seeds sown in a larger community structure (natural communities) and slowly develop into a church, defined as the presence of the Word and sacrament. Meanwhile nominal Christians are treated as equals and not as second-class citizens or "unregenerate." In Protestant church-planting we call people out from sinful social structures into a body

271

of believers which is defined not only by the Word and sacraments, but more importantly by discipline. This last point makes all the difference in the world, I suspect. . . . Nonetheless, I am not totally convinced that Protestant base communities are impossible, because they are happening spontaneously in Central America in a situation of tremendous violence as a defense against institutionalized violence and brutality . . .[10]

At times, the process of breaking the forces that create poverty calls for a Christian political response, using the power of the masses. It is difficult, however, to integrate this political response with the task of establishing new churches, since establishing the political processes requires broad support from a total community. The gospel does not always generate such a positive attitude from all within a community.

There are many other responses to poverty. Each kind of poverty requires a God-response. Each cause and each result require a different response. There is room for thousands of Christian organizations ministering to different groups of the poor.

Philosophical issues in development

We are focusing on poor people's churches as the center of economic uplift. We observe, also, that the financial base of middle-class churches helping the poor is generally at a level of assisting families or communities. Since there is a historical pattern of involvement of evangelicals in projects. at this level of capital, it is good for us to examine some key principles that have emerged over the last decades.

1. Personalized, not programmed

What is it that has caused the renown of Mother Teresa? It is how God has used her prophetically to declare to the world the character of Christ. She has demonstrated the caring, personalized, and incarnational nature of her Lord as he dealt with the multitudes. The poor of Calcutta do not talk much of other aid programs. They talk of Mother Theresa and her caring. The dignity of the poor is as important to them as the reality of their economics.

2. Incarnation—development from the center

By living among the poor there is a possibility that the outsider may develop an empathy and understanding of the issues faced by the poor. Success will be defined by the people, so it is wise that the worker seek definition of goals from the people at the center, not from office-bound executives.

Incarnation also leads to an understanding that the people have limited, simple, and realistic goals. Not for them is the fancy mansion, but instead a plot of land with the title in their hand, and then after a few years and careful skimping of finances, adding a few bricks every week, the building of a permanent home.

3. Priorities the poor perceive

There is a natural progression of development in any city. There is also a general pattern of perceived needs in the squatter areas throughout the city.

"First a foothold, then a job." Jobs are almost always the top priority in the people's minds. They take precedence over the need for housing or water. But if jobs are available, water and electricity are generally the next pressing needs, preceding such things as sewerage or roads. So we may go on and for each community, developing priorities 1, 2, 3, 4, etc.

The people's priorities are critical in the process of development—not the priorities of the outside development worker who perceives their needs and seeks solutions.

4. Expected percentage of failure

Sixty-eight percent of small businesses in Sydney fail within five years. By contrast, 25 percent of aid programs in one study in Manila were successful, another 25 percent were partially successful, 25 percent were total failures. While there are factors that are not comparable, these figures indicate that, as a rule of thumb, the development worker must reckon on a degree of failure—failure that is just as real as that dealt with by any business owner. If development workers are not business oriented, they are well advised not to get involved in this area of ministry. There are ways of operating that will increase the rate of success, and there is a great deal of available expertise in most cities.

5. Community involvement

To be effective, any group activity must be owned by the people involved in its implementation. They must feel it is theirs. This begins at the conception of the idea, the planning of its progress, and its implementation. Unless community leaders are involved in the decisions at the outset, the idea will eat up finances and produce little.

Many aid organizations enter communities, work with the people to define goals, and provide funding for specific projects and objectives. The difficulty is that the people are in process. They have no background for accomplishing these goals and hence need to frequently readjust through discussions. This often leads to a redirection of the goals and frustration of the outside funding agency.

Once, a co-worker invested a large sum of money in a grand development project a friend had devised. The friend revised the plan when the realities made the original one unworkable. The friendship was broken as the donor accused the worker among the poor of dishonesty.

Open-ended pilot projects are a wiser way to work with such communities. This enables the people to move a little distance in a certain direction, then rethink their priorities and goals in another without a continued sense of failure.

6. The multiplier effect

When faced with the enormity of the task of transforming poverty, why do we go on? With another billion squatters entering these cities over these next ten years, how is it we do not sink into a pall of discouragement?

The reason is because Jesus told us how a mustard seed multiplies and grows into a great tree. Spiritual life creates life. It has a dynamic to expand. The kingdom keeps growing, and even the gates of hell will not stop it. The small things we do today we know will generate many other things.

Similarly, in the natural sphere, life multiplies. From this comes wealth. When men with wisdom and gifts in practical matters handle money, it increases. (When people with eldership gifts handle money, it may or may not increase).

Projects begun with the poor, if they succeed, soon are copied. Even when our resources are limited, by faith we perceive a God who will multiply all we do. When blocked by corruption, oppression, envy, or human error, we have hope in an infinitely interested God. He likes his people to succeed.

Yet we are not unrealistic optimists. Our optimism is based on a great pessimism regarding human nature and the nature of the principalities and powers that increasingly sap the life of the world's poor. We know the script in the Scriptures, the prophecies of increasing oppression and increasing authoritarian controls. We see a world increasingly groaning in pain and know that Jesus must come soon—for he alone is able to save. Meanwhile we save all we can of the earth, her societies, and her people.

Patterns in the development of a diaconal team

Building on these principles, patterns can be developed. Bob Moffitt of HARVEST has developed an approach to use with existing churches in the slums of Central America. I will inadequately summarize this process, developed to a highly programmed level, for helping these small, isolationist churches to begin to relate to the issues of their community and as a result, begin again to let the gospel have an impact.

Begin by preaching the holism of the kingdom and show biblically how it affects all aspects of life. Then draw together the leaders of the church. From these a committee will be elected.

Get a blackboard, divide it into four parts, and dream with the people as to perceived needs in the community. A typical afternoon of discussions might cover the following:

Spiritual	Social	Economic	Political
Bible study on Kingdom	Youth football	Land rights	Land rights
New altar	Teach adults to read	Electricity	Godly community leaders
	Creche/day care	Jobs	
	Care for widows	Credit co-op	
	Recreation area	Herbal plants	
		Scholarships	
		Funeral co-op	

Prioritize these with the people, both in terms of need and in terms of the relative ease of accomplishing something. Then work with them to make plans for one of each of these areas.

For the highest priority needs, plan field trips, contact government authorities for information on their programs, contact NGOs (non-governmental organizations), make a plan, and work with other community leaders outside the church, possibly drawing them into this committee.

We may extend this community development approach into community organization with its goal beyond mere projects.

Defined in a Christian sense, the goal becomes enabling the people to understand fully their ability under God to effect change in the face of opposition from those who oppress them and deny their rights to basic human dignities.

In all community organization, it is important to start with realizable projects. Build the people's sense of ability to deal with those in authority through small and positive experiences. Lay a base for political action slowly. When negative experiences occur, work through issues that arise with them.

Marxists and those who choose a confrontational approach often will use these occasions to increase bitterness between the classes. Christians, during these times, will seek to train people in biblical responses to oppression. Thus, when negotiations break down, develop manageable confrontational techniques that defuse violence but effect change. Before they break down, make sure a thorough theology of dependence on the sovereignty of God in the midst of suffering has been internalized by the believers.

Roles of missionaries, elders, deacons

The key actors in the growth of the church need to have a clear understanding of their roles. The missionary is a catalyst, a change agent who has a significant role in introducing a theology, new ideas, networking both inside the community and with outside resources, and generating some degree of group dynamic. But he or she is a guest and an outsider.

The missionary will only be effective if some insiders take these ideas to themselves. Insiders must be the developers and implementers.

For years, I have taught that it is wise for the missionary not to enter a community with great sources of funding. For years, workers because of their zeal for the poor, have violated this teaching, only to realize later that the people perceive them as a source of finance. This has greatly hindered the processes of evangelism and development. Jesus taught his disciples to go from town to town preaching, dependent on the people. While we need to take sufficient provisions for ourselves, because we are less mobile and more foreign than those first apostles, we need to go with a level of income that results in some degree of dependence on the people.

During the first year of church-planting, as a nucleus forms, we will not be administering great amounts of money for aid programs. We may use seed money on a more personalized basis with individuals. During this time, any use of money needs to be discussed with key advisers from within the community. It means that often there will be emergencies during which we can help, and at other times we will have to get on our knees with the people and pray for the finances with them so that they too learn to look to God and see him provide.

We need to do enough in this economic area so that the new believers see that God is vitally involved in economics and so that they can discuss the biblical teachings on economic issues. We teach by life and word.

But we wait, until gradually among the new believers, it becomes evident that some are gifted in the economic areas, some in management, some in servanthood, and some in business. These need to be drawn together into an emerging diaconate.

Over a period of time, by experimenting with meeting various areas of need, these emerging leaders will learn how to lead the church to a point where each leader, and ideally each member, becomes economically self-sufficient. The exception will be some widows and orphans who will always have some dependency on the church.

Deacons are not the elders. Nor are they the pastor, although initially the deacon has to exercise strong oversight in the use of funds. Elders have very clear ministry gifts. Deacons have very clear economic gifts. Because the process of discerning these gifts takes time, it is advisable not to formalize these roles too quickly, but have a series of *ad hoc* committees form for different activities or projects.

An emerging diaconate

In the following report a middle-class team was involved in founding a church. They are now transferring their vision to a group of emerging disciples who, in turn, are initiating a cooperative loan fund.

Over the previous year the economic committee had consisted of Pastor Jun and Milleth, Jun II and Thelma (all from the middle class Kamuning Christian Fellowship). At the time of the following report a new committee of local believers is being formed.

Report on Tatalon Economic Projects 1983-84

Adel Payawan (now a professor) has continued the herbal plants project which she began here, at Central Luzon State University. Belle Celedonio has now copyrighted her Christmas card production and has become self-supporting in it to some extent. She has been unable to delegate it yet but has made simple designs and patterns for non-artists to help her. She has borrowed 300 pesos to implement this. Pastor Jun's vermiculture was a resounding success till the market disappeared.

Excess goods from last year's shipment of goods from Hillsborough Baptist Church in New Zealand were sold to provide initial funds for the loan fund. Twenty people have taken out loans of up to 300 pesos at a time for projects such as meat stalls in the market, sari-sari stores, transportation and costs for job applications, paint brushes, a pancake stall, buying a harvest of vegetables and selling it, and buying a motorbike. These believers are being encouraged to develop a more structured credit coop where gradually the collective capital will increase. The total turnover of a capital of 1,500 pesos has been 9,471 pesos during the year.

Over 2,200 pesos have been given away in acts of mercy for victims of stabbings, for medicines, to destitute widows, and for a desperately ill woman. Over the last month, another 1,500 pesos have been given for such needs.

Three university /technical courses have been sponsored from the scholarship fund, two in computing and one in electronics. Repayment will be sometime after obtaining a job. The work promised in computing by the University of Life did not eventuate.

The total ministry income from local sources has been 10,324.66 pesos over the last year. This excludes the pastor's support. Good accounts are now available and an accounting system is now operational.

Discussions with the Ministry of Social Services and Development are underway to pass long-term poverty cases onto them. A foster care program proposal has also been initiated. Melly is working on this.

Dressmaking is the next major project A group of interested people are being formed together. Melly and Jonel are working on gathering the necessary data. Nine sewing machines came with the gifts from New Zealand.

The remnant of the vermiculture capital will be spent on chicken-raising. It is a viable project, returning 400 pesos on 1,500 pesos after two months with a high initial risk.

Notes

1. McGavran, Donald, *Understanding Church Growth,* Grand Rapids, Michigan: Wm. B. Eerdmans Publishing Co., 1980

2. Alinsky, Saul, *Reveille for Radicals,* New York: Vintage Books, 1969.

3. Linthicum, Robert, *Empowering the Poor: Community organizing among the city's 'rag, tag and bobtail',* Monrovia, California: MARC, World Vision International, 1991.

4. Galbraith, John Kenneth, *Mass Poverty,* Cambridge, Massachusetts: Harvard University Press, 2001.

5. Harrington, Michael, *The Other America: Poverty in the United States,* Penguin, 1965.

6. Chowdhuri, B., "Bank Finance for Slum Dwellers in Calcutta Metropolitan District," *Calcutta Slums,* Calcutta: CASA, 1983, pp 130-132.

7. Ibid.

8. Kagawa, Toyohiko, *Brotherhood Economics,* New York and London: Harper and Brothers, 1936. Excerpts summarized, NASCO, P. O. Box 7293, Ann Arbor, MI 48107.

9. A group of weavers in 1844 in Rochdale, England, developed some basic principles for cooperatives.

10. Cook, William, *The Expectation of the Poor: a Protestant Missiological Study of the Catholic "Communidades de Base" in Brazil,* Ph.D. Dissertation, Fuller Theological Seminary, 1982

Chapter Twenty-one
The Role of the Affluent Church

Rich churches immediately think of giving financial help when they think of the poor. This is not the primary need. Far more important is giving personnel who can impart spiritual life and technical skills. Nevertheless, there is a place for the transfer of capital. It needs to be done in a such a way that it does not distort the local cultural situation, impose goals on the poor church by the affluent church, nor create dependency.

Having said that, in the case of widows and orphans, refugees, and others for whom the calamity is immediate, or for whom no long term solutions are available, direct aid is most appropriate. In such situations, dependency on the church is normative and not unhealthy. Thus child sponsorship programs, for example, are a good biblical response to what is generally an insoluble problem apart from continuing input from outside.

One of the underlying theses in the theory of capitalism is that creativity must be encouraged and released. This is derived from a cultural understanding of Genesis 1, where God created humankind in his creative image. A second thesis is that the availability of capital is a crucial factor in generating this release of creativity. In reality, seed capital for ideas generated by the people themselves is a means of fostering entrepreneurial ability. Long-term input to ongoing projects, however, results in dependent relationships that are not healthy.

Giving scholarships to the poor so that they may get training in fields that are expanding is another good way for the affluent church to serve the poor. Scholarships are generally not open to significant corruption nor dependency, and fit with cultural patterns that enable the poor to emerge from poverty.

Our aim needs to be to get the means—and control of the means—of industrial production into the hands of the poor. This involves transfer of expertise, work patterns, management skills, and capital. The diagram on the next page further explains what the upper and middle classes can do to fight against poverty and empower the poor.

As indicated in the diagram on page 286, transfer of seed capital through loans or a credit cooperative is a significant way to assist a poor church. This enables the poor themselves to decide on the use of the money for activities that people already may have initiated. The poor are wise. They know which proposals from other squatters have the potential for success or failure. The people can organize cooperatives in such a way that each person, as he or she repays a loan, gives an extra "thank offering," thus increasing the sum total of capital available and covering for cases of failure and non-repayment.

Transferring expansion capital for functioning businesses is another option at a higher level, as is the transfer of capital for small business development. Neither of these is easy to develop without the decision-making remaining to a large extent in the hands of the donor. Because of this, the failure rate is far higher than in cooperatives.

Funding for community leadership programs also increases the net level of skills in the community. This may pay for management courses, community organization courses, or field trips to observe projects in other communities that are models and can be copied. This kind of funding, however, while significant, can also lead to dependency.

The primary focus should be on the transferal of skills and

THE FIGHT AGAINST POVERTY
What the Upper and Middle Classes Can Do

1. JUST STRUCTURES

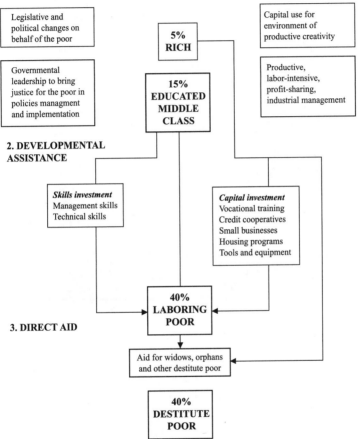

Legislative and political changes on behalf of the poor

Governmental leadership to bring justice for the poor in policies managment and implementation

5% RICH

15% EDUCATED MIDDLE CLASS

Capital use for environment of productive creativity

Productive, labor-intensive, profit-sharing, industrial management

2. DEVELOPMENTAL ASSISTANCE

Skills investment
Management skills
Technical skills

Capital investment
Vocational training
Credit cooperatives
Small businesses
Housing programs
Tools and equipment

40% LABORING POOR

3. DIRECT AID

Aid for widows, orphans and other destitute poor

40% DESTITUTE POOR

Aim: To transfer skills, technology, tools, and control of capital to the productive poor.

SACRIFICIAL, SIMPLE LIFESTYLES
Interchurch International Economic Justice
II Corinthians chapters 8 and 9

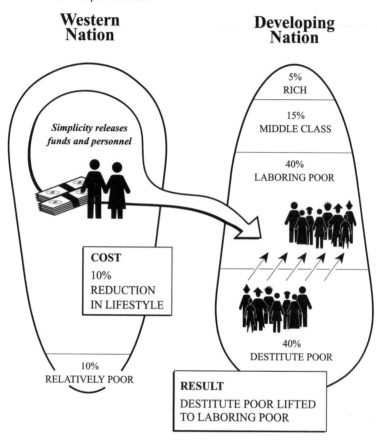

Western Nation

Simplicity releases funds and personnel

COST
10%
REDUCTION
IN LIFESTYLE

10%
RELATIVELY POOR

Developing Nation

5%
RICH

15%
MIDDLE CLASS

40%
LABORING POOR

40%
DESTITUTE POOR

RESULT
DESTITUTE POOR LIFTED
TO LABORING POOR

REMOVING BARRIERS
Migration barriers
Multinational controls
Usurious interest
internationally

CREATING OPPORTUNITIES
Financing credit coop.
Scholarships for vocational training
Transfer of tools and equipment
Transfer of technical knowledge
Transfer of skilled personnel

value systems. This can best be done by supporting an incarnational development worker in the squatter area.

Confrontation with injustice

For those in the upper echelons of government, industry, or military leadership, a Christian commitment to the poor involves working to restructure society for their uplift.

In the present world economic milieu, this commitment to the poor leads to a commitment to theories of democratic capitalism that have been transformed by ethics and social conscience to include many socialist goals.

While recognizing the demonic factors of capitalism, it has obviously been more effective in generating significant city-wide economic uplift for the poor than has socialism.[1] It provides more government capital for housing, education, and health than does socialism. On the other hand, capitalism has never provided sufficient housing for the poor,[2] so that in certain areas governments must take social responsibility.

As we reflect on the nature of God and humankind, we are led to severely oppose multinational control of economies, and to support cooperative patterns of profit sharing within industries as ways of protecting producers from foreign exploitation.

In terms of politics, a Christian posture means confronting corruption among rich politicians, military elite, and businessmen. It also means seeking long-term democratic structures that will enable the poor to have a voice, and hence to defuse violence. These roles are not dissimilar to those proclaimed by the prophets in the Old Testament.

It is important that movements of churches among the poor and among the elite have a strong theology of social transformation. One hundred years after his ministry began, Wesley transformed England because his theology dealt comprehensively with the issues of society that caused poverty. Sadly, in Brazil, where there are great movements among the poor, Pentecostal theology has not provided the twenty nine evangelicals in Parliament with the theology they need to transform their nation.

The outline of such a theology of social transformation is the genesis of another book. Meanwhile there is work to do among the poor.

Notes

1. Berger, Peter, *The Capitalist Revolution: Fifty Propositions About Prosperity, Equality and Liberty,* New York: Basic Books, 1987, p. 213.

2. Galbraith, John Kenneth, *The Nature of Mass Poverty,* Cambridge, Massachusetts: Harvard University Press, 1979, pp. 321-2.

Chapter Twenty-two

Finale

I dreamt of the dark murky waters that swirled down the river past the squatter settlement of Tatalon. Plastic bags and broken wood bobbed up and down beneath the oily surface. Each year the flood would sweep through the houses by the river, washing some away, causing havoc.

And in my dream I saw another river, crystal clear, flowing through the slum, and from here into the favelas and bustees and barrios of city after city. As it came it brought life and refreshment—and joy. Its stream kept tumbling and tumbling until it filled all of the slums and squatter areas of the earth with its gentle gurgling.

In the midst of the dust and carrion calls of the crows of India's bustees, and in the desert of Lima's pueblos jovenes, trees began to sprout along that stream, bringing a new green into the drabness. The leaves covered the garbage strewn around Bangkok's slums. The half-naked on Calcutta's streets found them good covering for their wrinkled, unwashed skin, as they cleansed themselves in the sparkling water. "The leaves of this tree were for the healing of the nations."

I saw the children, with their large eyes and protruding bellies, their limp hair colored red through vitamin deficiency, begin to reach up from their play and take the fruit of the trees. And as they ate, new fruit emerged—a new variety each month. The sores on their heads began to disappear. Their spindly arms began to fill out. New happiness took over from their old hunger.

The curses on the nations and on the poor were no more, and oppression dissolved before the beauty of a righteous throne.

Looking up at that throne were some servants—humble men and women in the sandals of the poor, still dusty, unknown. And suddenly his name was on their foreheads in all its glory. And they began to reign, along with their chosen companions from among the poor, and to rectify the injustices they had chosen to suffer.

The Lord was with them forever. In one caress he wiped away their tears. Suddenly before them, their squatter shacks turned into mansions of delight, for he will make all things new.

And the poor cry out, "Come quickly, Lord Jesus, come!"

About the Author

Following the Holy Spirit, Viv Grigg has been a prophetic voice, living among the poor, church-planting in Manila, Calcutta, Sao Paulo, Los Angeles, and other cities. The Lord has used him to catalyze several new apostolic orders (networks of communities) who live incarnationally in the slums of over 30 emerging megacities, planting churches and creating a plethora of ministries to transform poverty.

Lead by the Lord in the 90s to initiate strategies for citywide *transformative revival,* he coordinated the global AD2000 Cities network, networking city leadership teams with strategies for evangelism, reconciliation and transformation. He leads the Encarnacao network of urban poor movement leaders, whose training commission is developing forty courses on CD for urban poor workers.

He teaches on Urban Leadership Strategies, Transformative Revival Movements, Churchplanting Among the Urban Poor and other urban topics in seminaries as he travels, and is author of *Companion to the Poor, Transforming Cities,* and others. Director of Urban Leadership Foundation, he is married to Iêda, a gifted Brazilian motivational teacher. They raise three children, in Auckland, New Zealand.

For information or donations: Urban Leadership Foundation, P.O.Box 20-524, Glen Eden, Auckland, New Zealand.

Other books available from Authentic Media and World Vision

129 Mobilization Drive
Waynesboro, GA 30830

For a complete catalog of
Authentic publications, please call:

1-8MORE-BOOKS
ordersusa@stl.org

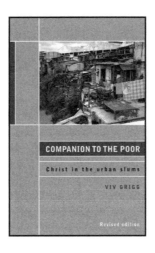

COMPANION TO THE POOR

Christ in the urban slums

VIV GRIGG

Revised edition

Companion to the Poor
Christ in the Urban Slums
(Revised Edition)

Viv Grigg

Viv Grigg challenges us to reexamine our strategies and design new approaches that will build Christ's kingdom among the poor—who comprise nearly half the world.

When he entered the Manila squatter settlement of Tatalon in 1979, Grigg knew what he wanted to do but not how to do it. The need was obvious—to establish a Christian church among Asia's forgotten people, the impoverished slum dwellers of its vast megalopolises. The challenge was to find a way that did not treat people's spiritual needs in isolation from their poverty, without simply becoming another economic or social relief program with no evangelistic component.

This book is the enthralling story of how the author met and solved this problem. But in a sense, it is an unfinished story. What has begun is but the beginning of the founding of a Christian community in a dark place.

(Published in partnership with World Vision Resources)
1-932805-133

The Hope Factor
Engaging the Church in the HIV/AIDS Crisis

Edited by Tetsunao Yamamori,
David Dageforde, and Tina Bruner

The Hope Factor discusses the role that the church plays in the growing HIV/AIDS crisis.

Each chapter is a summary from various academicians, pastors, AIDS patients, and physicians on how the church is addressing this pandemic in their country. They share hard-won insights that will help individuals, churches, and organizations make a difference in practical ways.

> *"I am delighted to introduce and commend this fine book. It offers models of good practice and will encourage and refocus practitioners fighting AIDS in the field as well as spur the giving and prayers of Christians in the West."*

Charles W. Colson
Chairman, Prison Fellowship Ministries and The Wilberforce Forum

(Published in partnership with World Vision Press)
1-932805-117